To Kill A Mockingjay

To Kill A Mockingjay

By

Tate Volino

ALCHEMY BOOK, LLC

Copyright © 2016 by Tate Volino

To Kill A Mockingjay is a parody and a work of fiction. Names, characters, places, and incidents are either the product of the author's imagination or are used fictitiously. Any resemblance to actual persons (living or dead), locations, or events is entirely coincidental.

Cover design by: Estella Vukovic
estella.vukovic@gmail.com

ISBN 13: 978-1540681232
ISBN 10: 1540681238

Thanks,
Austin Rockwood
Jarod Kintz
Martin Ruane

Special thanks to the Bush and Clinton families for their contributions to this work and our country. Now please stop running for president.

Also by Tate Volino

Gold Albatross
Pull the Pin
The Front Nine

Ilium Way #11
The Master of Time, Space, and Dimension
Meta Mobius

Part One

Lawyers, I suppose, were children once.
~ Charles Lamb

Adults are just outdated children.
~ Dr. Seuss

1.

It's not my fault!
~ My children, your children, everyone's children

When he was a kid, my brother Stone broke his leg at the knee. He was skateboarding in front of the mall where large signs clearly indicated the activity was not allowed. Friends brought him home and he tried to hide the injury, but the pain was too great. It wasn't like he'd scraped an elbow.

After returning from work and finding Stone writhing in pain, our father went through the normal spectrum of paternal emotions. He hurried Stone to the hospital and made sure he was okay. Then he gathered the details of what had happened. Shortly after that he filed suit. You see, he was a successful trial attorney and that's how he dealt with problems.

Our father's given name was Flatuous Pinch, but everyone called him Flats. From the time we were old enough to speak he also expected Stone and me to call him by this nickname. He never wanted to be Pa or Pappy, like many of the other dads in our town. It was peculiar, but that was his desire.

Flats reviewed the footage from Stone's GoPro and put together a case alleging the sidewalk at the mall was an attractive nuisance. He contended the property owner had not taken enough precautionary measures to prevent the accident, despite the numerous warning signs with bold, red lettering. The mall owner was more than willing to agree to a quick settlement and in response removed all sidewalks from the property.

I can vividly recall the conversation we had one evening after the accident. When our father sat Stone down in the study and asked me to join, I knew a morality speech was in the works.

My brother slumped in the chair across from me, his pale, impish face furrowed like a bulldog, his fists firmly planted against his chin. Too annoyed to move his hands, he periodically puffed a quick breath against his lower lip to clear the greasy, brown bangs washing low across his forehead.

Directly across from him, my father sat rigidly upright, fingers intertwined on his lap. After a long day, Flats's chalk-colored suit showed not a single wrinkle while his tie was not even a fraction of an inch from dead center. His dark hair, immobilized by a generous helping of Brylcreem, had a metallic sheen and was so stiff I doubt a twister could have moved it.

Flats was still upset with Stone, but not about the injury or the attempt to hide it. What was really bothering Flats was that Stone had tried to claim the accident was *his* fault during the settlement meeting.

"Stone, you just about blew it. Your instructions were to sit quietly and look injured. At most, let out a few groans of pain and anguish."

"I know and I'm sorry, Flats. But *I* was the one who messed up. It was my fault. They even had signs telling me not to do it."

"That's an admirable attitude, Stone, but we live in a time when fault is to be avoided and transferred whenever possible, preferably to a party with deep pockets."

"Jeez, Dad!"

Flats raised his eyebrow like Dwayne Johnson pondering quantum physics.

"Sorry. Jeez, *Flats*! Shouldn't you be teaching us to be responsible for our own actions?"

Flats got a faraway look in his eyes for a moment as he considered Stone's argument. He seemed to be having an inner debate on his position. It passed and he shook his head disapprovingly.

"That's not how the system works."

"Why not?"

"It's just not, son," Flats said, patting my brother gently. "Stone, what are the letters?"

"But..."

"Stone, I'm going to ask you again. What are the letters?"

2

"N...M...F..."

"That's right. NMF—Not My Fault. Stone, you're getting older and need to face reality. It's nice that you have all these dreams of how things should be, but you're going to have to let some of them go."

My brother searched momentarily for a rebuttal. When he opened his mouth to speak, Flats held up his hand and cocked his head to signify the discussion was over.

Stone knew better than to argue with our father, and he certainly knew better than to talk to the hand. He nodded compliantly and hobbled out on his crutches.

I wanted to plead Stone's case for him, but against Flats it would be an exercise in futility. Instead, I twisted my freckled cheeks and Spock-like eyebrows into a menacing scowl and stomped on my father's foot. I marched off to cheer up my brother with tousled, pageboy hair bouncing in perfect rhythm to the pumping of my skinny arms.

For the most part, Flats was a good dad. He tried. His legal career kept him very busy and being a single father with two rambunctious kids added plenty of strain. But when he encountered an unexpected problem, such as a broken leg, he reacted more like an attorney than a parent.

When we look back on that time in our lives, Stone and I would agree it was a low point for Flats, but also a turning point. He soon had cases that would change his view of the law and also the world. Over the following years, Flats would become a different person; we all would.

As for our mother, she disappeared when I was just a toddler. I don't remember her, but Stone was old enough to have more vivid memories. They were mostly of loud, alcohol-fueled fights. Stone said mom would break a lamp or a vase and yell: "Go ahead and sue me, asshole!" Flats would respond by saying she wasn't nothing but a gold digger. Later, Stone would hear them resolving the conflict in their bedroom. That part of the fight involved muffled moans and the rhythmic sound of the headboard slamming against the wall. Maybe it's best I don't personally recall any of those special moments.

Eventually their relationship reached the point of no return and my mother decided Stone and I were no longer her responsibility. One of our neighbors told me about the day she left. My mom was screaming in the front yard, saying she wasn't interested in raising the spawn of Satan. She slammed the door on her convertible Mercedes and drove off, never to be seen again.

During my formative years, many of the maternal duties around the house fell upon the broad shoulders of our housekeeper, Cornucopia. Flats joked that the name fit her perfectly because, like a cornucopia, she was full of crap. We all just called her Corn. She and Flats had a unique relationship, but it seemed to work and she provided a balancing force in our lives.

Corn could be sweet when called for and downright nasty if necessary. If we got out of line she would say motherly things like: "Girl, misbehave and I'll slap you into tomorrow!" and "Touch those cookies and they'll find your body in bed with a plastic bag duct taped over your head!" and "I'll waterboard your ass if you're lying to me!"

Corn had joined our family a few months before Stone's accident. Previously she worked for the Jeffersons, who owned the dry cleaning business in town and used to live over on Hauser Street. When they moved on up to the east side Corn thought the commute would be a drag and resigned. Stone and I loved Corn and thought we were lucky to get her.

Before Corn, we had a maid named Alice. She was funny, but totally incompetent. It was like she was an anachronism from another time. The poor dolt couldn't even figure out how to use a microwave oven. She also had a habit of spending too much time at the butcher shop getting meat and eventually Flats had to fire her.

Alice then got a job with the Brady family who lived out on Clinton Way. Flats represented the Bradys several times over the years. There was the time Jan didn't wear her glasses and ran her bike into a crowd of bystanders, killing several of them. Flats was able to plead to lesser charges, but she still served a couple years up in Tuscaloosa for that stunt. On another occasion, a boy at school was teasing sweet, little Cindy about her lisp. Instead of working it out she shanked him in the cafeteria with a spork. The kid nearly bled to death, but Flats mounted a bullying defense and got her off.

4

Unfortunately, the Bradys were too poor to pay the legal fees and compensated my father by leaving boxes of psychedelic clothing from the 1970s on our back porch. Mr. Brady was an architect, but Flats said no one in town wanted to buy the ugly-ass houses he designed.

As for me, my given name is Jean Luc Pinch. I was named after a distant *male* relative, but was always a tomboy, so I guess it fit. My typical attire was denim overalls and a button down shirt with the sleeves rolled up. On occasions when I did wear a dress most people didn't even recognize me.

Growing up, everyone called me Spy. Alice was actually the one who gave me the nickname. When I was little I had a habit of sneaking up on folks and listening to their conversations. Then I started sneaking into the bathroom and watching people when they were in the shower. One afternoon I caught Alice showering with her boyfriend, Sam the butcher. They were doing some sort of strange dance and I was afraid they might slip on the wet floor, so I warned them to be careful. Alice screamed and grabbed her towel when she saw me sitting on the toilet.

"Listen you little spy. Don't you dare tell your father about this!" Alice growled, while holding my face close to hers with a firm grasp on my pigtail.

"What were you doing in there?" I asked.

"Sam was making a meat delivery. The sausage was dirty and we needed to wash it."

"Oh, I see. Thanks for being so careful; we don't want to eat any unsafe meat."

Alice smiled and nodded. "I'm glad we got that straight, sweetie. Now run along and I'll make you some brownies in a little while."

"Thanks, Alice. You're the greatest."

2.

There's no doubt about it, earmarks are not very popular. There are good earmarks and bad earmarks. The good earmarks are the ones I get for my district.
~ Anthony Weiner

Looking back, it was clear the government and legal establishment had gone too far—that the pendulum had swung past its gravitational limits. I thought it started with the class action lawsuit where Republican voters were sued for electing an incompetent president. Luckily, voter turnout rates were so low that the class ended up being only a small fraction of the total population.

Stone, however, contended the departure from reality started long before that. In history books he had read about a time when individuals took responsibility for their actions. Back when you didn't always have to be looking over your shoulder. Back when kids could play in their yards without being afraid of creepy shut-in neighbors.

What we did agree on was that somewhere along the line sense and reason had gone out the window like the smell of Corn's cookin' on a cool, autumn night. We were headed for a day of reckoning when the pendulum was going to smack us all square in the back of the head.

We lived in Maybach City, the capital of the Southern Trial District. It was a wealthy town and luxury cars lined the streets, however, the ultimate symbol of achievement was the Mercedes Maybach. Flats had two, which were normally parked in the car-house. He preferred to walk to work. On any given day there was a long line of the stylish sedans parked in the valet lot next to the stoic justice building. Maybach City was initially a snide nickname for our town until the egomaniacs in charge changed it to the formal title.

The district was made up of the former states of Mississippi, Alabama, Louisiana, Arkansas, and Texas. Mississippi had long been considered the gold standard of favorable venues for trial attorneys. Louisiana and Alabama were also near the top of the ranks. After the three states agreed to merge they needed a new common name. The top candidates were: Ole Miss, New 'Bama, and Bayou Bengalis. Each of these was particularly offensive to the other members so they settled on the Southern Trial District or STD.

The legal profession celebrated with an extensive media campaign. The smiling faces of attorneys danced through the airwaves and were splashed across billboards. During that timeframe legal commercials began to consume more airtime than actual television shows.

The Chamber of Commerce mounted a counter campaign alerting people to the dangers of the STD. They warned that if people didn't take precautionary measures it could spread. The campaign received additional support from the Centers for Disease Control and Prevention as well as the Trojan Condom Corporation.

Sure enough, around the same time, former Presidents Clinton and Clinton were driven out of their adopted state of New York for being too honest. After loading up the El Camino, they returned to their home state of Arkansas. They were looking for a new income stream and liked what they saw in the nearby STD. They took over a run-down law firm called Whitewater and Associates and re-launched it with their names and faces. The Presidents had a thing for white roses, so a rose became a symbol for the firm.

The entity grew like bamboo in a sewage pond and the firm soon had its tentacles wrapped around the state of Arkansas. After a period of furious negotiating and lobbying—buttressed by a bevy of bribes and blackmail—Arkansas became the fourth state admitted to the district.

The STD then set its sights on the massive neighbor to the west. Texas battled valiantly and held strong for a while, but was eventually overrun by the law firm of: Antonio, Santa, and Ana LLP. They were more than happy to mess with Texas after the state's economy withered during a downturn in the oil industry. Following the annexation, the five member states consolidated power in the central location of Maybach City.

With their base established, the leaders of the district shifted their focus toward increasing their power relative to the rest of the nation. They built a well-trained army of lawyers, lobbyists, and political wonks to carry out the assault. The force descended upon Capitropolis, the national capital of Pander, and made annual crusades to procure funds from a group known as the Lawmakers. This body had been a representative group of citizens from across the nation of Pander, but that changed after The Ohio Compromise, which merged the legislature into a unicameral house with no term limits. It was the first thing the members had agreed upon in years. To commemorate the truce, they voted themselves a pay increase.

The Lawmakers knew this process was a problem, but instead of fighting they decided it would be easier to simply throw money at it. None of them had the courage to turn down the party; the cleanup would be somebody else's problem.

Initially, district leaders tried to cover up the strategy's grotesque spoils. The embarrassment, however, soon faded and the leaders began to fight for bragging rights. They took to the talk shows to let voters know what mamma bird had brought home to the nest.

"Who deserves a bridge to nowhere? You do!"

"Who's entitled to clean energy tax credits for their Hummers? The citizens of the district, that's who!"

I was young, but can still remember Pete Rose cutting the ribbon in front of our new multibillion-dollar, taxpayer-financed baseball stadium. It didn't matter that we didn't have a major league baseball team and couldn't entice one to come to our city. Maybach's Little League team played a few seasons there before the structure was imploded to make way for a hockey arena.

The celebration of the booty they'd extracted eventually became a formal, annual event also funded by Pander's taxpayers. A lobbyist had attached it to an appropriations bill as a joke, but it was passed without comment so the district threw a party.

As part of the festivities, my school held The Pork Pageant to show our appreciation. Older students used large appliance boxes to make elaborate costumes representing government structures that had been built in the district. Elementary students like myself were dressed up as various cuts of pork. One year I was bacon, another year the tenderloin. The pageant wasn't too bad until the year I was picked to be the ham. The costume was bell-shaped and had a big bone sticking out above my head. I was extremely constrained and could barely move while wearing it. It felt like one of those inflatable sumo wrestler suits.

Stone had to walk me to school that night and taunted me the whole way.

"Who's your date for the dance tonight? Green eggs?" Between snorting sounds he'd yell, "Suuu-ee, suu-ee. Here suu-ee, suu-ee!"

A few times he pushed me over and laughed while I rolled on my back and flailed my appendages. Once he'd had his fill he'd stand me upright.

"That'll do, pig. That'll do…" followed by more snickering.

After the show—which was a total hit, I nailed the Macarena despite my costume—I was ready to change when I realized there was a problem. Because the costume was so hot, I'd only worn my skivvies underneath and had forgotten to bring a change of clothes. I wanted to leave, but Stone insisted we stay for the dance. I agreed to stay for a little while and followed him to the gym. I fell over several times on the dance floor and each time kids would start spinning me like a top. I nearly threw up.

"Stone, please take me home," I pleaded.

"Okay, th-th-th-the-the-that's all folks!" Stone said, roaring with laughter and slapping his knee.

By that point I couldn't wait to get the costume off so I could beat the hell out of my brother. My revenge was going to be sweeter than a honey and brown sugar cured ham.

Outside, it had gotten dark. I wanted Stone to call Flats to pick us up, but he pointed out that I wouldn't even fit in a Maybach while still wrapped in fake meat. Grudgingly, I began the march homeward.

We took a short cut across a vacant lot and I shuffled as fast as I could. Halfway across the property I noticed a sound behind us.

"Do you hear that, Stone?" I whispered.

"Uh-huh."

I could sense the fear in his voice. We paused and the noise stopped. Inside the ham, my heart was pounding.

"What should we do?"

"Keep moving. We'll be okay, Spy," he said, taking my hand. I felt cool sweat on his palm.

The noise behind us grew louder and closer.

"I'm scared, Stone. How can it see us?"

"It's your bone, Spy," Stone said, smacking the shimmering, white protuberance with his free hand. "It sees your bone, Spy. Hide your bone!"

Seconds later the pursuer was upon us and made a guttural pronouncement. "I'm going to eat you!"

I tried to run, but went straight down. My hand lost grip of Stone's.

"Help me!"

"Sorry, Spy, every chicken—I mean, ham—for themselves!" Stone yelled as he sprinted away.

"Asshole! If I don't die out here I'm going to kill you!"

I felt a heavy weight land on top of me and smelled the pungent scent of alcohol on the man's breath. I tried to fight, but was helpless. In typical, little girl fashion I yelled, "My daddy is Flats Pinch and if you know what's good for you…"

"I know exactly who your daddy is," he snarled. "Now, come here little darling. I've wanted to eat you for so long!"

As he began to gnaw on my costume I noted another set of footsteps approaching. I hoped it was Stone returning to save me.

My rescuer raced in and plowed the attacker clear of me. "Get off of her, you fat sack of shit!" said a voice I didn't recognize.

My ears were keen in the dark. I heard the sound of muffled kicks hitting the assailant's body followed by the uneven clicking of a stun gun. The hot light from electrical waves arching toward a fat, triple chin burned into my eyes.

"Ow! That hurts!" the attacker cried. "Don't taze me, bro'!"

Whoever had rescued me began to drag the attacker off toward the street. A moment later he returned and pulled me to the sidewalk by my ham bone. It was bad for attracting muggers, but it did make a nice handle.

When my eyes adjusted to the light, I caught a glimpse of my rescuer running around the corner. He was dressed head-to-toe in black and, although I couldn't be sure, I had an idea who he was…

Looking up, I saw another man dressed head-to-toe in black. It was Rabbi Kravitz.

"Oh, shalom, Rabbi."

"Shalom, Spy," he said, helping me to my feet. "Are you okay?"

"Yeah, I think so."

I looked around and saw a disheveled, overweight man in a suit lying on the sidewalk next to us. I realized it was Mayor Levinson.

"Why did you attack me?" I asked, my blood still boiling.

"I'm so sorry, but it wasn't my fault. I couldn't control myself and lost my mind; I just needed a little taste."

I could smell the making of a temporary insanity defense as I listened to the mayor grovel.

"Are you drunk, Eli?" the rabbi asked.

"I had a couple of drinks at the pageant."

Rabbi Kravitz reared back and smacked Mayor Levinson in the side of the head with a hardbound copy of the Torah.

"Ow! That hurt!"

"Your hand is going to hurt when you're sitting in temple transcribing Deuteronomy. How could you do this to an innocent, young girl?"

"I was so hungry. I wanted to try a bit of ham and she looked so tasty. Come on, look at the little temptress. She shouldn't be allowed to dress like that."

The mayor flinched and held up his hands as Rabbi Kravitz prepared to take another swing.

"This girl is not kosher!" he said, shaking his head.

"I know. I'm sorry."

Behind me I heard a commotion and turned to see Corn and Stone running our way. Corn was wearing a robe and looked excessively sweaty, despite the short distance from our house.

"Where's Flats?" I asked.

"Oh, he was, uh, kind of busy, uh, in the bathroom," Corn stammered. "He'll be along in minute. More importantly are you okay, sweet pea?"

"Yeah, I think so. No thanks to this jackhole," I said, swinging my arms impotently at my brother.

"Settle down, HoneyBaked. I went to get help as fast as I could."

"What happened?" Corn asked, looking at the rabbi and mayor nearby.

"The mayor got liquored up and tried to eat me."

"He did what?" Corn said as she slid past me and pounced on the mayor. "You tried to eat my little girl? Get ready for a whoopin' fat man." She landed on his chest and slapped his face repeatedly.

"Ow! That hurts!" the mayor cried.

Rabbi Kravitz intervened and wrestled Corn off him. As Corn struggled the top of her robe came loose and exposed her light brown breasts. Stone's eyes grew wide and he pointed with embarrassment before looking to the ground.

"Eh-hem, Corn," he mumbled.

"Oh, sorry, baby," Corn said as she worked her way loose from the rabbi and pulled her robe closed. "A little wardrobe malfunction."

The rabbi stepped in to take control of the situation. "I know you're upset, Corn, but I think the mayor just had a little too much to drink tonight. Why don't you get the kids home and I'll deal with Eli."

"Okay," she said, herding Stone and me toward our house. She turned and delivered some parting words to the mayor who'd quickly sobered up. "You better stay away from the Pinch kids. You so much as look at 'em funny and I'll burn your career down in scandal."

The mayor held up his hands defensively and nodded. As we walked away Rabbi Kravitz pulled a phone from his robe and called a cab.

Flats was coming down the steps when we got to the house. His pajama bottoms were on backwards and he too was sweaty. I didn't know why everyone seemed to be perspiring. It was a pleasant night and they weren't even wearing a ham costume.

12

"Are you okay?" Flats asked as he tried to throw his arms around the girth of my meat suit.

"Yes, I'll be fine. Can we go inside and get this stupid costume off?"

"Sure, sure."

Corn held my ankles while Flats yanked on the bone to free me from my pork prison. I told Flats I didn't want to talk about what had happened and headed up to get ready for bed. After washing up, I called for Stone to come over to my room.

"Stone, can we talk?"

"Sure," he said.

As he came closer I kicked him hard in the groin. He doubled over and moaned. "What was that for?"

"You know damn well."

"I'm sorry, Spy," he said, rubbing himself tenderly.

"Apology accepted. Now, I do have a question for you. Did you see the man in black tonight?"

"Johnny Cash?"

"No, you idiot. The one who rescued me."

"Oh, him. Yeah, but only for few seconds."

"Everything happened so fast it was like a blur. He kicked the mayor's ass and then was gone before I could even thank him. Do you think it was *him*?" I asked, inferring that my rescuer was our mysterious neighbor whom we had speculated about for years.

"I don't know, Spy. It may have been. I doubt we'll ever know for sure. Get some sleep."

I drifted off while replaying the evening's events over and over in my head. I was simultaneously scared and thrilled by my memories of the man in black.

3.

Summer will end soon enough, and childhood as well.
~ George R.R. Martin

Like our primitive ancestors, when Stone and I didn't know the answer to something we usually made one up to suit our purposes or scare the other into doing what we wanted. Mirroring the weeds in our yard, these tales grew particularly tall in the long, hot days of summer. Without the distraction of school our minds and bodies wandered freely through the neighborhood.

For the most part Stone and I got along during those days that seemed to last forever. We played nice knowing we had to tolerate each other or else play alone. Our immediate neighborhood had few kids our age. Rather than pick on one another it was easier to invent rumors about our neighbors. We often incorporated them into the movies and TV shows we liked to act out.

Our little microcosm took a strange turn the summer I turned nine. That's when Pyckle (pronounced: *pickle*, like a dill) arrived.

One slow morning Stone and I were hanging out in the treehouse when we heard voices in the neighbor's yard. I looked through a peephole and spied a young, black child standing by their back porch. I nudged Stone and motioned for him to come take a look.

"Should we introduce ourselves?" I asked.

"Let's go check it out," he said, shimmying toward the ladder.

We made our way to the ground and crept over to the hedge. The boy had his back to us and appeared to be doing a chore.

"Well?" I whispered.

"He looks about our age. Maybe he's here visiting the Cosby family for the summer."

"It would be nice to have another friend around. And it would mean we'd have another actor when we do our movies and shows. I get tired of having to play three or four different roles."

"You're very versatile, Spy," he complimented.

"Okay, let's at least go say hi to him."

"Go ahead, ladies first."

"No, you go. You're older."

"Yeah, but you're less threatening."

"All right, I'll go, Stone. Sometimes you're such a pussy."

I stood up and dusted off my overalls. Decisively I marched to a break in the bushes and walked into the Cosby's yard with Stone shadowing me. I stopped short of the boy and cleared my throat to get his attention. When he turned I saw his face and took a quick step back.

"Oh, dear!" I blurted.

He scowled and examined me and then Stone.

Stone moved forward to my side.

"Uhh, I think what she was trying to say was: sorry for disturbing you. We didn't, uhh, realize that…"

"Realize what?" he said indignantly.

"Well, just that you're a…"

"A what?"

"How old are you?" I asked, my curiosity overtaking my embarrassment.

"I'm twenty-five."

"Jeez, you're right puny, aren't ya'," Stone noted.

"I'll still pound you silly," the man-child said, taking a step forward.

"Hey, settle down little fella."

"Little fella?"

"Sorry, we've never seen a black little person before. What should we call you?" he asked honestly.

"When you look like me you get called all kinds of things. The crafty ones think its fun to call me 'midga' or 'nidget'. How about just using my name?"

"Sure, what is it?"

"I'm Pyckle."

Stone and I both had to stifle giggles.

15

"Pyckle, eh? More like a gherkin!" I said, elbowing Stone.

"Hey, don't think I won't hit a girl," he said, edging toward me.

"Try it, baby dill," I taunted. "My dad will garnish a portion of your wages for the rest of your days."

"Oh, I see, another spoiled lawyer hatchling."

"You're not very friendly."

"Yeah, that's why they revoked my membership in the Lollipop Guild."

"Okay, let's keep cool, guys," Stone said, stepping between us. "Spy, come here a second."

We moved back toward the bushes out of earshot.

"Spy, let's make friends with him."

"Why?"

"Think about all the other shows we could act out if he joined us. *Webster, Different Strokes, Fantasy Island.* We could even do more modern stuff like *Austin Powers* and *Game of Thrones.*"

"Hmm, good point."

We walked back and employed some of the negotiation skills Flats had taught us.

"Mr. Pyckle, I'm sorry we got off on the wrong foot," I began. "We want to be friends. I'm Spy Pinch and this is my brother Stone. Would you like to come see our treehouse?"

He eyed us suspiciously and then glanced up at our fort.

"It does look pretty cool. What do you all do up there for fun?"

"Lots of things. We read, play cards, and put together our plays—we like to act out TV shows and movies we've seen. Kind of like live reruns."

"What card games do you play?"

"Hearts, Go Fish, Crazy Eights. All the good ones."

"No poker?"

"No, but you could teach us," I suggested.

"I've got a feeling there are lots of things I could teach you two bumpkins. All right, I'm stuck here for the summer helping my Aunt Mame since the old bag refuses to go to an ACLF. I guess I can pass a few hours babysittin' you kids."

16

"Great," I said, excited by the prospect of learning new things.

We didn't know it then, but that was the start of a lifelong friendship. We stayed close even after Stone and I hit puberty and outgrew Pyckle. Gradually we learned that poor Pyckle had never really had a childhood of his own. He spent his early years being tossed from one family member to another. Instead of being treated like a guest they normally made him serve as a houseboy and he rarely had a chance to interact with other kids. The summers he spent in Maybach allowed him to make up for some of the lost time. He always acted like he was babysitting us, but we were really just friends.

"Let me go change Aunt Mame's oxygen canister and then I'll meet you up in your treehouse in a few minutes," he said, climbing the back steps.

"Wait, we need to give you the password," Stone said.

"The password?"

"Yeah, to get into our clubhouse. Everyone has a password."

"Okay, what's the password?" he asked, rolling his eyes.

"Bosco."

"Super. We'll be changing that too."

Stone and I returned to the treehouse and tidied up a bit to prepare for company. When Pyckle arrived at the base of the tree he yelled, "Bosco!"

"Permission granted," Stone said, lowering the rope ladder.

We looked down through the trapdoor and watched as Pyckle flew up the rungs.

"Wow, you climb like a..." I started, before catching myself.

"What? A monkey? Were you going to call me a monkey?"

"No, a...a...a Sherpa!" I declared.

Pyckle pushed my shoulder playfully. "I was just screwin' with ya', girl. I am what I am. My grandma taught me long ago to do the best with what God gave you. I always knew the NBA wasn't an option, but I've got other plans—despite my appearance."

"Good for you, Pyckle. What's in the bag?"

"This?" he said, holding up a brown paper bag with a spout protruding at one end. "You've never seen a forty?"

"Oh..." Stone said, startled at the presence of alcohol.

"Come on, kids. Time to grow up and turn up!" he said, handing the bag to me.

I looked skeptically at the bottle and then glanced at Stone. He shrugged his shoulders like I should give it a try. I hesitated and then took a quick swig, considering it for a moment as the carbonation tickled my sinuses.

"It takes just like Coke."

"Really? Maybe that's because it is!" he said, cracking up and pulling a Coke bottle out from the bag. "Malt liquor is nasty, but I have to try and look tough to keep up appearances with my brothas. You two are gullible. Maybe I'll have some fun this summer after all."

He handed the bottle to Stone and sat back to evaluate our treehouse. "So this is the Maybach VIP room. If you want to make this a real man-cave, Stone, you need to throw up a flat screen, get a little recliner, and a mini bar. You could put a satellite dish on one of the branches up above."

"Our dad doesn't let us bring our electronics up here. He wants us to read and engage our imaginations, says it's still important and something kids are missing."

"Yeah, I 'spose he's right. Still..."

"We do have a great view of the whole neighborhood," I said, pulling him toward one of the windows. "Right across the street is Mrs. Simpson's house, we call her Mrs. Marge. Her husband was a big shot nuclear scientist, but he died while doing a consulting project in some place called Chernobyl. She had kids, but they're gone. She pretty much just tends to her yard now. Aren't her flowers lovely?"

"Yeah, I've met her. Aunt Mame sent me over there to pick up some of her special 'medicinal' flowers. I kept a few for myself," Pyckle said, producing a Ziploc baggy. It contained something that looked like a rolled paper maggot. "Don't worry, you don't have to inhale if you don't want to. Just in case you ever become president..."

"Next door is the Fredericks. Under a wood cover in their front yard is a big pipe that leads straight down. We think it goes all the way to China," I said.

18

"Sure, if China is the name of the local sewage treatment facility you're probably right."

"Down the road a little way is Mrs. DuPont's house, the one with the green roof. Her family was in the chemical business. She is very well off, but very mean. We've got our eye on her. Some sketchy characters come and go at strange times of the day."

"Maybe she's a hooker?" Pyckle guessed.

"She's not real attractive," Stone said.

"Hey, that's not always the deciding factor."

"She's old too."

"Listen, if a sailor's got an itch he'll swing into any port."

"And then there's the *Baaa*-ddley place," I said, accenting the first syllable to convey the spookiness.

"What's up with that joint? It looks more like a factory than a house."

"It's the oldest building around here. A man named Duval 'Dew' Baddley owns the property. We've heard lots of stories about him, but have never seen him in person. We're not sure if he even still lives there on a regular basis, but there's a constant procession of UPS and FedEx trucks coming and going."

"Maybe he's staying out of the spotlight on purpose. Could be a government informant."

"Nah, he was some kind of businessman and then one day he just closed the gates. Or so they say."

"Was he in the candy business by chance?"

"No, I don't think so."

"So does he do all the work himself?"

"That's another mystery. We see the silhouettes of people moving around in the windows. They seem to do a lot of work at night."

"Interesting. It sounds like we've got a mystery on our hands. We may have to find a way to sneak in there," Pyckle said.

Stone and I exchanged glances. We had been curious about the Baddley compound for years, but were always afraid to investigate. Flats said not to bother him—leave a sleeping dog lie.

"All right, enough sightseeing for now. Let's play cards."

Pyckle turned out to be an excellent card player. He knew all of our games and beat us easily. Then he taught us poker. Stone and

I were fast learners, but we realized it would be a while before we could compete with the teacher. Pyckle quickly pocketed our allowances and then acquired Stone's wristwatch in a climactic final hand.

We were hoping Pyckle would participate in a play after he finished cleaning us out, but he said he wanted to see our skill level before joining in. Stone and I were glad to put on several sketches from an episode of Downton Abbey. One of the characters Stone played was named Atticus Aldridge. Those Brits sure come up with funny names.

When we finished Pyckle gave us a standing ovation. Because he was a little person, he could literally stand up in our treehouse without even bumping his head.

"Wow! You guys are good. That was beautiful," Pyckle admitted while rubbing his eyes with his sleeve.

"Are you crying?" I asked.

"No! It's my allergies. There's a lot of pollen up here in this tree. Your clubhouse needs an air purifier."

"Well, thank you for the praise, Pyckle."

From outside we heard Corn call our names. Stone tried to check the time, but realized his wrist was now bare.

"What time have you got, Pyckle?"

"Almost noon."

"Already? We must be having fun!" I said.

Pyckle looked out the window and spotted Corn down below.

"Hello, sweet brown sugar! Is that your maid?"

"Yes, but we think of her as part of the family. Her name is Cornucopia, we call her Corn."

"That's some nice lookin' Corn ya'll got there."

"I've seen her boobies," Stone blurted out, trying to impress our guest.

"Boy, don't tell me you're already taggin' that."

"No, not anymore. We stopped playing tag years ago."

Pyckle rolled his eyes yet again and shook his head. I was starting to wonder if it was some kind of physical tic.

"Pyckle, would you like to be our guest for lunch?" I asked.

"Will Corn be there?"

"Absolutely."

20

"In that case, count me in."

We climbed down and walked across the yard where I introduced our new friend. Corn looked him over with skepticism.

"Hmm…how old you be?" she asked.

"Aged twenty-five years, like a good whiskey."

"You best not be a bad influence on mista Flats's kids now," Corn warned. I noted how Corn's vernacular changed when she addressed Pyckle. The same thing happened when she saw her church friends down at the Jitney Jungle.

"Nah, we cool. Just chillin'. And don't go judgin' the book by the cover my Nubian princess," Pyckle added as he held her hand up and kissed it.

Corn yanked it back like he'd bitten her.

"Take it down a notch, Billy Dee."

"No worries, sista. I've got all summer to work my magic."

"Pyckle, eh? I think I'll just go ahead and call you *Trouble* from the get go. You kids—and your friend Trouble—get on in there and wash up."

4.

All the world is full of suffering. It is also full of overcoming.
~ Helen Keller

The prior year, Flats thought he would broaden our horizons by sending us to summer day camp. Stone and I were excited by the opportunity, but that lasted for about five minutes once we arrived. The thrill turned to fear and we soon had one goal: survival.

Our fellow campers were primarily the dregs of our school and they were making a seamless transition from detention hall to the camp. Stone checked to be sure we were in the right place, wondering if perhaps we had accidentally been assigned to a prison camp.

Meanwhile, the counselors appeared as if they were in need of counseling. Talk about patients running the asylum. They possessed two traits: apathy and disdain. Many of the campers checked in and then disappeared until the end of the day at pickup time. This didn't bother the counselors; in fact they encouraged it—fewer faces to deal with each day.

The first week featured lots of "free play." To the boys this meant wrestling and MMA fighting. At some point a supervisor visited and asked the counselors to come up with an alternate activity. In response they moved the matches to a clearing in the woods, which they called the octagon. The intensity of the battles increased further when the counselors began wagering on the action. It may have been the only time I saw them show an interest in the campers.

I was strictly a bystander until a boy named Jerry decided to start running his mouth and insulted my dad. He said Flats was probably home shucking some corn while we were at camp. I didn't know exactly what he meant since corn normally wouldn't be ripe until late in the summer, but I wasn't about to take it. I rolled up my overalls and had a tumble with Jerry. I messed him up pretty good so he didn't have much to say to me after that.

All of the combatants had their share of scrapes and bruises, but the bigger problem was the fact that the octagon was chock-full of poison ivy. Over the next few days a good portion of the campers arrived with oozing sores; it had the feel of a young zombie colony. I almost felt bad for Jerry whose face I'd rubbed into the ground. Who knew you could get poison ivy on your eyeballs?

The lice bugs were considerate enough to wait until the second week before arriving. Parents responded with mandatory buzz cuts. When we arrived at camp the following Monday it looked like a neo-Nazi youth gathering. I'd never seen that many angry, agitated skinheads in one place before.

I cried when Corn took me in the back yard and shaved my head. But when I finally looked in the mirror I realized it was pretty badass. Kinda like Sigourney Weaver in Alien 3 or maybe Britney Spears when she had her little "breakdown."

Things were getting bleak after a drowning, a lightning strike death, and an abduction. The final straw was a mini-outbreak of measles. At some point a surprising number of otherwise rational parents had stopped vaccinating their kids. For some it was a moral issue, others based it on faulty findings by a quack in the UK, while the rest heard it was bad from an email that quoted a blog post about someone's tweet who may have been a doctor—possibly a veterinarian.

It turned into a legal quagmire and of course no one would take responsibility. Patient zero died and, as if that wasn't enough, his folks then had to deal with lawsuits from other parents. But skipping the vaccine did at least keep them from getting…well…nothing…

Needless to say, Flats decided we had stuck it out long enough and yanked us. This summer he was content to let us stay home. For the first few weeks we did a decent job of staying busy and keeping out of trouble. A lot of the credit goes to Pyckle, who fit right in to our little acting group. On days we would do episodes of *Different Strokes*, Stone and I would go home with bellyaches from laughing so hard. We couldn't control ourselves when Pyckle would lay down a perfect delivery of: "Whatchu' talkin' 'bout, Willis?" while pursing his lips and looking sideways.

Still, restlessness eventually reared its head. That's when we started to focus on our common obsession: the Baddley place. We were an unstoppable force and it appeared to be an immovable object. Something had to give.

We saw it as a castle and we were going to lay siege before the end of summer. The fact that Flats didn't want us playing there made it even more tantalizing. We wanted to know what was going on in there, but most of all we wanted to see Dew Baddley in the flesh.

Rather than an all out assault, we talked about minor incursions to get our feet wet. Get on the property and then see what happens.

One night after dinner, we were sitting on the wall that faced the Baddley place looking around the neighborhood and thinking up new lies and rumors. In the waning dusk we saw the blue lights glowing in the back rooms of Mrs. Marge's house. She was always complaining about the amount of money she spent on electricity to keep her precious flowers alive. Pyckle had grown very fond of her flowers and confirmed they were worth every penny. I said I thought she was doing experiments on human cadavers; using all that power to create her own version of Frankenstein. Pyckle said he liked my story, but was pretty sure she was only growing plants, not people.

Eventually the conversation rolled around to the impenetrable castle of Dew Baddley.

"Why won't you go over there, Pyckle? Dude, you're twenty-five, time to man up," Stone goaded.

"Two things for you to consider, Stone. First, I got here a few weeks ago. You two have been procrastinating for years. Second, and more importantly, look at me. I'm a young brotha wearing a hoodie, baggy jeans, and a crooked baseball cap with the tag from the store still on it. Folks tend to treat someone fitting that description a little differently than two white kids who just jumped out of a Norman Rockwell painting."

"By the way, Pyckle, it's like ninety degrees out here still. Why do you have a sweatshirt on?" I asked.

"Representin'."

"And the underwear sticking out?"

"Same thing."

"Well, I'm getting you a belt for Christmas."

"Very thoughtful of you, Spy. Anyway, Stone, it's what they call a double standard. That means *you* need to be the one to man up."

"What do you think, Spy?" Stone asked, trying to deflect Pyckle's challenge.

"I've been working on a bold plan. We start with a Trojan horse—like a brown delivery truck. Then we drop off a large package with Pyckle hidden inside. He can take the GoPro and film everything once he's inside the house."

"And when they find me walking around?"

"You'll be wearing a disguise."

"A disguise?"

"Yeah, Corn will make a cute little pair of white overalls and we'll make you up in orange face," I said, conjuring up my image of Mr. Baddley's workers.

My plan resulted in a slap from Pyckle.

"Ow!"

"Girl, haven't you heard: orange is the new black. Next time you get knuckles."

"I'll take that as a 'no' vote on my plan. What happened to you being okay with who you are?"

"It only goes so far as Oompa Loompa Land, little girl. I can make jokes about my characteristics, but you can't. Again, it's called a double standard. Besides, who's gonna drive the truck?"

"I could work the pedals, while Stone steers."

Pyckle shook his head in frustration. "I may need to find some new friends."

"Yeah, maybe they'll have a better plan," Stone said indignantly.

"What's gonna be sad is if Spy beats *you* to it, Stone. Think about it: losing out to a girl...who also happens to be younger than you. Oh hell, that's gonna be a wreck. All the boys at school will be rattlin' your chains."

Stone was feeling the pressure build.

25

"I *dare* you to go ring the doorbell and then run back here," Pyckle said slowly while looking my brother in the eye.

Silence.

"Ding-dong, ding-dong," Pyckle sang. I joined in.

More silence.

Finally, he broke. "All right! I'll do it."

As with so many childhood choices, it came down to a dare, which is often a poor way to make decisions. Now that it had been accepted there was no turning back. I was amazed when Stone hopped off the wall and began to walk at a measured pace toward the fence surrounding the Baddley home.

"Dead man walking," Pyckle called.

"Stop it, Pyckle," I whispered. "I don't want him to chicken out now."

"Damn! I can't believe he's doing it."

"Flats is gonna skin him," I said, staring as if I knew a train wreck was about to happen.

Stone looked around as he approached a section of the wrought-iron fence we'd already scouted as a weak point. The area didn't appear to be covered by one of the security cameras. He turned, gave us a thumbs up, and started to climb.

I half expected him to be blown back in a shower of sparks, but apparently the barrier wasn't electrified—something else we probably should have scouted.

Within seconds Stone made it to the top and then flopped down on the other side. He was in! We saw him roll behind a nearby bush as he stopped to plot the remainder of his course.

Stone was like a secret agent, weaving his way from one landscaping bed to another. As he neared the home, the excitement rising in Pyckle and me was palpable.

"I can't believe he's really going to do it," I said with wide eyes.

"He's almost there."

Stone was within twenty feet of the main entrance, attempting to gather his courage. He leapt forward and ran toward the door, but his movement triggered a sensor and the front floodlight turned on. Stone stopped in his tracks, frozen in the beam of light.

"Oh no!" I cried.

26

"Our man's in trouble," Pyckle replied. "Get out of there, Stone," he added in a loud whisper.

I could sense my brother was still considering making a dash for the doorbell when his survival instincts kicked in. He started running again, but on a different path. He ran toward a corner of the building and slapped it. He waved his hand in our direction to make sure we'd seen what he'd done. After that, he bolted toward the fence. Halfway back he stumbled in a bed of rocks and fell forward. He got up, but was looking around on the ground for something. Right when it looked like he'd found it a light went on inside the house.

"Run!" Pyckle yelled.

Stone abandoned his rescue and sprinted flat out toward the fence. Once again he was up and over in an instant. After rejoining us, we all ran to the treehouse for safety. Our hearts were pounding and we were panting like tired dogs. We peered out the window at the Baddley house to see if anyone would come out. Nothing. A minute later the security light turned off and eventually the inside light was also extinguished.

"Oh my God, Stone. That was a close call," I said.

"Did you see me? I touched it! I touched the Baddley house!" He was flying high from his accomplishment.

"I gotta give you credit, Stone. That was bold," Pyckle said, soul shaking my brother's hand and pulling him in for a man hug.

"Did you rip your pants on the fence?" I asked.

"My pants? No. But I dropped my phone."

"Oh no…"

"Yeah, I saw it next to a rock and the screen was shattered. Hopefully, it broke completely and no one will be able to turn it on."

We hung out for a bit longer and retold the story of Stone's run many times over, each time augmenting and exaggerating more details.

When we finally headed in for the night, Flats stopped us in the sitting room where he was reading. "Did you have fun this evening?"

"Ah, yeah, you know, same ol' stuff, Flats," Stone said, exchanging grins with me.

"Great. Oh, can I borrow your phone a second, Stone? My battery died and I want to look something up."

Stone literally turned to stone. It was as though Flats somehow knew what we'd been doing outside.

"My phone?"

"Yeah, let me borrow it for second. I want to Google something quick."

"I…uh…" he replied, patting his pocket in vain. "I think I left it at school," he blurted. I slapped my hand on my forehead in disbelief.

"School?" Flats said, doing the thing where he raised his eyebrow really high. "But it's summer vacation."

"Oh yeah. I meant…the Cosby's. I left it over at their place."

"Well, okay. Be sure to get it tomorrow."

"Will do. Goodnight, Flats."

"Goodnight."

***

Stone's small victory turned out to be a big victory for us. Although Stone had been the one to do it, Pyckle and I felt as though we had overcome some previously unconquered barrier. The neighborhood was the same as it had been, but the atmosphere felt different. The next day the sun appeared to be shining a bit brighter and it sounded as if the mockingbirds were singing a tad louder.

Walking past the Baddley home that afternoon Stone stood a little taller. All of us tried our best not to mention it or look toward the house, hoping to prove we'd broken its spell over us. Honestly, I had to force myself to keep my head from turning. We were almost to the other end of the lot when we heard a strange, muffled noise.

We froze in our tracks and waited for a moment before we heard it again. It sounded like it was coming from a nearby tree. We edged closer and determined it was originating from inside a large knothole in the stout oak's trunk.

"Is that a phone? What's that ringtone? It sounds like *Ice Ice Baby*," Pyckle said.

"It is! That's my phone," Stone said, looking at me with surprise.

Stone shoved his hand inside, quickly located the phone, and fished it out. It was still ringing, but when he swiped his finger and tried to answer it the line was dead. The screen said the call had come from a blocked number.

"Is that your phone, Stone?" I asked.

"I think so. This is my case." He popped the shell and held the back up so we could see it. When I saw "Stone" etched in the back, chills climbed my arms and spine.

"That is so bizarre!" I said, still marveling at the phone in his hand.

"What? Having Vanilla Ice as his ringtone. Yeah, that is bizarre," Pyckle scoffed.

"No, wise guy. That his perfectly repaired phone started ringing right when we were walking past."

"Yeah, that's kind of messed up too."

"But how?" Stone asked.

"Divine intervention?" I postulated.

Pyckle shook his head and we all turned simultaneously to look at the house. We couldn't be sure, but it looked like a dark silhouette moved behind the curtain in one of the windows. Had someone been watching us the whole time?

Stone pocketed his phone and we shuffled away toward the treehouse.

In an instant the mystery returned to the Baddley home, but it had a different vibe—a positive one.

5.

We are living in a world today where lemonade is made from artificial flavors and furniture polish is made from real lemons.
~ Alfred Newman

The next few weeks moved along as usual. The one thing that did change was the temperature; the mercury rose as a record heat wave swept the district.

Our games were getting repetitious and we were looking for new ideas, but struggling to find the right one. Pyckle had long since cleaned out our piggy banks playing cards and we all agreed strip poker would be way too weird. Inspiration finally struck one afternoon during an episode of *SpongeBob SquarePants*. As always, Mr. Krabs was formulating a moneymaking plan and had SpongeBob dress up as a little girl and open a lemonade stand.

"That's what we can do," I proclaimed.

"Cross-dress?" Stone said.

"No, a lemonade stand," I replied.

Pyckle stroked his chin in thought. "I like that idea."

Stone, however, looked dubious. You see Stone was a born inventor and salesman. He loved to tinker and experiment and from the time he was little he wanted to start businesses and sell things. He wondered if it was something genetic, perhaps inherited from our mother. Flats said he doubted it given the only things she'd ever sold were her body and her soul. He reckoned it had more likely traveled through the Pinch blood from our ancestor, Willy Pinch.

Flats didn't like to talk about Willy, but over the years I was able to piece together a reasonable history. Willy bounced around between the used car industry and homemade liquor sales before heading south and getting into the knife business. He was able to secure the exclusive regional sales territory for a knife that could cut right through a can and still be sharp enough to perfectly slice a ripe tomato—the legendary Ginsu.

He started going door-to-door, wearing makeup and sporting a Fu Manchu mustache to add authenticity. Over time he built a multi-level marketing structure that fed him a steady stream of profits. Sales tanked, however, after a female serial killer named Clove began decapitating her victims with a Ginsu. Following her arrest, she bragged that she would never have been able to kill so many people if not for the ridiculous cutting ability of her trusty knife. Attorneys for the victims pounced on the connection and eventually bankrupted Ginsu's parent company. Clove later put out a line of T-shirts with her likeness and catchy sayings such as: *Knives don't kill people. I do!* It was messy endings such as this that caused Flats so much concern.

Willy was the kind of person who woke up each day with a new idea dancing through his head. Unfortunately, he often couldn't concentrate on just one—probably some undiagnosed adult ADD—and had difficulty taking his projects to fruition. Still he saved enough from the Ginsu venture to purchase a large parcel of land about twenty miles east of Maybach. The property became known as Pinch's Point and remains in the family to this day. Over the mantle in the great room is a massive portrait of Willy dressed in full Samurai attire with a long Fu Manchu dripping from his jowls. I once asked Flats if the sword Willy was holding was an authentic katana. He said, no, it was just a really big Ginsu.

As for Stone, several of his early business attempts were questionable—yet still successful. After seeing ads in the back of magazines and on the Internet, he determined that penis enlargement and breast augmentation were fertile, growing markets. Like most kids, his first client base consisted of classmates at school. For the boys, he charged a dollar and gave customers a box with a few random pictures pulled from a copy of *Hustler*. The girls received a gift bag with two tennis balls and a roll of duct tape. Although not what they expected, the kids could not argue with the results and Stone had no returns under his money back guarantee. The principal caught on after teachers complained about the massive uptick in requests for bathroom passes. Stone's business was shut down, but for a second grader you had to give him points for creativity.

Stone also had a paper route for a while, but ended up dropping it voluntarily. He tired of Flats's daily grilling as to whether or not he had been injured in any way while on someone else's property.

My brother's inventions, however, were what really scared Flats. Like most young boys, Stone often made weapons so there were the obvious concerns about injuries. But even when Stone came up with something beneficial or innocuous Flats still worried more about the risk than the potential for success. It's not that he didn't want to see his son succeed, rather Flats saw demons of liability around every corner. "Businesses are dangerous enough in the hands of adults," he would say. "How can a child be trusted to run an enterprise? If someone gets hurt it will be my neck on the line."

In light of this history, Stone, Pyckle, and I spent the next few days focusing on prospective risks in our business plan. Compared to knives, lemonade seemed relatively harmless.

We began our preparations in secret and decided to wait until right before our grand opening to bring Corn into the fold. As for Flats, rather than asking permission, we would beg for forgiveness if and when he found out.

Our window of opportunity opened the following week when Flats left town to conduct discovery work on a new case. We would have the weekend without him and the forecast for Saturday was sunny and hot—the perfect combination for lemonade sales.

To cover a broader market, we decided it would be prudent to offer a selection of choices. Our menu included low-price instant lemonade, premium hand squeezed real lemonade, and lemonadeX with Red Bull mixed in—to really get the kids juiced. To placate the granola crowd we sourced several bags of organic lemons. Of course there was no way to prove they were truly organic other than the word of a guy with a pick-up truck full of fruit and melons.

Our team divvied up the tasks and I was put in charge of production, mixing, and pouring. Stone was the CFO, handling the books and monetary transactions. He still had reservations about the project, but was feeling bolder after the Baddley house touch—as though he had acquired some newfound power. He entered the zone as soon as he heard the first coins ringing in the cash drawer.

Pyckle was the head of marketing. He had been complaining about Mrs. Marge raising the price on her special flowers and was eager to make some extra money. Therefore, he was giving our business one hundred and ten percent.

His primary duty was to serve as our human signage—standing along the road to garner attention. Some sign guys dance or spin a big neon arrow; others hide behind their sign and pray to be overwhelmed by car exhaust. Pyckle tried to veto the idea, but Stone and I used our sibling voting block to overrule him.

The biggest issue was the required uniform. Stone and I had retrieved my ham suit from the basement and painted it bright yellow. We painted the bone dark green to look like a stem. Pyckle probably wouldn't have made the team for a Fruit of the Loom commercial, but it got the point across. To counter his objections, Stone and I agreed to give him an extra share of the profits for serving as our spokesmodel. Trust me, it was worth every penny to see someone else having to wear that silly thing.

Pyckle was steaming mad on an already hot opening day as he wobbled out toward the street corner. "This is ridiculous. I'm going to sweat to death."

"Here, have a sample," I said, holding up a cup with a long straw.

"Give me that," he said, grabbing the plastic cup.

Pyckle took a couple of sips and then spilled some on the ground. "That's for my homies."

"Huh? Stone and I are your homies. Now quit wasting our juice and get out on the street."

"This is humiliating."

"At least as a lemon no one is going to try to eat you."

Our other marketing efforts included handing out flyers to our friends and neighbors and posting signs. We were counting on strong word-of-mouth referral business. The stand itself was simple and elegant—a long, folding table clad in a red and white checkered cloth. I carefully stacked cups and made sure our containers were filled with properly mixed product. At eight o'clock sharp our stand was up and running.

Corn was our first customer. We had given her a heads up on our project and she agreed to deny all knowledge of it if Flats interrogated her.

"It looks great, kids. I bet you're going to sell a bunch today."

"Thanks, Corn."

"I can't believe you got Trouble to wear your lemon suit. He looks so silly."

"Shhh...he's very sensitive about it, but we need him out there to bring in the car traffic."

"Oh, he's an attention getter for sure."

"What flavor would you like, Corn?" I asked.

"Hit me with the high octane, darling. I'm feeling a little sluggish this morning." She chugged the contents and put the cup back down on the table. "Oooh, that's nice. Pour me a refill," she said, slapping down another bill.

"Don't get carried away. That stuff's pretty potent."

"Yeah, good thing Flats is away, I might hurt the man if I get my buzz on," she mumbled.

I figured she might get hyper, but didn't think she would become dangerous to anyone in our family. Still, this was something we hadn't thought of. We would definitely need to limit the number of Red Bull cocktails each customer could drink. For kids we would need to make sure they had a designated bike rider.

Corn couldn't help herself and wandered out to see Pyckle.

Trying to act cool, despite his predicament, Pyckle attempted to wax philosophic. "Is your lemonade glass half empty or half full, sista?"

"Depends if you're drinking or pouring, Trouble."

"True that..." he said, nodding his lemon in agreement.

Corn snapped a picture with her phone before he could react and then ran back laughing.

"You better delete that!" he yelled.

"Corn, please don't upset our Pyckle," I pleaded.

She was still chuckling as she went up the steps and back into the house.

A few minutes later a group of teenagers drove past and hollered, "Dance for us, lemon-boy!"

"Dance on this!" he retorted while pointing to his bulbous, lemon crotch area with his middle fingers.

"Stop, Pyckle." I called. "They could be customers. Just do a little dance."

He flipped me off as well.

Later in the morning a cute girl stopped at the stand and asked if he would dance. This time he smiled and started to move. It would be best described as the cabbage patch in a straight jacket.

Our sales started solid and gained strength by mid-morning. Then, like a door slamming, traffic stopped dead. After a half hour without a single customer, Stone and I knew something was up.

I tried to prime the pump. "Dance some more, Pyckle. Think about Mrs. Marge's flowers." He proceeded to drop the Dougie like a wrapped sausage.

The cause of our problem arrived on a bike minutes later. A hipster-looking, twenty-something pulled up on his single-speed, cyclo-cross cruiser. He parked in front of our stand and glared down at us without saying a word.

"Would you like a lemonade, sir?" I said sweetly.

"No, I'd like for you trolls to shut down this illegal enterprise."

My heart sank and tears welled up in my eyes.

Stone stood up and assumed the roll of big brother. "Don't talk to my sister that way."

"I wasn't just talking to her, boy."

Pyckle could sense there was trouble and slowly shuffled our way. The visitor saw him and cracked up.

"This is sad," he said, shaking his head. "Even more reason to shut it down." He shifted his khaki messenger bag around and pulled out a stack of pages, throwing them on the table before me. "Here you go, kiddies. It's your cease and desist order."

"What!?" Stone cried. "Who are you?"

"I represent an interested party," he said. His bag was still open and I could see a Starbucks apron inside. It made my stomach crawl.

"We just opened! How can you already have a legal order prepared?" Stone asked.

"We keep a template in Word. It takes a few seconds to fill in the blanks. Besides, we're living in real time, little boy. This is what happens when you try to mess with the big boys."

"Really? Are you in first grade or something?"

"No! Second year law."

Stone rolled his eyes.

"There's a whole list of infractions in there," he continued. "You don't have a retail license posted, your manufacturing facility hasn't been inspected, your recycling program for plastic cups doesn't meet the Green Council guidelines, etc., etc. If you can rectify all of the listed items you're free to reopen. Good luck."

I turned to the order's addendum and saw at least twenty items listed.

"Oh, also I went ahead and collected these for you as well," he said snottily, tossing the torn pieces of our signs on the table. I'd spent hours working on the signs.

"Why are you doing this?" I said through tears.

"We recently introduced a new line of lemonade spritzers— they're totally delish—and we can't have you interfering with our roll out. Our store is a beta site."

"Which one? There are like a dozen Starbucks within a one mile range."

"None of your business. And lemonade is no longer your business either."

Pyckle had arrived and could see my emotional distress. "What the hell's going on over here?"

"He's shutting us down," Stone said, looking completely deflated.

"My ass! I'll shut him down." Pyckle leaned forward and charged the hipster. He drove the lemon stem into the man's chest and knocked him sideways. The man caught his balance and easily shoved Pyckle onto his back. He began to flail his arms helplessly and swear.

I was now crying and laughing at the same time, making sort of a hiccup sound. Pyckle's shame was one I knew well.

The man mounted his bike and rode off.

"Oh, so that's how it is? You better ride fast, hipster-bitch. I'm gonna bust you up good," Pyckle yelled.

An evil competitor was another threat we hadn't fully considered. Stone jogged down the street and found that the signs that hadn't been destroyed were defaced. Starbucks didn't mess around.

After standing Pyckle back upright (I pushed him over once more to cheer myself up) we gathered around the stand to figure out what to do. We'd made a modest profit, but not achieved our full potential in the lemonade industry. There was still plenty of product on ice and only so much would fit in our fridge, the rest would go to waste.

I was now in that post-crying phase of sniffling and uneven breathing. A strange sensation ran across my body and I instinctively looked toward the Baddley house. Once again I had the feeling someone was watching us.

A moment later we heard a text message arrive on Stone's phone. He was so despondent he didn't even bother to check it. When the second reminder chimed, he fetched the phone from his pocket.

His faced screwed up in a confused look when he read the message. "That's weird."

"What's it say?" I asked.

"It says: 'Don't close yet.'"

"Who sent it?"

"Don't know. It's from a blocked number."

"Just like the phone call that day by the tree!"

"Yeah..."

In unison, we all turned slowly toward the Baddley house.

"Do you think?" Pyckle asked.

"I don't know."

"Well, what should we do?" I asked, suddenly feeling better.

"I think we stay open," Stone said decisively. He picked up the cease and desist order and tore it into small pieces. "I don't see any order."

"Yeah, boy," Pyckle said and we all high fived. Actually his was more like a mid-five due to his limited mobility.

Then we saw it. A wave of people headed in our direction.

"Oh...my...God..." I mouthed. "Is it?"

"I think so," Stone answered.

"Zombies?" Pyckle asked with wide eyes.

"No, you idiot. A flash mob."

"What should we do?"

"SELL!" Stone said triumphantly.

A mass of smiling faces queued up in front of us. I poured and passed as fast as I could. I didn't even have time to ask where they'd come from. Stone was pulling in one-dollar bills like a stripper with a Dyson vacuum.

"How many glasses?" I asked a woman with two kids. She simply held up her three middle fingers without saying a word.

Then three boys stepped up. They also held up their three middle fingers.

They were followed by Siamese triplets. Again, the one on the end did the three-finger thing.

Next came a pimp with greased-back hair and a girl on each arm. He held up the three fingers, but also gave me a dirty look, which made me feel as if he had more interest in me than just my lemonade. I thanked him and moved on to the next customer.

Three cups became a surprisingly common order. It was weird, almost like some kind of sign. We joked about it being a salute to our revolt against the establishment.

When we finally caught up with our backlog, I asked where everyone was coming from. The first wave of people said they'd received broadcast texts telling them to check out Maybach's coolest lemonade stand ASAP.

As a second wave of new customers arrived, I started getting a different answer. They told me they'd tried to beat the heat with a new lemonade spritzer from Starbucks, but all of the locations had abruptly closed. There were rumors of a bomb threat and a group of Peacekeepers in EOD suits were operating around the locations on Main Street. Suspicious looking scones and biscotti were being removed and detonated with trigger explosives. Someone had unleashed chaos upon our tormentor.

When I heard about the bomb threat I looked askance toward the Baddley house. But then another possibility dawned on me: Corn. It was just the kind of thing she would do to help us.

I hoped we'd get answers later, but my more immediate concern was restocking our supplies. I ran to the house and grabbed all the lemons Corn had in the kitchen. I gave her a handful of cash and she headed down to the Jitney Jungle to buy even more.

Business continued at a torrid pace through mid-afternoon. We barely had time to eat the sandwiches Corn had made and then she brought out a plate of cookies to keep us going.

Around four o'clock we received a visit from the local head of the Peacekeepers, a person they used to call the sheriff. His name was Hell Tate and he happened to be good friends with Flats. The two had lived in Maybach their whole lives and known each other since they were children.

"Good afternoon, kids," he said, tipping his hat. He looked over at Pyckle and nodded with a wry smile.

"What can we do for you, sir?" I asked.

"Is Flats around?"

"No, he's out of town today, sir."

"I see. Well, I'm investigating a bomb threat against Starbucks. Some flake over there with a patchy, wannabe beard said he suspected a couple of kids running an illegal lemonade stand. I followed the crowds and ended up here. Do you know anything about it?"

"Oh dear!" I said, putting my hands on the sides of my face like Munch's *The Scream*. "I don't know anything about mixing up explosives. All I know about is mixing up the sweetest lemonade this side of the Mississippi. Do you have any clues?"

"Just the phone message, which was recorded."

"What did the person sound like? Was it a black female in her thirties with a hint of island lilt in her voice?"

"No, more like a middle-aged white guy."

"And you didn't get a phone number?"

"No, it was a blocked number. Couldn't trace it."

"Hmmm. That is strange indeed and I don't know anything about it. We've been out here selling delicious lemonade all day."

"It does look mighty fine. I'll take a glass for the road."

"This one's on the house," Stone said. "For Maybach's finest."

"Thank you, son."

I looked around and then slipped him a cookie. "And Flats doesn't need to know anything about this, right?"

39

"Sure thing," he said with a wink. "Have a good evening, kids."

When we heard the church bells strike six we decided to wind down. It had been a wild day, but we'd managed to pull it off. Our hard work had resulted in success and profits. It was an amazing feeling.

The smell of success lingered, while our profits were promptly redistributed in our next poker game with Pyckle. The wealth transfer continued when we saw him run across our yard in his hoodie, heading to Mrs. Marge's house.

As for Stone, he reaped another dividend. The business had rekindled a spark inside him. In the coming years it would turn into a raging fire.

6.

Those who can, do; those who can't, teach.
~ George Bernard Shaw

The summer ended before we knew it and soon it was time to head back to school. We said goodbye to our beloved Pyckle who was going back to college. After the lemonade stand we kept a lower profile. Flats eventually found out, but by that point we were able to pass it off as a non-event. Our questions about the bomb threat and flash mob organizer faded like green leaves in the fall.

That year I began the fourth grade. I fully expected to get Mr. Holland, who had been Stone's teacher. He was easygoing and thought the world of my brother, so I figured the year was going to be a breeze. To my surprise when I entered the room there was a young, perky lady greeting the arriving students. A starched, white button-down shirt and black pencil skirt accentuated her ample curves in all the right places. As she spoke, her dimpled cheeks danced between curtains of freshly styled black locks. She was the kind of girl Flats would say was *nicely put together*.

"Good morning," she said, reaching down to shake my hand.

"Hello," I replied. "Who are you?"

She pointed to the name written on the chalkboard behind her. "I'm Miss Fisher, the new fourth grade teacher."

"Oh," I said, with clear disappointment. "What happened to Mr. Holland?"

"He died this summer," she answered, the cheery smile never leaving her face.

"What!?"

"Yeah, he was brutally murdered."

"That's terrible," I said, my emotions doing a complete one-eighty.

"Ahhh-ha! I got ya'," she said, pinching my cheek playfully. "You should have seen the look on your face."

"So...he's not really dead?"

"No, he's taking a sabbatical. Spending time writing a play or opus or something silly like that. Couldn't get it done with all the demands of teaching, blah, blah, blah..."

"Why would you say such a horrible thing?"

"I was getting tired of everyone asking me about this Holland guy. And I felt like messing with you. This year is going to be so much fun. I can't wait to get my hands all over you little balls of clay," she said, squeezing my shoulders so hard it hurt.

"Okay...cray-cray..." I said under my breath as I took my seat.

The bell rang and Miss Fisher addressed the class rules and expectations. While she covered the boilerplate issues I looked around and surveyed my classmates.

It was a mix of new and familiar faces. There were a number of kids who were technically much older than me. I say *technically* because they were born years ahead of me, but their birth certificates had been altered to meet fourth grade requirements. The school did this to avoid a loss of funding for children who didn't progress adequately. In turn, numerous boys had full mustaches and goatees, while many girls had D cups. It made me feel very self-conscious when we changed for P.E. in the locker room.

I felt a tap on my shoulder and turned to see Chucky Smalls sitting behind me.

"What do you want?" I hissed.

"Look at her name."

"Yeah, what about it?"

"It says Miss Carrie Fisher."

"And?"

"Wasn't she in *Star Wars*? I wonder if it's the same lady."

"Seriously, Chucky? Like she'd be teaching here in Maybach? Besides, that movie came out like a million years ago. She'd be older than Yoda by now."

"Oh. I guess you're right. Still, I'd like to see *this* Carrie Fisher rocking a metal bikini."

"Dream on, Chucky."

I turned back and saw Miss Fisher staring at me. "You, young lady," she said, pointing.

"It's Spy Pinch, ma'am."

"Your name is Spy? Are you one of Bruce Willis's kids or something?"

"That's what people call me, ma'am. My given name is Jean Luc."

"Well, Jean Luc, it looked like you and your boyfriend had an important topic to discuss. Would you like to share it with the rest of us?"

"Uhh, we were just saying...uhh...how pretty you are. And he's not my boyfriend."

"Are you sassin' me?"

"No, ma'am."

She grabbed something from her desk and moved aggressively toward me. "Cause if you are I'll cut your tongue out with these scissors. They're super sharp," she said, standing over me with her arm cocked like Mrs. Bates in the motel bathroom.

I reared back, pinned in my desk chair. "I'm sorry, Miss Fisher. Please don't take my tongue. I don't want to be an Avox!"

"Ahhh-ha! Got you again! Maybe I need to send you down to third grade. You're not a real fast learner, Jean Luc," she said through evil laughter.

"Are you nuts?"

She turned and looked at me with wide, crazy eyes. "Don't you ever say that again," she warned while snapping the scissors at me. I had no idea if she was still joking or not. I clamped my mouth and slouched in my chair.

Miss Fisher returned to the front of the class and continued as though nothing had happened. I had a sinking feeling that fourth grade was going to be a lot worse than I'd expected.

"Now, we've been told that everyone needs to start moving up each year. Let me tell you about our new curriculum. There are two primary components. First, is the standardized test to measure student progress. I have an advance copy of it here," she said, holding up a light blue test booklet. "Our studies will focus exclusively on passing this test in the spring. Instead of teaching you how to fish, I will be jamming the fish down your throat. When the time comes you damn well better be able to regurgitate it. Is that clear?"

The room was silent.

"The second part will be career tracking. We used to wait until high school or college to let you figure that out, but in order to better compete in a global economy the Lawmakers of Pander have decided your lot in life will be determined in fourth grade. The intent is to stamp out any traces of childhood. Time to man—and woman—up! Isn't that exciting? And since I'm your teacher, the rest of your lives are pretty much in my hands," she said, clapping with rigid elbows like one of those toy monkeys with cymbals.

A boy I didn't recognize raised his hand.

"Yes?"

"Ma'am, why are they changing this? My pa wanted me to learn readin', writin', and 'rithmatic this year."

"I don't care *why* they are changing it. It's the law and if y'all achieve a certain level I'll get a bonus. Pretty simple."

I tried to hold my tongue—in part for fear it might be severed—but the words just came out. "Shouldn't elementary school provide a broad base of knowledge? Flats thinks we should know about lots of things?"

"Who is Flats?"

"He's my father."

Miss Fisher gazed around wildly, but didn't say anything. She looked under her desk and began opening and closing the drawers. Then she walked over to a file cabinet and did the same thing. She even picked up the trashcan and peered inside.

"Miss Fisher?" I asked cautiously.

"Yes?"

"What are you doing?"

"I'm still looking for your daddy, Jean Luc. Can't seem to find him anywhere. I guess it means he's not teaching this class."

"Oh, I get it. But..."

She picked her scissors back up and clicked them viciously. That was something the entire class learned the first day. When you saw or heard the scissors it was time to shut the hell up. Pavlov would have been proud.

44

Her smile reappeared and she went on unfazed by our interruptions. "Now let me explain the five factions you can consider. Everyone please listen, this is important if you care about the rest of your lives."

We were stunned when Tristan Yule stood up and headed for the door. He was about six foot two with numerous tattoos and piercings. I'd estimate his real age was about twenty-two.

"Where do you think you're going?" Miss Fisher asked as she stepped in front of him.

"I'm not hanging around for this crap. The only reason I came to school was so I could dominate in kickball at recess. If we have to do all this other garbage then screw it. I want to get home in time to watch *The Price Is Right*."

He was taller than Miss Fisher, but she held her ground. I saw the scissors in the hand behind her back. She could've used them to cut the tension in the room at that moment.

"Tristan, please don't diverge from our program yet."

He looked directly in her eyes and tilted his head, like he was trying to figure something out. Then it got weird. I thought for sure she was going to stab him in the leg with her scissors. Instead, she reached up with her free hand and ran her fingers through his long, wavy hair.

"Tristan, I think you'll enjoy my class once you get to know me better."

"Well…"

She touched his arm and turned her eyes toward his seat.

He hesitated for a second and then sat back down.

Another student leaned over and whispered, "Looks like your going to learn after all, Tris'."

"Ha! She'll be the one learning…"

Miss Fisher returned to her desk, picked up a stack of papers, and handed them out.

"Here's our first test. At the top you'll see Tippy the turtle and a pirate. You need to pick one—see, you still get choices—and in the blank space below draw that picture the best you can. If you do a good enough job you may be an artist. That's the first faction."

We had an hour to finish, but most kids were done in minutes. I peered over my shoulder and saw Chucky had drawn pairs of stick people in strange positions. Later, after we'd taken a sex-ed class, I understood what those positions really were. Chucky wasn't a particularly good artist, but he was very creative.

Miss Fisher collected our renderings and mailed them to a place in the Northern District called Minnesota.

The second test was outside. Miss Fisher led us to the playground where a large grill was rolling with flames. She handed each student a beef patty and a spatula and we took turns trying to make hamburgers. This test was meant to identify the burger-flipping faction. Sadly, a number of students suffered severe burns and were sent to the nurse's office.

Back in the classroom, Miss Fisher set up lab stations with traditional school subject projects. There were areas for biology, chemistry, geometry, and others. The activities were engaging and most of the kids participated, *doing* all kinds of worthwhile things. However, several kids dropped out and sat together at a table in the rear of the room.

Miss Fisher approached the group and we watched closely, expecting her to go off on them for quitting.

"How's it going, kids?" she asked calmly.

"I couldn't *do* any of those things," one boy pouted with his arms crossed.

"I *can't* either," whined another.

"Don't you see? That *is* the test. Those who can, do; those who can't, teach. Welcome to the academia faction!" she exclaimed and gave them all big hugs.

"Seriously?" Chucky Smalls muttered before jamming a scalpel into his frog at the dissection station.

It had been a stressful morning and we thought we were finally getting a break when Miss Fisher announced we would be heading to the gymnasium. On the way I decided to chat her up.

"Excuse me, Miss Fisher."

"Yes, Jean Luc."

"Am I doing all right so far?"

"I think so. No burns from the grill at least. Some kids are easy to pick, but you are a bit trickier. What do you want to do with your life?"

"Honestly, I hadn't given it much thought until a few hours ago."

"Have you ever had a job?"

"Oh, yes. This summer we ran a lemonade stand. I was the head of production."

"Well, Jean Luc, aren't you *enterprising*. We'll see how the rest of the tests go."

"Thank you, Miss Fisher," I replied and then dropped back in the line not wanting to push my luck.

When we arrived, the gym was set up for a game of dodgeball—one of my favorites. Teams were picked and we lined up on opposing sides. The whistle blew and all hell broke loose. Bowling balls had been substituted for the usual rubber balls.

The first victim was a nerdy kid named Harry who yelled, "Let's play quidditch instead! I'll get the broomsticks."

Several of the big kids hit him with balls simultaneously, shattering numerous bones and putting him in a full body cast. A high shot snapped his glasses and left him with a jagged scar on his forehead.

As the blood bath continued, it became clear this was a test for the warrior faction. The winners would be directed toward positions as Peacekeepers, soldiers, and New Jersey housewives. The only way us smaller kids survived was by hiding behind our massive janitor, Mr. Hagrid.

Mercifully the final whistle blew and the wretched remains of our class staggered back to Miss Fisher's room for the final test. Everyone breathed a sigh of relief when we saw it was a written test and didn't involve flaming hot coals or twelve pound projectiles.

I scanned the exam papers and saw a long list of moral and ethics questions such as:

If no one were looking, would you "borrow" another student's lunch money?

Bribery is an integral part of doing business (true/false).

If you could get away with murder, would you consider it an option?

Did you have sexual relations with Ms. Lewinsky?

It was the craziest test I'd ever taken. *What the hell is this?* I wondered. I answered the questions honestly, turned in my paper, and waited for Miss Fisher's explanation.

"Well done, students. That was your final test for today."

"Those were terrible questions. What faction is that for?" a girl in the front row asked.

"If you were destined for the final faction I would hope it would be obvious to you, dear."

The girl shrugged in frustration.

"The most devious, dishonest, and incompetent will of course be tracked toward politics," Miss Fisher clarified.

It was like a group light bulb went on over our heads and we all nodded in unison.

The girl in the front asked a follow-up question that was on a lot of our minds. "What if you don't fit into any of the five factions?"

"Those individuals will go to a category called: potpourri—like on *Jeopardy*. They can be placed in any random job. Freelance writers, concert security guards when the Taylor Swift tour comes to town, and workers in those tiny kiosks at the mall. Stuff like that."

She glanced at the clock and then rang a brass hand bell sitting on her desk.

"Time for lunch everyone. Single file line down to the cafeteria please."

I was so discombobulated I could barely eat. I nibbled on an Uncrustable and sipped my Capri Sun. When my friend Gomer offered me half of his jelly donut I turned him down.

Back in class, Miss Fisher allowed us to watch a movie because it was the first day. She even let us pick between the two she'd brought in. We voted for *Full Metal Jacket* over *The Silence of the Lambs.*

When the final bell sounded I sprinted to meet Stone on the front steps. As we walked home I recounted the details of my bizarre day. His old curriculum had been grandfathered in under a provision in the No Child Will Survive bill, making for a far less eventful day.

A later amendment changed the legislation to the One Child Will Survive bill. To commemorate it they held a big festival in

Capitropolis featuring two students from each district. I was totally bummed when I didn't get selected to go.

Stone could tell I was feeling down so he started talking about all the fun things we'd done over the summer. Our route took us past the Baddley compound and he stopped to point out the exact spot where he'd touched the house.

"I've never felt so alive," he recounted.

"Yeah, that was pretty awesome, Stone," I said, feeling a little better. "And how about finding your phone in the tree?"

"I know, right? You know what, Spy? We should check the knot again to see if anything else is in there."

"Huh? Why would there be anything in there beside squirrel scat?"

"Come on, you never know."

He raced over to the tree as I followed. I wasn't tall enough to reach the spot so Stone stretched his arm up into the dark hole. He felt around for a second and found something.

"It's soft and furry, like a rabbit's foot."

He pulled it out slowly, but as soon as he saw the item he flung it on the ground.

"Oh God!"

"What is that?" I shrieked in horror.

"Eww. It looks like a dead mockingbird."

"This was a bad idea, let's go."

Stone was furiously wiping his hands on his pants. "Yeah, that was gross. But, Spy, I felt something else in there."

I was shocked when he began fishing around in the darkness again.

"Got it!"

This time he produced two colorful pieces of card stock.

"Are those what I think they are?" I asked.

"iTunes gift cards!" he cheered. "Fifty bucks each! Score! One for each of us, Spy."

He handed me one of the cards, but then I had a change of heart. "Stone, what if somebody lost these? Maybe we should put them back."

"What!? Are you high? Who would *lose* two gift cards inside a tree? A squirrel with an iPod? If you don't want yours I'll take it," he said, reaching for my card.

"No, I guess you're right. Finders keepers."

We skipped the rest of the way home and ran to our rooms to download some new music.

7.

Proof of our society's decline is that Halloween has become a broad daylight event for many.
~ Robert Kirby

Early October brought the first chills of fall. The weather triggered changes in the environment and also in the minds of children. It was a reminder that the "big three"—Halloween, Thanksgiving, and Christmas—were on deck and chemicals in our brains dialed up the excitement.

With the daylight hours getting shorter we spent more evenings inside, usually watching TV with Corn. By that point the fall television season was in full swing and we could count on the major networks to keep us enthralled with fresh episodes of our favorite sitcoms and dramas.

After years of production, *NCIS* and *CSI* had made their way through all the major cities and second tier locations now had their own versions of the show. We watched *NCIS: Wichita Falls* religiously. The biggest mystery was what Navy investigators were doing in a landlocked city in Texas. However, we couldn't get hooked on *CSI: Sarasota*. It was mainly just old people dying of natural causes.

Luckily, the "reality show" craze had finally run its course. The shows became so extreme that viewers grew desensitized. It got to the point where they ran a program about kids killing each other in an arena and no one was even fazed by it.

While we gathered around the tube, Flats was usually reading in his study. Sometimes he read for pleasure, but most of it was business related—what he called his *investigative* work. He said he was looking for people to help, but Stone and I interpreted that as people or entities to sue.

He read medical reports looking for cases of people suffering from unusual syndromes or unreported side effects. ED drug warnings mentioned the risk of a four-hour erection, but Flats once located a guy who had a woody for four weeks! When the man *finally* returned from Las Vegas they filed suit. Unfortunately, the client decided to take the drug again and suffered a heart attack in week two. The man died with a smile on his face and Flats obtained a large settlement for the family. Flats called it a win-win, overlooking the man's irresponsible behavior.

As Stone and I grew older we began to question much of the work that Flats pursued. We believed our father had started in the legal profession with benevolent expectations. He wanted to fight on behalf of the underdog, but somewhere along the line that mentality was lost. Instead of controlling his career path, the cases were shaping the type of lawyer he became.

His victories became progressively larger, but each was hollower than the last. There were also wider swaths of collateral damage left in his wake. Even though we knew it was eating at him, he did his best to keep his feelings buried. That Halloween some of his demons began to crawl out of the ground.

Each year, Stone and I spent countless hours picking and designing our costumes. Corn and Flats were good sports and would dress up as well, often complimenting our outfits. The prior year, Stone was Batman and I was Robin. Yeah, I know, pretty cliché. Anyway, Flats was Alfred the butler and Corn squeezed into a tight, shiny black outfit to portray Catwoman. We were the envy of the neighborhood.

After Stone and I went to bed, Flats and Corn kept up the act. I heard Corn sneak in through Flats's window. She cracked her whip and asked him, "Trick or treat?" It sounded like they had a lot of fun.

Departing from the superhero craze, Stone and I decided to go as evil ghouls. Stone had originally suggested I repurpose my ham/lemon costume as a human heart with real flowing blood. It sounded cool, but I knew it would hinder my gathering abilities. Corn was going to be a ghost; she loved the irony of walking around Maybach at night wearing a white sheet. Flats had been procrastinating, but with All Hallows' Eve rapidly approaching we finally had to force the issue one evening.

"Yo, Flats! Come here," Stone hollered.

"Yes, Stone, is something wrong?" Flats said as he entered.

"Have you decided what you are going to be for Halloween?"

"No, I haven't. What's our game plan this year? Fun or scary?"

"We're all going spooky."

"How about a zombie?"

"Nah, they're way overplayed."

"Vampire?" he suggested, bearing his teeth in a menacing manner.

"Played..."

"All right, what do you suggest?"

"Hmmm..." I thought. "Maybe something to compliment our ghouls and Corn's ghost. Perhaps one of our undead victims. Stone, what do you call a creature with no soul?"

"Flats," he answered without hesitation.

Corn let out a hearty laugh, but I still remember the look on my father's face. Stone might as well have given him a sucker punch below the belt. It was an existential slap of disrespect that no parent wants from his or her offspring.

"I'll just be a corpse," Flats said before turning and walking out.

I shot Stone a look, knowing he'd said something to upset Flats.

"What? Did I do something wrong?" he asked, turning to Corn for an answer.

"Oh, don't worry yourself, Stone. It's just that he tries his best to fit in with ya'll. He's older than your friends' dads so it can be tough. Halloween is one of the times when he can still participate."

"But he doesn't do anything else with us. All Flats knows about is the law," Stone complained. Unlike other boys, Stone had never tossed a baseball, thrown a football, or flung a pelota in a jai alai fronton with his father.

"Now, Stone, don't be too hard on him. You know he's sensitive about his work. He tries to do the right thing, but he has to deal with the system. Underneath that three-piece courtroom suit

Flats is a good man."

"But what's he good at besides suing people?" Stone pushed.

"Oh, your daddy's good at lots of things," Corn said with a far-off look and dirty grin. "He's doing what he has to do. You'll understand better when you're older. Kids and grown ups can see the exact same thing quite differently."

"Why?"

"Just the way it is. Always has been and always will be. Now run along and get ready for bed."

***

Our house had been decorated, which looked cool and spooky, and then liability proofed by Flats, which looked lame. He'd placed orange reflective tape along the front sidewalk to avoid potentials falls. Motion sensors triggered massive floodlights capable of generating enough lumens to kill a real vampire. There were faux headstones in the yard that said: *Beware! Enter At Your Own Risk!* Below in fine print they read: *Seriously, by entering these premises you agree to waive all liability against the property owner and bear all risk for any injuries sustained thereon.*

Halloween fell on a Wednesday night, which sucked because we had school the next day. After classes let out, Stone and I had a few friends over for a small party. There we laid out our plans for crisscrossing the surrounding neighborhoods in order to optimize our haul.

When the sun finally disappeared for the day we embarked upon our journey. Following our typical procedure, Flats the somber corpse stayed at the house to be a distributor. Corn chaperoned our group. It was good to have a ghost watching your back in case another crew tried to run up on you for a nasty trick.

In movies I'd seen how Halloween used to be. Kids would walk around and gather candy from random people, most of whom they didn't even know. For children in Maybach, however, the rules had changed. For a while all trick-or-treating had to take place *before* sunset, usually in the form of a parade. Parents loved it; kids not so much. Then they even tried to change the name from Halloween (too spooky and satanic) to Voluntary Sharing Day. That was the straw that broke the camel's back. The following year kids boycotted the treat part and focused solely on a massive campaign of tricks. When Maybach's residents awoke to a town covered in eggs, toilet paper, and flaming pet feces they reinstated the old policies.

The candy issue, however, remained a point of contention. Leaders wanted to maintain control over all that sugar; there were simply too many risks.

The solution was the voucher system. Here's how it worked. Residents would purchase bulk quantities of their favorite sweets and then take it to a local collection center. There they would exchange it for vouchers, which in turn could be handed out to children. We still went through the normal door-to-door process, but our bags were filled with little slips of colored paper instead of actual candy. We then returned to the collection center to trade our vouchers for the candy, which had been X-rayed and inspected by the Peacekeeper Safety Authority or PSA. Of course the bastards were skimming the best stuff for themselves, just like they did at the airports they were supposed to be protecting. Yeah, Halloween had become a royal cluster hump.

The program did have a caveat. If you were not satisfied with the candy options in your neighborhood you could use a voucher to get your candy in another neighborhood with better offerings. Luckily we lived in a top-performing neighborhood already. Still, I always felt bad for the kids in those "other" neighborhoods who got stuck with bad candy if they didn't use their vouchers. A lot of it just got thrown away and candy is a terrible thing to waste…

We scurried from house to house with unbridled enthusiasm, determined not to let the system ruin our fun. The vouchers listed what type of candy they could be exchanged for so there was still the thrill of getting something special. Up and down the street you heard kids calling out their spoils: "I got a Snickers!" and "They're giving out Three Musketeers over there!" and "Skip that house, they're unloading generic hard candy."

Horse-trading soon commenced during the trips between houses. I was happy with a variety of candy and didn't make a lot of transactions. Stone, however, was a sugar man. He would dump all of his chocolate to pick up some SweeTARTS, Nerds, or Bottlecaps.

With costumes on, many of the kids were unrecognizable. Others, though, were easy to identify. After turning onto a new street, I spotted a boy from school who suffered from alopecia. He was carrying a set of drumsticks so I assumed he was dressed as Phil Collins again.

I called out to him as he walked away from a house I had yet to visit. "Hey, Charlie Brown, what did you get?"

"I got a voucher for a rock," he said in his normal, dejected voice.

"Bummer, dude," I said before hurrying past.

We had been on the move for roughly two hours when Corn the disgruntled ghost started to moan. "Spy and Stooooone. It's time to gooooo hooooome."

"Just a few more streets? Please. We'll share some of our candy when we pick it up."

"Okay. Fifteen more minutes and then we start heading back. And you're both into me for a KitKat—full size, not one of those puny fun sizes."

"Deal," we said in unison.

Heading further west, we heard an increasing amount of noise up ahead. Based on the screaming and yelling we assumed someone had set up a haunted house. Our group was drawn to it like zombies seeking human flesh.

Rounding the corner onto Mockingbird Lane, we finally saw the source of the disturbance. We moved cautiously down the street, slowly approaching the intersection with Cemetery Lane. There, two of Maybach's strangest families lived directly across from each other.

The Addams and Munster families seemed to think every day was Halloween. They were all totally Goth—even the parents, grandparents, and cousins. And they weren't Goth posers; they lived it. The kids rode black bikes and the parents drove black cars. When Eddie brought his pet in for show-and-tell at school it was black. He said it was a hamster, but it was obviously a large rat with the tail cut off.

Both clans lived in towering, gray mansions. The only creepier house in town was the Baddley place. Given their inclinations, October 31st was a high holiday and they always tried to outdo each other in terms of spookiness. Normally it was good spirited, but that year it had turned ugly.

Our group stopped and watched with a combination of terror and amusement as Lurch and Herman Munster went toe-to-toe in the street. A brutal head-butt dropped Lurch like a sequoia and then Mr. Munster was on top of him. Mr. Munster let out a disturbing laugh while stomping on Lurch's skull with his thick-soled jackboots. I can still remember that haunting, "Hauh-hauh-hauh-hauh!"

We jumped to the curb as the DRAG-U-LA roared down the street. Grandpa Munster was driving and as he passed we heard a gruesome mix of jingling chains and high-pitched screams from Cousin Itt, who was being dragged from the rear bumper.

The rest of the family members were engaged in hand-to-hand combat using an assortment of medieval weapons. Overall, it looked like the Munsters were kicking the Addams family's asses.

"Damn! It looks like *The Purge* up in here," Corn said. "We better be gettin' back, kids."

"Corn, can't we stay for a while to watch?" I pleaded.

"All right, but not too long."

We could tell she was interested in the macabre tableau as well.

"Thanks," I said, giving her a big hug before taking a seat on the curb. We watched from the sidelines as the carnage continued. When a severed head rolled past us Corn said it was definitely time to leave. She would run us out to the collection center and then home. On the way, we finally heard the wail of Peacekeeper sirens heading toward the brawl. Somebody always had to spoil the fun.

***

An hour later, Stone and I were sitting on our front porch, surrounded by a debris field of empty candy wrappers. The mainlining of thousands of sugar-derived calories had offset our exhaustion from the night's march.

Flats had stepped inside for a moment and our attention turned to the Baddley house. Across the way we could see its harsh outline in the dim evening light.

"You know, I've been thinking about it, Spy. Maybe Halloween is our chance."

"For what?"

"To get to the door. Trick-or-treating provides the perfect scenario. We'd have costumes on and a valid reason for going up there."

"But everyone already knows *not* to go there on Halloween, Stone."

"Even better. It'll be like a sneak attack."

"I don't think I could do it," I admitted.

"What if there was a bunch of us though? If we had ten or fifteen kids who all went together. Safety in numbers."

"That sounds like a better idea, but you'd have to be sure some of the kids didn't chicken out. If one of them suddenly bolted the rest would follow."

"Yeah, you're probably right. Still, I'm going to think about it some more. We have a whole year to figure it out now."

Flats returned to the porch and we recounted more of our evening exploits with crickets providing background music. Our stories were interrupted when a Peacekeeper cruiser pulled up in front of our house. Hell Tate climbed out and walked up the front steps.

"Evenin', ya'll," he said.

"Evenin', Hell. Everything okay?" Flats replied.

"Just fine. I was out this way and thought I'd stop by to say hello. Hadn't seen you in a while, Flats."

"Busy as ever and my cases have kept me traveling. Why don't you come on up and sit a spell on the porch with us?"

"Thank ya', Flats. Don't mind if I do."

Corn heard the voices and came out to greet Mr. Tate.

"Evenin', Corn," Mr. Tate said, tipping his hat.

"Well, howdy do, Mr. Tate. I still have a little pumpkin pie and apple cider in the kitchen. Could I interest you in some?"

"Oh, I'd be very interested indeed. It's been a long night."

"I'll be back in a jiffy."

"This must be one of your favorite nights of the year," Flats observed.

"Boy, oh boy," Mr. Tate said letting out a long sigh.

"Sometimes kids will be kids."

"Unfortunately, the adults are just as bad or worse. We may need to go back to daylight hours again."

Stone and I both let out groans of disapproval.

Corn returned with a plate and glass and handed them to our guest. "Here you go."

"Thank you."

After shoveling down a big bite and chasing it with cider Mr. Tate proclaimed, "That's delicious. It'd be hard to have a better combination for Halloween. It's like cold lemonade on a hot summer day." He looked our way and winked.

"You're welcome. So, Mr. Tate, I've always wondered, where did you get such a crazy name?" Corn asked.

"Well, my family came from the panhandle of Florida. There's a big forest there called Tate's Hell—named after one of my ancestors. My folks wanted to pay homage and my mom had a twisted sense of humor so my given name was going to be Heck Tate, not quite so edgy. Then she spent six days in labor with me. When the hospital lady came around my mom supposedly said, 'I've just been through hell with that boy. His name shall be: Hell Tate.' The rest is history."

"And he earned it growing up. I can't believe he became a cop," Flats said.

"I bet you got hassled growing up," Corn said.

"Yeah, people gave me grief when I was the age of these here youngins," he said, motioning toward us. "Not so much anymore. If any of our prisoners try to get cute with me they get a baton to the head and a week in the hole. It pretty much keeps things in check.

"Teachers at school had the toughest time. They always tried to avoid calling on me. We had one lady who darn near lived at church. I think she washed my desk with holy water everyday after I left class. Do you remember Mrs. Smith, Flats?"

Flats nodded and smiled, joining Mr. Tate for a walk down memory lane.

"I was really talkin' 'bout your last name: Tate. I bet people called you Tater, and Po-Tate-O, and Tater Tot," Corn said chortling like she was the first person to come up with the nicknames. "Tate-Tate-Banana-Nana-Fo-Fate-Me-My-Mo-Mate—Tate."

Flats gave her a look like it was time to stop talking. She kept giggling to herself.

"So what was going on out here?" Flats asked him.

"We had to break up a brawl over on Mockingbird Lane. The Addams-Munster feud boiled over."

"We saw them in action," Corn said. "It was gettin' nasty."

"It took us a while to get there. We were already dealing with a drunken fight over in Victors' Village—a bunch of people with lots of money and no class," Mr. Tate said, shaking his head.

"When I saw a head roll down the street I knew it was time to leave."

"Oh, that. It was a real head, but from a cadaver the Addamses had placed in the yard as a decoration so at least I didn't have to deal with a murder charge. We gave them a group drunk and disorderly. Sooner or later we're going to have to Baker Act that Grandpa Munster. Heck, maybe all of 'em need to be committed."

"Things in Maybach are a lot different than when we growing up here," Flats waxed nostalgically.

"You said it, Flats, especially the last few years. The criminals have changed. Instead of headin' into the woods to blow up the occasional moonshine still I'm working on meth lab cases. I wanted to be a small town cop, not a narcotics agent."

"Times change, Hell. We just do our best to adapt and survive."

"I know, but we should be able to hang on to some of those small town ways. Like this. Sitting down and chatting with neighbors."

"I'm with you Mr. Tate. There're lots of days I'd like a big taste of the simple life." Corn said while looking down at pictures on her iPad.

"Stop by any time you want, Hell. You're always welcome here," Flats assured him. "But there ain't no going back. The future's up to them, not us," he said, swinging his head our way.

Stone and I were starting to feel like props, being referred to by everyone on the porch but not directly addressed.

"I 'spose," Mr. Tate said, staring off into the night. A moment later the Peacekeeper communication device on his wrist went off. He let out another sigh and stood up to leave. "Yep, sure miss the good ol' days. Tomorrow is another day, I guess. Thanks for the pie. Good night ya'll."

After Mr. Tate drove off we sat quietly for a spell before Flats announced it was bedtime. He was pensive that night. The way he talked about the big picture was different than his normal approach. Typically he acted like he controlled his world, not the other way around. When he spoke to Mr. Tate it seemed liked he was addressing a paradigm that had already shifted.

8.

Double, double, toil and trouble; fire burn and cauldron bubble.
~ Shakespeare

Around midnight the weight of my eyelids was finally too much for the candy high to fight. I wandered into an initial state of black unconsciousness, but soon passed through the door of dreams into a strange and wonderful world.

On the other side was a breathtaking scene where the inhabitants wore bizarre outfits and outlandish makeup. It looked like a costume party or Halloween, but this was their everyday life. Unlike the monochromatic lives of Maybach's goth kings, everything was in vivid Technicolor. I wandered around, an unnoticed bystander taking in the surreal scenery of the amazing city.

Along one of the streets I found and ice cream parlor and went in to get a snack. The man behind the counter dug out a heavy scoop of butter pecan and packed it into a waffle cone. Returning to the street I took a big lick. The flavor was delicious, but something about the texture was wrong. I looked down to see my cone filled with little scraps of paper, which looked like Maybach's vouchers. Picking one out, I read the writing. It said, "A dream you have will come true." *Hmm, maybe these are fortune cookie slips instead of vouchers*, I thought. I looked on the back and sure enough, there was a set of lottery numbers.

The beaming sun began melting the flavored papers so I licked feverishly. I made my way to a nearby park and took shelter under a sprawling shade tree.

From my vantage point I watched a group of children playing nearby. They were playing a modified version of hide-and-go-seek. Anyone could find anyone else and when they did locate another player they beat them unconscious with tree branches and rocks.

Names probably wouldn't have hurt them, but the sticks and stones broke a lot of bones.

A particularly resourceful boy set a trap and then yelled, "Olly olly oxen free!" When the others came skipping out he mowed them down with malice. While he was doing a celebration dance a hidden snare caught his ankles and yanked him upward. Dangling upside down from a branch he looked like an angry piñata. A svelte girl dropped from the tree, put on a blindfold, and then used a pipe to beat the stuffing out of her prey. When his abdomen ripped open, entrails and an assortment of wrapped candies spewed onto the ground. The survivors crawled over and helped themselves to the bounty.

Watching the display of uninhibited, carefree fun was comforting. I finished most of my cone and tossed the remaining stump in a trashcan before leaving.

The streets were free of cars, but a procession of horse drawn chariots was passing nearby. I hopped on board one of the carts and rode down the wide boulevard. Random people on the street cheered as I passed, although I had no idea why. I was simply a girl in flame retardant jammies.

The ride was so pleasant I kept going straight out of town. When the paved road turned to rough rock I finally disembarked and walked into a wide meadow. Even though it was a warm and sunny place, I felt drawn toward the dark, sinister forest in the distance.

When I entered the tree line the atmosphere changed drastically. The air became damp and earthy. The dense timber reduced the daylight to a bluish glow. I clambered and climbed over twisted roots until I arrived at a clearing with a massive oak in the center. The tree produced a humming noise and drew me closer. More specifically, a dark knothole in the trunk entranced me. It was at shoulder height and when I looked inside I could see a galaxy of stars. The opening seemed too small, but I was able to pull myself through and plunged into the emptiness beyond.

As I fell, the points of light moved faster and became more numerous. I forced my eyes to remain open as the brightness intensified. It was getting hotter, too, as though my body was somehow creating friction with the air surrounding me. I curled into a tight ball and accelerated further. Just when I thought I'd hit terminal velocity, I came to a complete stop. Allowing my limbs to relax and uncurl, I found I was in the midst of a raging fire. The flames had me surrounded on three sides so I jumped up and ran toward the opening. Every time I reached the edge, the fire progressed and created another tunnel in front of me.

Running full speed, I couldn't manage to escape. The tunnel began to narrow and the opening ahead of me shrank. The blaze was leading me toward a rapidly closing door. Determined to break free, I ran harder and leapt forward as it slammed shut. The flames stopped me like a concrete wall.

When I opened my eyes I saw the ceiling of my room bathed in swirling orange light. Had I arrived in Hell? Had I just passed through Tate's Hell?

I had to consciously remind my lungs to function and started taking deep, forced breaths. The seconds ticked as I debated whether or not I was awake or still dreaming. Sound started to return and I heard Stone's voice.

"Wake up, Spy!" he said, charging into my room. "There's a fire and we need to get out." He pulled back the covers and spun my legs off the edge of the bed.

Putting on my slippers, I still wasn't fully convinced I'd exited my candy-induced dream. As my senses slowly returned to full functioning, I accepted that I was indeed running down the stairs and out the front door of my own house, Flats and Corn's footfalls pounding right behind me.

After making it down the front steps I realized we were actually running *toward* the fire. I stopped on the sidewalk and looked back at our house, which didn't appear to be burning at all. Across the street Mrs. Marge's house was engulfed, creating the light I'd seen on my ceiling.

"Flats, is our house on fire?" I asked.

"No, Spy, but it's always best to get out first just to be sure. In case it does spread to other houses we need to be ready to run."

"Is Mrs. Marge okay?"

"Yes, I see her over there by the fence."

I saw our neighbor talking to the firemen who'd arrived on the scene, but didn't appear to be doing much to stop the fire. She was flailing her arms and yelling at the men to no avail. When she turned and saw Flats she came running toward our house. She was wearing a worn, terry robe and had a scarf pulled over her blue hair.

"Oh, this is terrible. My dear buds are burning, Flats! Please help me," she moaned as if her children were on fire.

"What can I do to help, Mrs. Marge?"

"The damn firemen aren't doing their job!"

"It'll take me a while to get a court order forcing them to work."

"No, all they've been doing is breathing in the smoke. Now they have the munchies. I need all the Doritos you've got!"

"Jeez, it sounds like a Cheech and Chong movie. All right, Corn and I will get the chips. Kids, I want you to go over there and stay out of the way."

We edged toward our property line with the Baddley place while they ran inside to raid the pantry. It was hard to look away from the inferno across the street, but I still managed to take a peek behind me. The flames reflected off two parallel windows on second floor creating a pair of ominous, orange eyes staring down at me. It was already a cool, October night and the image gave me a second layer of chills. I wished I'd had time to grab a jacket before we ran out and now Flats was busy helping Mrs. Marge. I wrapped my arms tight and tried to stay warm.

Moments later Flats and Corn delivered several bags of yummy, Frito-Lay products to the team of firefighters. They popped the bags and ate by the handful.

"Now get back to work!" Flats commanded.

"Hey, dude, if we burn, you burn with us!" one of them replied.

"Are you talking about the fire or the weed?"

"Uhhhhh…"

"Just point the damn hoses at the house. It's not that complicated."

Slowly they organized their equipment and got back to firefighting. As they started to spray water, the amount of smoke increased significantly and the fireman high-fived each other.

"Shouldn't they try to avoid the smoke?" I asked Stone.

"I thought so. Maybe this is a new technique they're using."

Once they were all back on task it didn't take long to extinguish the fire. When things appeared under control, they dropped their hoses and gathered near the back of the home, constantly staying on the downwind side. Obviously proud of their work, their faces were draped in smiles and contented looks.

Flats and Corn finally came to retrieve us.

"Why did we have to stand outside, Flats?" I asked.

"Yeah, I guess that was pretty stupid. Next time I'll let you go back inside."

I had stopped shaking and felt much warmer. Initially, I thought it was simply the heat from the fire radiating our way. Flats, however, was giving me a funny look.

"Where did you get that?" he asked, pointing straight at me.

"Get what?"

"The shirt you're wearing."

I looked down at my arms and saw I was wearing a long-sleeve, black mock turtleneck.

"I...I...I don't know, Flats. Honest, I don't know where it came from."

Stone rolled his eyes. "Seriously? How could you not know someone pulled a shirt over your head?"

"I swear. I don't know. And you need to butt out, Stone. It's none of your business."

"Awfully defensive aren't you? Last week that filthy Linus kid tried to drape his blanket over my shoulders—that boy's got some issues. Anyway, I knew immediately and threw it to the ground. If I could tell that someone had put a blanket on me you should have certainly known that someone had dressed you in a long-sleeve shirt."

"I said butt out, jerk!"

"Hey, I'm just saying, Flats. I think she's lying."

"Enough you two. It's been a long night and it's time to get back to bed. We'll worry about the shirt another time. Now move it."

Upstairs, I was glad to crawl back into bed. After everything that had happened in the past few hours I was exhausted. My new shirt was so comfortable I decided to sleep in it. I even wore it for the next few days in a row. Flats eventually made me take it off. He said people were going to think I was a weirdo if I wore the same thing all the time.

I didn't want to agree with Stone, but he was right. It was strange that I didn't know who had put the shirt on me that night. At the time I had my theory; only later would I get a definitive answer.

9.

I stopped believing in Santa Claus when I was six. Mother took me to see him in a department store and he asked for my autograph.
~ Shirley Temple

After the Halloween excitement, our lives quieted down. Then Christmas and New Year's were upon us. That meant time with extended family, which for most people also means chaos and angst.

Our two closest relatives were my father's siblings, Jacques and Emily. Aunt Em was the current resident of Pinch's Point so we still saw her on a regular basis. Uncle Jacques lived way out west, but made a point to get back to Maybach every year for Christmas. His given name was Jack Pinch, but he changed it to Jacques Pinchot when he started acting in theater. He wanted something with more pizazz in order to stand out when he moved to the entertainment district.

Both siblings had their own unique personalities, so when you added Flats to the mix the Pinch holidays were always memorable.

We were already on break from school when Uncle Jacques arrived at our house one afternoon. Stone and I saw his car pull up and we ran out to greet him. There were two reasons for our enthusiasm: one, we loved Uncle Jacques; two, he always brought us the coolest presents.

When he popped the trunk and handed Stone and I each a long, skinny box we about burst with excitement. Unless he was messing with us—which he was prone to do—we knew exactly what we would be opening on the twenty-fifth of December: guns.

Our uncle and father shared a definite sibling resemblance, but I always thought of Jacques as a smaller, hipper version of Flats. The captivating facial features and thick, black hair served him well in obtaining rolls in his acting career. Although Flats's walking kept him in good shape, Jacques made a conscious effort to stay trim and his fashionable clothes were always tailor-fit to his body shape. With no gut to hide, he tucked his shirts in even when he was dressed casually.

After stowing our presents in the front room, we helped Jacques with his luggage. Corn met us on the porch.

"Well, well, look who's back. I can't believe it's been a year since we last saw you, Mr. Jacques. And somehow you keep getting better looking," Corn said, welcoming him with a big hug.

"Bonjour, Blé, mon amour," Jacques said, putting his hand behind Corn's neck and kissing her slowly on the cheek.

"Don't be teasin' an ol' lady now. Every year you show up here and get my blood boiling. Then I have to face the facts that Santa ain't bringin' me none of your lovin'."

"Sorry, my dear. You'll just have to make do with a pinch of something else."

They had a good laugh and walked inside together.

Uncle Jacques kept us engrossed with stories of his life out west until Flats arrived home from the office. We were all sitting in the kitchen when he came in the back door carrying his briefcase and a large, cardboard box. He set his items on the counter and greeted his brother.

"Hello, Jack," he said, extending his hand formally. Our father still insisted on calling him by his original name.

"Flats," Jacques said in a dull voice, mocking our father. He shook hands and then yanked Flats in for a hug. They patted each other the back to break the ice of not having seen each other for a year. As they released, Jacques further shattered the ice by leaning in and giving Flats a kiss right on the lips.

"Cut it out, Jack," Flats said, shoving Jacques away in embarrassment.

"Oh, Flats, don't be such a prude. They may have a homophobic streak a mile wide down here in the Southern Trial District, but last time I checked incest is fully embraced and even encouraged."

"See, you're the one who's prejudiced, Jack. We've been making great strides to become more progressive. In fact, spouses now have to be at least *second* cousins," Flats joked.

"Oh, my bad!" Jacques scoffed. "So what's in the box?"

Flats shook his head in disgust as if the box contained a rabid skunk that sprayed tear gas.

"It's my legal fee."

"For what?" Jacques asked as he peeked inside.

"Those damn fools the Bradys. Their daughter got picked up for solicitation again. Marcia! Marcia! Marcia! That slack-jawed tramp can't keep her legs together," Flats said, banging his fist on the counter. "She said she was lonely, having to take care of all those other youngins. One night last month when her folks were away she saw a guy walking past their place. She invited him in and asked if he would help brush her hair."

"What's illegal about that?"

"After they finished one hundred strokes through the hair on her head she lifted her mini-skirt and showed him another area that needed tending to. She said it would only cost him a quarter."

"Wow!"

"Crazy, huh?"

"Yeah. Only a quarter? Things are still so much cheaper back here in Maybach," Jacques observed.

"The john was an undercover cop, Officer Robinson of the Peacekeepers vice unit. I tried to work an entrapment angle, but he captured the whole thing on video. It was sad to watch. He's handcuffing her and she says, 'That's fine, but it'll cost you an extra ten cents.'"

"What kind of sentence did she get?" Jacques asked.

"So get this. Judge Trinket calls out Marcia's name and starts to read the decision. Her sister, Jan, stands up in the gallery and volunteers! There's a rarely used clause whereby a sibling can take the place of the convicted. Apparently Jan's rationale was that if she couldn't *be* Marcia she would at least settle for impersonating her in prison. An interesting play—one I did not see coming. Jan's going to be doing a few more years up-district."

Jacques was rifling through the box, which was full of clothes. He held up a patterned shirt with an enormous, pointed collar. "Damn, Flats, this stuff is vintage. Can I have it?"

"Help yourself. There's more of it in the garage. I was going to burn it, but was afraid of the polyester fumes. Now that Marcia's free and back on the prowl I may be able to get you some more before New Year's," Flats said, only half-kidding.

"Sweet. Whatever I don't keep I'll blow out on eBay."

Uncle Jacques settled right in and we spent the next few days finishing our Christmas preparations. Stone and I monopolized much of his time making him be our audience while we acted out our favorite skits, cajoling him into joining us whenever possible. It was nice having a professional actor to provide advice and coaching. We told him about Pyckle and all the fun we'd had together over the summer. We also started lobbying him to come for a visit more than once a year.

***

On Christmas Eve we loaded up one of the Maybachs and made our pilgrimage out to Pinch's Point. Corn had gone to spend Christmas with family in another part of the district so it was just the four of us. The layout of the property was typical for a southern plantation home. A long driveway, bordered by rows of evenly spaced pecan trees, led to the main house. Watching the dark trunks flash repetitively past my car window made it feel like I was taking a trip back in time.

When we climbed out in front of the house everything appeared just as it had the prior year. Aunt Em had arranged the holiday decorations the exact same way. Her displays were very traditional—a nativity scene, wreaths, and real Christmas trees. She became visibly angry when she saw the giant, inflatable Santas, snowmen, and snow globes from The Home Depot. One year a neighbor accused her of stabbing holes in his inflatable Rudolf. It made me sad when I saw the saggy, half-full reindeer with duct tape bandages all over his body.

Flats and Jacques exchanged a silent glance as we headed up the front steps. It was as though they were both preparing to deal with something unpleasant—putting on their game faces. Despite being about thirty minutes from our house, we only went to Pinch's Point a few times a year. Flats had a tenuous relationship with his sister, Emily, who was the current occupant of the home. He liked to say that Pinch's Point was close to our house, but not *too* close.

Aunt Em was a proud widow who told everyone her husband had died in the Civil War. Only when asked, would she clarify that it was the annual football game between Oregon and Oregon State. He was there for homecoming and while tailgating he was run over by the Oregon State mascot—a giant beaver—who was driving a golf cart while intoxicated. Flats cleaned their clocks in court.

My aunt carried herself as a religious woman and I don't recall a single instance of her smiling. Perhaps it was the anguish of the internal battle between her personal beliefs and the bonds of family. The lingering conflict was always simmering under the surface, but would rear its head when she tried to pass judgment on her brothers, whose lifestyles she didn't approve of.

Flats knocked on the door and then went inside. "Emily, we're here!"

A moment later Aunt Em arrived in the foyer wearing a green, plaid apron. Although only two years older than my father, she looked much older. Her thinning blond hair was shifting toward light gray and her frail arms looked like sticks protruding from a skinny snowman.

"Hello, Flats, Jacques, Merry Christmas," she said giving them each hugs. She turned our way and examined us like a couple of urchin children from Les Misérables.

"Hello Stonewall and Jean Luc." Aunt Em also didn't approve of my given name and definitely not my nickname. She often told me I should have a respectable girl's name, like Dorothy.

"Hello, Auntie Em," we replied.

"Come on, Spy. Let's get the presents and put them under the tree," Jacques said, taking my hand. He called me Spy intentionally, knowing it bothered Aunt Em. The Pinch family chain rattling had already begun.

One thing we could never criticize Aunt Em for was skimping on the Christmas tree. The great room at Pinch's Point had twenty-foot ceilings and the tree always stretched to the top. She had a company bring it in and used a lift to decorate it. Entering the room, the fragrant pine triggered olfactory memories of past Christmases. I looked at the massive fireplace and thought about the years I'd spent imagining Santa sliding down after we'd all fallen asleep. Two years prior, Stone had passed down the sacred childhood knowledge of Santa's non-existence. I spent another year in denial searching for ways to prove him wrong. When I questioned Flats he tactfully told me Santa was whatever you thought he was no matter your age. Stone was right, but I preferred my father's explanation.

Above the fireplace was the portrait of Willy Pinch. He stared down upon me with a roguish grin, brandishing his deadly Ginsu. I wondered what Christmas with great-great-grandpa Willy would have been like. My guess was a lot of fun.

Stone and I spent the afternoon re-exploring the property and working up an appetite for Aunt Em's Christmas Eve feast. After dinner our tradition was to gather around the television and watch a sampling of holiday classics. To Aunt Em that meant some sappy black and white movie, while to the rest of us it involved stop motion animation shows.

"Let's watch something that celebrates the joy of Christmas," Aunt Em announced.

"Sorry, Em, too late. Christmas has been hijacked. I'm thinking more like *Frosty* sponsored by GE Refrigeration Products or *Santa Claus Is Coming to the Mall* sponsored by Macy's," Jacques said, scrolling through the program guide. "We could watch *Rudolf, the Red-Nosed Reindeer* for the millionth time, although I just love how that little elf Hermey shows his pride...in dentistry. Here's something called *Santa, Baby!* Never heard of that one. And of course we have *A Christmas Story*, but really, who gives a kid a gun for Christmas? Ha! So what's your pick, Stone? Spy?"

We looked to both of them, not wanting to take sides. We compromised and ended up going with a new classic: *Elf.* It was chocked full of commercialism, but I assured Aunt Em that the ending was happy and celebrated the joy of Christmas. It did, however, have one adverse side effect for me: I was now completely freaked out by jack-in-the-boxes. Uncle Jacques knew this and popped up from under a blanket when I wasn't paying attention, totally rattling my nerves.

The movie was on regular television so it was loaded with commercials. Jacques could fast forward through most of them, but not the legal ads. The district had passed a law requiring the cable companies to show all legal advertisements. The rationale being it would assure that citizens were not deprived of needed representation. Paid attorney spokesmen would be heard no matter what.

Shortly after the movie started, a commercial for the firm of Fairchild and Fairchild—one of Maybach's largest—appeared showing a chubby lawyer in a Santa hat.

"Oh look, there's one of your friends, Flats," Aunt Em said facetiously. "I'm not sure why he's impersonating Kris Kringle. He should have horns and a pitchfork—Satan Claus."

"I can't argue with you there, Em." Flats replied.

Attorney Fairchild was pointing at us from the screen. "Have *you* been injured by a car, motorcycle, bus, dump truck, scooter, Segway, unicycle, bicycle, tricycle, quad-runner, Big Wheel, wagon, boat, jet ski, snowboard, skateboard, or even on foot? You may be entitled to substantial compensation. Call now. We are standing by on Christmas Eve to help you."

I saw Stone rub the scar on his knee from his skateboarding accident and knew he still felt guilty about it.

"We will also be open tomorrow in case you are injured in any way while opening presents. Pay close attention to puppies in boxes; they can be especially dangerous. Happy Holidays from our family to yours."

"Where's your commercial, Flats?" Emily proded. "Maybe you could dress up as Jesus celebrating his birthday in the courtroom."

Flats glared at her but didn't engage, not wanting to spoil the mood. We sat silently until the show resumed.

Within an hour Stone and I were the only ones still awake. When the movie ended we poked our sleepy elders and headed off to our rooms with visions of sugarplum fairies.

Unfortunately, my night was filled with dreams of Attorney Fairchild dressed in fur from head to foot. He dropped down the chimney and slung over his shoulder was a red sack bulging at the seams. When I ran to see what he'd brought I was disappointed to find a bag full of legal documents—reams and reams.

"Here, this one's for you, Spy," he said, handing me a subpoena.

"Oh, thank you Satan Claus! And this is for you," I said, handing him a box. When he opened the lid I no longer had anything to dread. The malicious puppy flew out and went straight for his head. After the beast took off a chunk of his nose, Fairchild gave me the finger and up the chimney he rose.

"I'll get you and your little dog, too," I heard him exclaim as he drove out of sight.

"Oh yeah? My daddy is Flats Pinch," I said and then laughed with delight.

10.

I grew up in Kentucky, but I did not grow up like that. I had heat, and I didn't have to shoot my dinner or anything.
~ Jennifer Lawrence

Even after I'd accepted the fact that Santa didn't come in the flesh, Christmas morning at Pinch's Point was always magical. And despite my disturbing dreams, I still felt like he had come in spirit overnight.

The adults were all awake before Stone and I arrived downstairs. They'd gotten each other minor gifts, but Christmas morning for them was now a spectator sport. They were eager to see the excitement on our faces when we tore into our presents.

As always, we saved the best for last. We set down the presents Uncle Jacques had brought and everyone gathered around. There was no question as to what was inside, but Stone and I were both tingling with anticipation.

For years I'd been lobbying for a gun. Flats countered that I was too young, however, it was a well known fact that he was given his first gun as a small boy. He also said it was different because I was a girl; an argument that held no water. Even though he teased me about being a tomboy, he relished having the equivalent of two sons.

My enthusiasm was contagious and Stone moved a rifle to the top of his wish list. Together, our ongoing pleas had gradually worn down Flats's resistance. Around Thanksgiving he'd finally made the ultimate statement of acquiescence, "We'll have to see what Santa brings."

We knew Santa meant Uncle Jacques. You see, guns were no longer sold in the Southern Trial District. All firearm sales had been banned years ago due to the number of ignorant people shooting innocent people. After hundreds of years of this behavior, the media spun into an uproar and demanded action—while taking no responsibility for their involvement in the glorification of violence. Flats said they were casting stones at the Second Amendment while hiding behind the First Amendment. He also argued that there were always going to be some people with screws coming loose—always had been, always would be. Whether it was guns, knives, explosives, or tainted Kool-Aid they'd find a way to kill people. I still remember when a teenager named Marvel went on a killing spree down in the small town of Arena *after* his gun had been taken away. He used a spear, an ax, and a knife to butcher a number of other kids. And God only knows how many creative ways the Munsters and Addamses could've killed people if the urge struck them.

Nonetheless, following a lengthy debate the ban on sales finally passed. It would have been defeated, however, minutes before the vote a gunman showed up at the district capitol building and shot several of the lawmakers who were opposed to the legislation.

Once enacted, the law basically did nothing to limit the number of guns in the district. As with all reactionary laws, there were loopholes and unintended consequences galore. Every special interest imaginable was able to obtain an exemption and kids were covered under several of those. The Unisex Scouts made sure their members were still able to pack heat. Scouts could even carry weapons in public in order to protect cookie sale proceeds. Although I wasn't a scout, I was covered by a subsection called "Barney's Law." It empowered children to use deadly force to defend themselves against annoying purple dinosaurs.

Uncle Jacques had recently been working on a project in the Rocky Mountain District where you could still buy guns everywhere—including the corner 7-11 store. He was the obvious person to buy guns for us and he didn't need to worry about bringing them into our district because guns as gifts were perfectly legal. This activity was covered under the Santa clause. (Aren't those lawmakers clever?)

We tore off the wrapping paper to find the gun boxes inside and everyone acted surprised. My eyes dilated when I saw the image of a Black Widow .22 rifle with a laser scope. My excitement ebbed momentarily when I turned and noticed Stone had received a different gun. His was a Red Ryder advanced semi-automatic assault rifle. Flats saw the pout on my face and quickly addressed it.

"Spy, Stone is older. Be happy with the weapon Santa chose for you."

I knew he was right and jumped up to hug and thank my father and uncle. After carefully cutting open the box, I felt the smooth, black gunstock in my hand. When I hefted it, the weight felt perfect. I locked the butt against my shoulder and aimed at the portrait of Willy Pinch. Peering through the scope I saw his face smiling back at me, a red laser dot sparkling on his forehead.

"Bam!" I said, faking a shot and the modest recoil.

"Now, Spy. Not in the house," Aunt Em said.

"Sorry," I replied, lowering my weapon. "Can we go shooting today?"

"Please! Can we?" Stone seconded.

"I think that can be arranged," Flats said, a broad smile carved across his face.

"I've got plenty of ammo down in the cellar," Aunt Em said.

"It's a bit cold out this morning, but it should be nice this afternoon. So if the two of you behave you can go after lunch."

"Thank you!" we said, dishing out more hugs to everyone.

***

We were now impatient kids with an agenda, so the rest of the morning dragged on mercilessly. I kept checking the thermometer outside the kitchen window, my enthusiasm rising along with the mercury. By noon it was creeping into the fifties, the sun reaching full power outside. We shoveled down our lunch and went out back where Flats had set up an array of targets.

Stone and I had shot at Pinch's Point in the past, but having our own guns was completely different. I felt a sense of connection with my new rifle. We wouldn't be able to shoot at our house, so I resolved to enjoy every minute until then.

Flats examined everything closely before giving us the green light. He was highly knowledgeable about guns; however, he never shot with us. When I offered him my gun to take the first shot he declined politely. Even Uncle Jacques and Aunt Em would normally squeeze off a few rounds. For whatever reason everyone in our family was fine with guns. I assumed it was a Southern thing, going back to the times when my ancestors hunted their meals and needed to defend their property from encroaching Indian casinos.

Our practice range consisted of bottles on the fence, assorted produce from the garden, and a fifty-five-gallon drum with a stick person drawn in chalk on the side. After a patient warm-up, we both quickly became more comfortable and aggressive. Flats gave Stone the go ahead to try his semi-automatic capability. When my brother finished blasting the mix of melons and squash it looked like the aftermath of a Gallagher show.

Despite not having shot for a while, Stone and I were nailing everything. I could sense a feeling of pride as Flats watched closely, standing nearby with his arms crossed, giving occasional pointers.

"A couple of chips off the old block," Uncle Jacques said, patting Flats on the shoulder.

"Flats, can we go out in the woods? Please, it's Christmas; we'll be good," I asked.

The look on his face said no, so I was shocked when he uttered, "Okay."

"You're going to let them go out alone?" Em asked.

"They'll be armed. There's nothing real dangerous out there this time of year."

"Still…"

"Do you want to go along as chaperone?"

I looked at Stone with fear. Aunt Em was not part of our plan.

"I've got cooking to do."

I breathed an audible sigh of relief. Uncle Jacques would be fine, but I could tell he was supporting Flats.

"I've got a big nap planned for this afternoon," Jacques said when Flats looked his way.

"So they'll be fine."

Aunt Em walked off, talking under her breath. "Can't believe they let you raise children; the district should take 'em away from you."

"Chill out, Emily," Flats called after her. Turning to us, he clarified the rules. "You two better behave. Be back before dark, make sure your phones are charged, and don't shoot each other."

"We will...and won't."

Stone and I grabbed water bottles and scurried off before Flats could change his mind.

Heading into the woods, I was filled with a feeling of freedom and independence. Romantic images of our long-dead ancestors setting out across the wilderness danced through my head. Pinch's Point covered several hundred acres, much of it thick forest. With guns in hand, Stone and I both knew our destination, an area we were no longer afraid to explore. We crossed the meadow, which had served as our former boundary, and then wriggled our way through an old barbwire fence. Hanging at intervals were badly rusted warning signs.

Stone and I planned to focus on target shooting, but if a small, unsuspecting animal crossed our path we'd take it down. Aunt Em would get angry if we left a large carcass lying around, so our general rule was: Bambi—no, Thumper—yes.

We took a few random shots as we went, striking action poses and adding our own sound effects. When we came across an ancient, downed cypress Stone flipped a switch to semi-auto and unloaded a clip into the dead tree. We both watched in awe as splinters of wood sprayed like smoke.

"Whoa!" Stone said, taking in the scope of his power.

"Don't waste all of our ammo."

"Sorry, Spy, it had to be done."

"Yeah, that was pretty cool," I admitted. I popped a few precision shots and we moved on. The afternoon was still early and we wanted to go as far as we could.

Soon we came to a lake we'd seen on the satellite map, but never visited in person. Steep, gray rocks surrounded the water like a wall of towering tombstones. We sat down on a flat boulder to take in the stirring vista. Among the birds and other sounds of nature we heard something strange—a girl singing. We couldn't quite make out the lyrics, perhaps something about a hanging tree.

After scanning the shore with our riflescopes we located a figure on the far edge. Stone and I hadn't anticipated meeting anyone on our journey so this was an added surprise. We walked back into the tree line and picked our way around the lake.

Nearing her location, we heard what sounded like a four-note mockingbird whistle and I began to echo it back. It was like a homing device drawing us closer. We finally punched through the thick brush and found the young girl who'd been singing.

She was pretty, but nothing special in my opinion, and I would've guessed her age to be around twenty. Long bangs of chestnut hair framed her face. The girl had a quizzical look, her pouty lips tensed, as though she was expecting someone else. "Who are you?" she asked. When she realized we had guns she drew her bow and arrow.

Stone and I exchanged amused glances.

"Seriously?" he asked. "Who do you think you are, Robin Hood? Who shoots with a bow and arrow?"

"It's a noble and dignified weapon. Besides I'm pretty good with this," she said, throwing her shoulders back proudly. She rotated and shot toward a large turkey vulture in a low tree branch. The arrow hooked and missed badly. The bird flew off, squawking as though it was laughing at the failed attempt on its life.

I turned to Stone and he nodded, giving me the go ahead. I looked way up in the same tree and located a chubby squirrel nibbling away at a pinecone. I shouldered my rifle, landed the laser dot on his white belly, and squeezed off a round. There was a faint plunking sound as the carcass bounced through the limbs on its way to the ground. It landed with a final thud by the base of the tree.

I shrugged at the girl waiting for her to acknowledge our superior firepower. She lowered the bow looking disappointed.

"We didn't come here to fight," Stone said. "We only wanted to say hello and wish you Merry Christmas."

"Oh."

Hearing a noise coming through the woods, we all turned in the same direction. It sounded like a large animal approaching.

Stone and I readied our guns. A moment later a handsome, young man popped out from the bushes near the girl.

"Is everything okay? I thought I heard a gun shot."

She motioned her head our way.

"Oh, we have visitors," he said.

We waved to him like the little kids we were.

"Hey, guys. Don't mind her, she can be a paranoid, drama queen."

"I am not, Dale!"

He raised his eyebrows and swirled his index finger by his temple, implying that she was a lunatic. As he came closer we lowered our guns. For me, watching the tall stranger approach was like viewing a film scene in slow motion. His dark eyes were simultaneously mysterious yet inviting. As though they were hiding secrets you were welcome to ask him about. His thick, wavy hair looked like the only styling required was a quick run through with his fingers.

"I'm Dale and this is Cattricks," he said.

"Nice to meet you. I'm Stone and this is my sister Spy. We are visiting our aunt over at Pinch's Point," Stone said, pointing in the direction we'd come.

"We live over there," Dale said, pointing in the opposite direction. "We were out here doing some videos. I got a new GoPro for Christmas and we wanted a natural setting."

"Is that the new model?" Stone asked.

"Yeah, it's pretty sweet."

"Cool."

"We were out here searching for the hidden treasure of Willy Pinch," I said, trying to enter the conversation. Stone elbowed me, indicating my comment was too juvenile for our present company.

"Cattricks and I are finished out here and were about to head to the Nub to pick up something from my cousin. Would you two like to come with us?" Dale asked.

"What's the Nub?"

"It's an industrial park, out that way," Dale said, gesturing to the west.

"Dale, I'm sure they need to get going," Cattricks interjected. She didn't sound interested in travel companions.

I deferred to Stone. "About how long will it take to get there? We can't stay out too long."

"It's not far. We'll get there in about fifteen minutes."

"We're in."

"Great. Let's get going," he said, picking up a nearby backpack. Cattricks leaned down and picked up a large handbag that had been moving.

"What's in there?" I asked.

"Oh, just my dog." She pulled back the flap and a tiny, tan Chihuahua poked its head out from the bag. "His name is Butterfinger."

"He's so cute. Can I pet him?"

"Well, he's kinda protective." She scooped the dog up and held him firmly across her forearm as she approached.

I held out the back of my hand for him to sniff. When he was within inches he bared his thin, pointed teeth and snapped at me. Cattricks pulled him back just in time. The animal began to shake and squirm trying to get loose. It growled and made a hissing noise. The angry beast looked more like a snake than a dog.

Instinctively, my hand slid down to my gun grip.

"Don't worry, that stupid dog hates everyone," Dale assured us. "Let's go."

Cattricks returned Butterfinger to the purse, which calmed the mini monster.

On the walk to the Nub we continued to talk mainly with Dale. "Do you know who she is?" he asked, when Cattricks was a safe distance ahead.

"No."

"Yeah, you guys are probably too young. Not part of our target demographic yet."

"Who is she?"

"She's a budding Internet sensation. Her online show has really been blowing up, the girl's on fire."

"What's the show about?"

"Honestly. It's about nothing. She just rambles about random topics and looks pretty and people tune in," Dale admitted. "Today we were out here doing a bit on the Paleo diet she has been on, eating like primitive man: meat, nuts, and berries. That's why she was hunting with the bow and arrow."

"Did she kill anything?" Stone asked.

"God no, not even close. The footage of her trying will get some good laughs. On the way home we are going to stop at McDonald's and she'll eat a burger without the bun, you know, show how humans have evolved."

"Are French fries okay?"

"Definitely not."

"You can count me out then," Stone said.

Cattricks had stopped ahead and was sitting on a stump waiting for us to catch up. I saw her nibbling on something as we approached.

"Are you guys hungry," she asked, holding out a handful of plump berries. "Dale found these in the woods earlier. They're delicious."

"How do you know they're not poisonous?" I inquired.

"Good question, young lady. Dale looked them up on his phone and the picture looked pretty close to the ones they sell at Whole Foods. We're still alive so they must be fine."

We turned and Dale nodded to indicate they were okay to eat. Stone and I each had some and they were indeed quite tasty.

After a brief rest we were back on the move. Once Cattricks had separated from us Dale grabbed me by the shoulders and whispered, "Don't worry, I bought those berries at Whole Foods yesterday. I made up the part about finding them. Don't tell her." We both nodded, happy to be in on his secret. I wasn't sure about Cattricks, but so far I liked Dale.

We picked up the pace to keep up with Cattricks. "Your girlfriend sure walks fast," I observed.

"She's not my girlfriend. We're just friends."

"Oh...sorry, I just assumed..."

"Don't worry, Spy. It's cool. I'm fine with the friends part. Although, ideally I'd like it to come with some *benefits*," he said, watching Cattricks strut down the path in dark pants and knee-high boots, her braided ponytail bouncing on her spine with each step. The footwear was perfectly accessorized to her brown leather hunting jacket. "Besides, there's another man," he added.

"Who's that?"

"A dude named Chip. He's an heir to a wealthy family in the food business. They own one of the biggest baking operations in all of Pander. The company bakes potato chips, corn chips, even pita chips—you name it. He and Cattricks have a crazy relationship and are always fighting over something stupid. She's been jerking him around for years. Of course, he probably says the same thing about me."

We soon crested a ridge and saw the industrial park spread out before us. It consisted of about two-dozen non-descript, tan buildings clad in corrugated metal. The complex was rather sedate and I assumed most people were off for the holiday. A few folks were milling about in different areas and a lone semi-truck was departing.

Dale took the lead and we walked toward one of the larger buildings on the perimeter. He opened the front door and we entered a small reception area. We sat down on the well-worn couches while Dale was escorted back to his cousin's office. Cattricks was content to check her social media accounts while we waited. I, however, was hoping to find out more about her.

"Is Cattricks a family name?" I asked.

"No, my real name is Jane, but no one calls me that anymore. I was using it when I started my Internet show and couldn't get much of an audience outside of my friends. Then one day I was at the salon and my stylist was laughing out loud about something on her phone. I asked what she was watching and she showed me this cat playing a keyboard," she said, bursting into a fit of giggles from the memory. "Oh, that keyboard kitty still makes me laugh. Then she showed me a bunch of other clips and they were almost all of cats doing tricks. It turns out cat tricks were huge. Only porn was getting more hits on a daily basis. So that's when Cattricks was born. We did a little wordplay, see?"

"Yeah, we get it."

"Almost overnight our views and ratings spiked. Everyone looking for those silly cat videos found me. It was total SEO— search engine optimization."

"That's amazing."

"Isn't it though? Someone like me with no skills or talent can become a huge star simply by riding someone else's wave. Ya' gotta love the Internet."

"I guess," Stone said, sounding unconvinced.

Cattricks's bag wiggled on her lap and she retrieved Butterfinger. Stone and I cringed as she held up the dog in front of her face and kissed him on the nose while his tongue shot out and entered her mouth. I had no idea why Chip and Dale would possibly want to kiss this girl.

Dale returned and introduced his cousin Vic. "Dale thought you might like a quick tour of the facility."

"That sounds cool," Stone replied. He was always interested in how things were made.

"We're running a skeleton shift since most of the workers are off for Christmas. I was afraid you might be here to rob us," Vic said, motioning toward our guns.

"These? No, we only use guns for target shooting, hunting, and self-defense," Stone said.

"Why aren't you off today, Mr. Vic?" I asked.

"I run the place so I end up working on holidays. Come on and I'll show you around. We need to leave the guns out here though."

Stone and I looked hesitant.

"Don't worry, we'll set them in my office. No one will touch your guns," Vic assured us.

After securing our weapons, the four of us followed him to the end of a hallway. He put his three middle fingers together and held them up to a sensor pad on the wall. A red light turned to green and the door unlocked. He pushed it open and ushered us onto the production floor.

The small door led to a surprisingly large room. The space was full of hulking machines and equipment. Hoses, conveyor belts, and conduits snaked in every imaginable direction. There was a hum of white noise and the air smelled of petroleum products.

To Stone it was like entering a candy factory, his eyes racing to absorb all the sights. The complicated contraptions entranced him. "Wow! I've never seen anything like this."

"Pretty cool, huh?" Vic said, taking pride in his facility. He handed us all white hard hats and safety goggles. Mine were way too big and made me look like a bug.

"What do you make here?" Stone asked.

"Everything. We fabricate and manufacture all kinds of things no longer made elsewhere in Pander. Many of them are products from companies driven out of business by frivolous litigation. Follow me."

We walked down a flight of metal stairs and he led us to a machine being fed small ingots on one side and spitting out gold lapel pins on the other side.

"Here's an example. A customer wanted these gold pins with some kind of pointy-headed bird holding an arrow in the middle of the circle. I have no idea why anyone would want these silly things, but I don't care. They send the request, I make and ship the pins, and they pay. I set up a different company for every order. If someone dies because of a gold lapel pin only that company is on the hook. Everything else is insulated."

"That seems ridiculous," I said.

"Even better, we often add stickers that say 'Made in China' in order to mislead people as to the origin of the products."

"For something made right here? That's crazy."

"It is, but that's the world we live in." Vic handed me a sample. "Would you like one, Spy?"

"Sure. Thanks." I clipped it on my jacket and followed as he walked us around the floor. Right away I noticed Cattricks taking an interest in it, blatantly eyeing the pin on several occasions.

Vic showed us all kinds of things we never knew existed. Stone was particularly impressed by a milling machine creating 3D renderings. Metal shavings flew in all directions as the cutting head swung around like it was possessed. "You weren't kidding. You really can make anything here."

"As long as we can keep the machines running. Unfortunately we have power supply problems. It used to be reliable until the government nationalized the companies. Now our leaders decide who gets it and when.

"Even worse, all of our power in this part of the district comes from a single hydroelectric project. It's so short sighted, what if something happens to the dam? We'll all be in the dark."

He directed our attention to a corner across the way. "Do you see that mess over there?" It was a partially completed piece of equipment surrounded by spare parts.

"What is it?"

"An energy project we were working on, it's supposed to be some kind of engine. I had a guy here who said he was going to get us all the power we needed and we would no longer be at the mercy of the government. He was a genius and it looked to have real potential, but the plans were all in his head. Then one day he disappeared, no trace whatsoever. I know it sounds like conspiracy theory, but I still wonder if the government had something to do with it. Maybe someday he'll return…"

Vic let the black helicopters fly away and went back to being a tour guide. Toward the end he stopped by a station and picked up a brown paper bag, which he handed to Dale.

"Here's your order."

"Thanks, Vic."

"So you have a separate company for that bag?" I asked.

"You bet! Hopefully my cousin won't sue me, but you never know."

Vic led us back to the offices where we thanked him for the tour and said goodbye. Outside we retraced our path back into the woods until we came to the spot where Dale and Cattricks would head north and we would go south.

"Thanks again for taking us to meet your cousin, Dale. It was very nice of you," I said.

"Yeah, that was one of the coolest places I've ever been," Stone added.

"No problem. It was nice to meet you guys," Dale replied.

"Sorry I was bitchy at first," Cattricks said. "You're a pretty good shot with your gun, Spy. Maybe next time we can include you two in my show."

"That would be awesome." I thought about Stone and I doing one of our skits and getting it in front of a huge audience.

She smiled at me warmly, her eyes drifting toward the pin on my jacket. It was neat, but something I could easily live without.

"Oh, by the way, Cattricks, I want you to have this," I said, unfastening the pin and holding it out for her.

"Really?" she said.

Dale rolled his eyes in disbelief that Cattricks would take it from me.

"Yes. The bird is holding an arrow so I think it fits you better. If it was holding an assault rifle it might be more my style."

"Oh, thank you so much, Spy," she said, grabbing it quickly and putting it right on her lapel.

We exchanged numbers and contact information, assuring her that we would like and follow her show. After that there was an awkward moment when we weren't sure if we should hug or shake hands or what. Instead we all made timid half-waves goodbye and walked in our opposite directions.

A short distance down the trail I glanced back over my shoulder. Dale turned a moment later, giving me a nod and wink of acknowledgement. My head spun back around, a strange flushing sensation spreading across my cheeks. At that moment he became my first official crush.

***

The sun was hanging low and the crisp air was tickling my nostrils so we picked up our pace on the way back to Pinch's Point. We did, however, squeeze in a little more shooting. Approaching an open, rocky patch we saw two male chipmunks chasing a female. She was leading them round in circles and I couldn't help but imagine it was Chip and Dale blindly following Cattricks. The female stopped on top of a stump and watched the other two race below her. The short pause was all I needed to take the rodent down. The bullet sent her body spiraling backwards, her tail flapping in circles. The act—and the sense of satisfaction it gave me—was my first display of romantic jealousy.

"Are you okay?" Stone asked, noticing my demeanor.

"What?"

"You seem a little…angry."

"I'm fine. It's just a chipmunk. No big deal."

"You're sure?"

"Yeah. Come on. I'll race ya' the rest of the way."

We clicked on our safety switches and sprinted off, our rifles flailing ahead of us, like soldiers charging across the battlefield. Even though I lost, the run was just what I needed to clear my head of the strange feelings I was having.

Back at the house, we stopped on the porch to unload our guns and take off our boots before entering through the kitchen. Following a long afternoon in the cold air, the warmth of the kitchen and the smell of dinner in the oven embraced us like a smothering hug.

Flats called to us from the living room and we raced in to tell him about our expedition. Stone and I had already agreed to limit the details about Dale and Cattricks and our visit to the factory. We didn't want him to get worried and put restrictions on future trips into the woods.

The next few days flew by as we continued to explore new parts of the woods. We looked and listened for Cattricks and Dale, but didn't see them again. On New Year's Eve we said goodbye to Aunt Em and took Uncle Jacques to the airport. We returned home and celebrated the New Year with Corn. Flats let us stay up until midnight and we toasted with sparkling apple juice. Ushering in the year, I had a shortage of personal resolutions, but an abundance of optimism for the days and months ahead. At the time I had no inkling of the tumult lingering just over the horizon.

PART TWO

The first half of our lives is ruined by our parents, and the second half by our children.
~ Clarence Darrow

11.

Behold, my friends, the spring is come; the earth has gladly received the embraces of the sun, and we shall soon see the results of their love!
~ Sitting Bull

In January I saw snow in Maybach for the first time I could remember. It was only blowing flurries, not enough to stick. Still, it felt like magic dust dropped from heaven and we were content to run around catching flakes in our mouths.

The cold weather didn't last and soon the signs of spring in the Southern Trial District began to appear. Green buds pierced crusty tree branches and anxious flowers erupted from the ground like the rising dead.

That spring I witnessed the beginning of two other major changes. Seeing that they involved my brother and my father I had a front row seat for both metamorphoses. At the time, my proximity made it difficult for me to discern the incremental adjustments. It was like watching someone lose weight. When you see them everyday the changes are often imperceptible. However, if you don't see someone for a period of months the transformation can be shocking.

Additionally, on a day-to-day basis I was distracted by yet another progression, one that had begun earlier in the school year: the downward spiral of my teacher Miss Fisher. With our year-end, standardized test nearing on the calendar, we watched with dismay as her enthusiasm declined by the day. The idea of not passing the test was scarier than a goblin on Halloween. I dreaded the thought of staying back and desperately wanted to leave fourth grade before I needed a bra.

What had started as occasional issues snowballed after the

holidays. Her once tidy hair and makeup became clown-like. We tracked her outfits and confirmed she was wearing the same clothes for several days in a row, undoubtedly sleeping in them as well. The one constant in her life was a pair of Ray-Ban sunglasses, which never left her face. When another teacher confronted her about them, Miss Fisher claimed they contained prescription lenses.

As difficult as it was to believe, her behavior became even more erratic. Between her regular naps she would address us with slurred speech and had no qualms about including obscenities. She could drop F-bombs like a stuttering rapper. When she became angry she was vicious, but it was difficult for her to sustain the tirades. She appeared too tired to fight.

By February, pretty much all teaching had ceased. Her curriculum became a two-pronged schedule of movie watching and quiet reading time. Students who couldn't read were allowed to listen to music.

The reading list featured titles such as: *The Most Dangerous Game*, *Arena*, *Deliverance*, *First Blood*, and *The Long Walk*.

Our movie options followed a similar theme. *Bloodlust!* was an older film featuring people hunting people. The special effects were so bad I'd really have to classify it as a comedy. The movie starred some guy named Robert Reed, who bore an uncanny resemblance to Mr. Brady.

One of my favorites was *The Running Man*. The film had some great one-liners, many of which we started using in class. When someone would go to use the bathroom they would stop at the door and say, "I'll be back!" It always got a laugh. Two of the stars went on to become the governors of other districts in Pander. Their acting skills likely served them well.

Every Friday we watched the same movie, Miss Fisher's (and Quentin Tarantino's) favorite: *Battle Royale*. It was a Japanese film with subtitles so her argument was that she was exposing us to foreign culture. We weren't buying it. *Battle Royale* was the story of a group of Japanese students taken to an island and forced to battle each other to the death, resulting in a single survivor. The level of graphic violence was completely over-the-top; still we couldn't help but watch. The battle was choreographed and managed throughout by a game master and as each student died his or her name was broadcast across the island. I'd never seen anything like it.

After weeks of this conditioning, her objective became clear: she wanted to reduce the class size. Lucky for us she lacked the energy to do it herself. Instead, she was hoping recess would devolve into a bloody culling of the class.

At first I thought she simply didn't want to deal with so many students. Then Stone figured it out. Her bonus was based on the *percentage* of students that passed the final test. If she could weed out some of the weaker children she would increase the odds of obtaining a higher percentage. She was also attempting to stack the odds by playing favorites. Her wrath was never directed at the two boys she knew would pass the test with ease: Ken Jennings and Brad Rutter—they seemed to know the answer to everything. I have to give her credit; it was a crafty strategy.

***

The mystery of Miss Fisher deepened one spring afternoon when Stone and I were walking home from school. We were taking our normal shortcut down an alley next to Mrs. DuPont's house when Miss Fisher's car came to a screeching halt behind us. The red Chevy looked as bad as she did; besides being filthy it was missing a hubcap and the front bumper was partially detached. The interior was filled with a haze of smoke.

Despite almost hitting us, she didn't even notice Stone and me standing there when she got out. She exhaled and shook her head like a dog flapping its ears.

"Hi, Miss Fisher," I said.

"Huh?" she said, startled. After getting her bearings she figured out who I was. "Oh, it's you, Jean Luc. What are you doing here?"

"We live just up the street."

"Oh, yeah, of course."

"What are *you* doing here?" I asked.

She looked around nervously. "Me? Well…I'm here…to see…Mrs. DuPont."

"Is she a friend of yours?" I couldn't imagine what the two would have in common, other than being crazy bitches.

"Well, sort of."

The screen door slammed and the specter of Mrs. DuPont appeared on the porch.

Miss Fisher dropped her voice and continued, "I...uhh...read to her. I come here to read books to Mrs. DuPont. Now run on home, Jean Luc."

"Why, isn't that nice of you, Miss Fisher. What are reading to her now?"

"Uhh...it's uhh...right now I'm reading...*Fifty Shades of Mauve*."

"I've never heard of that one."

"It's more of an adult book, a little above your head. I better get going. She gets cranky if story time gets off schedule."

"Oh, look it's Maybach's teacher of the year and her apt pupils," Mrs. DuPont called. "Are you back for another fix already? Get your butt inside and we'll hook you up."

Miss Fisher cast her face down and ran obediently up the stairs.

"What are you two degenerates looking at?" Mrs. DuPont hollered as we stood staring up at her. "Why are you bothering with school, Spy Pinch? You're going to grow up and work the pole down at the Risqué Cafe. Why not change your name to Diamond or Jade? *Next up on the main stage: Diamond Pinch.* How do you like the sound of that? I'm sure your good-for-nothing daddy will be real proud. Maybe you'll save enough dollar bills to buy a pick and shovel. Then you can dig gold like your mama." Finishing the monologue, she laughed herself into a coughing fit.

I had the vision of a red laser dot dancing on her forehead. Why was she so nasty? We'd never done anything to her. I couldn't understand how some people could be pure evil.

Stone sensed my anger rising. "Let it go, Spy. That old bag's not worth it."

"One shot, Stone. That's all I need. One shot, one kill. For something that evil I might need to use a silver bullet though. I swear I'd do it in cold blood," I said through gritted teeth.

"Come on, let's go," he said, pulling me away while giving Mrs. DuPont his best stink eye.

"Yeah, you better run on home."

Stone and I both stopped when we realized the jeer did not come from the porch. It was a male voice from the sky. Taking a couple steps back we could see the outline of a man standing behind the white parapets along the roofline.

"Your mother was a gerbil and your father smelled of scuppernongs!" the man yelled with an obnoxious, French accent. He was dressed as a knight, which was strange since the Medieval fair normally came to town in the summer. A string of obscene hand gestures followed so we ran off before he could taunt us a second time or do anything seriously crazy, like pelt us with livestock.

Over the past months we'd noticed an increasingly strange cast of characters at Mrs. DuPont's house. After the taunting incident we resolved to start taking the long way home.

Later that night I recounted the story to my father.

"Flats, why is Mrs. DuPont so mean to us?"

"Spy, you have to understand we're all humans, but each person is different. Some of it's nature and some of it's nurture. We are born pre-wired with certain personality traits and then during our lifetimes we are shaped by our own unique set of experiences. Some things can be controlled and some can't. Does that make sense?"

"I guess. Do you think Mrs. DuPont was born mean or became mean?"

Flats smiled. "I don't know her very well so I can't be sure. However, I do know she's had some tough issues to deal with so she may have been a good person who grew angry at the world."

"You've had to deal with lots of bad people, Flats, but you don't holler at kids on the street."

"Only *my* kids," he said, patting me playfully on the knee.

"She could *choose* to be nicer, right?"

"I suppose. Listen, Spy, I try to love all my brothers and sisters in the world..." his voice trailed off and I noticed he was looking across the room at Corn who was bent over, wiping the table. Her round posterior was waving in the air, wrapped in leopard print, spandex leggings. "Where was I?"

"People making choices," I said.

"Oh yes. Anyway, before passing judgement you have to try and appreciate where they are coming from. To understand a person like Mrs. DuPont you have to climb into her skin and walk a mile in her shoes."

At the time it seemed like he was being literal. Mrs. DuPont was a tall woman and I didn't think I would fit in her skin. I had a vision of a baggy, tattooed epidermis suit dripping from my limbs and clown-sized shoes flapping on my feet.

He could see the consternation on my face. "What I mean is see things from her point of view, Spy."

I was still stuck on the skin suit image. "Didn't you have a client who tried to climb into people's skin?"

Flats thought for a second. "Oh, Dr. Lector? No, not him. He was eating people. It was a patient of his who was walking around in other people's skin. But please don't ever go to those lengths to try to understand people, Spy."

"No worries, Flats. What ever happened to Dr. Lector?"

"After he was released from the asylum they gave him his own show on the Food Network. In fact, the liver and fava beans dish that Corn makes is one of his recipes. Anyway, we're getting a little off topic, Spy. Just give Mrs. DuPont her space and I think you'll be fine."

"Okay, Flats. I'll try." I gave him a hug and left him to his evening reading.

Shortly thereafter we would find out what was really going on at Mrs. DuPont's house and it explained a lot of things.

12.

Failure is the condiment that gives success its flavor.
~ Truman Capote

With all the excitement in my life, I initially overlooked the changes Stone was going through. He had arrived at puberty and became far more concerned with his privacy. Also, the visit to Vic's factory over Christmas had sparked something in Stone. He'd thrown himself into working on his school science fair project and spent a lot of time working alone in the basement. When I did occasionally snoop, he made it clear he wanted to be left alone. He also spent a lot more time in the bathroom. I wasn't sure what was going on in there either.

Corn told me it was just a phase and warned that I would soon be going through the same thing. With Flats busy at the office and Stone locked down in the basement, I started spending more time with her in the kitchen. She assisted me with schoolwork and I helped her with dinner.

Flats and Corn were content to let Stone be, but curiosity was killing me. I had never been so excited for the science fair to arrive. I finally saw Stone's finished product the day before the fair when he practiced his presentation in our kitchen. Even though I didn't understand all the details, it seemed like a sure winner to me.

On the evening of the fair we arrived at school early. The contestants were required to stand next to their projects and describe them to the attendees. The judges had already done a preliminary evaluation, but also wanted to hear about the students' work directly. The kids were wearing formal dress and most of them looked exceptionally nerdy, swaying nervously with their hands in their pockets. Stone, however, appeared right at home. He engaged with the judges, looking them in the eye and talking fluidly about his work. His sales skills were on full display.

Stone explained how the air was full of electricity—from tiny discharges like the shock on the end of a finger to massive releases like a bolt of lightning. Stone had designed a small device that created a static charge when rubbed, capturing and amplifying the electricity. The unit could then be used to run small appliances and charge batteries in electronics. Stone's prototype was crude, but showed lots of potential.

In terms of comparison, several other students had electricity-related projects. One kid had built a potato battery while another had gone with the lemon-powered version. Both wasted a lot of produce and were only able to light a single LED—certainly not the solution to tomorrow's energy needs.

One boy had hooked up a generator to a hamster wheel and was initially able to harvest a slightly higher yield. Unfortunately, the hamster died of heart failure halfway through the show and the project was disqualified for animal abuse.

The team of Billy Masters and Ginny Johnson submitted another project that didn't make the cut. They conducted experiments in the back of Billy's dad's custom van and developed equipment to facilitate human reproduction. They were both expelled.

As the night progressed the buzz around Stone's project continued to grow. I saw lots of jealous parents pointing and whispering. When our principal finally took the podium to hand out the awards we knew a win for the Pinch family was all but assured. He gave out an assortment of participation ribbons and runner-up awards before arriving at the main event. Even though I knew it was coming I screamed, clapped, and jumped up and down when I heard my brother's name called. I was so proud of what he'd done.

Stone beamed when he accepted the trophy and posed for pictures. Then the principal announced a special added prize and Stone's excitement went off the charts. As the overall winner he would be given a guest appearance on the television show *Remora Tank*. He was going to get the chance to pitch his product to some of the biggest investors in all of Pander. The remoras had huge fortunes, the size of which was eclipsed only by their egos.

***

When Stone began scripting his presentation for the program he decided to use me as a prop. My thick, black hair worked well for generating static and everyone agreed that I added to the cute kid factor. I was super excited to be on national television and after the recent exclusion I was glad to be working with my leading man again.

Two days before the show, Stone showed me the latest version of his generator. It was now smaller and more stylish.

"Did you make that?" I asked.

"The innards, yes. The case, however, I contracted out."

"What do you mean?"

"At first I was going to see if Dale's cousin Vic could make it. Unfortunately, I didn't think there was enough time. Instead I left a list of the specs in the hole in the tree by the Baddley house. A few days later I checked and there it was."

"Whooaa…" I said, stroking the smooth, shiny metal.

"Crazy, huh?"

"I can't believe we have a magic tree."

"Don't use it without asking me, Spy. It might be like a genie's lamp and I don't want to waste any wishes on unimportant things."

"Okay," I murmured, still marveling at the object. "It was good before; now it's great. You're going to have the remoras fighting to work with you, Stone."

"We can't get overconfident. The remoras can be pretty fickle. Sometimes they like to chew up contestants just for the fun of it."

***

Two weeks after the science fair we were on our way to the facility where *Remora Tank* was filmed. Sutherland Studios was a massive complex where, in addition to shows, they filmed the constant stream of government propaganda and attorney commercials.

Inside, Stone and I were taken to make-up to get the glam treatment before rejoining Corn and Flats in the reception room. A producer gave us a briefing and said we would be called shortly.

Stone quietly ran through his pitch speech. He was excited, but exuded a confident level of calmness. I was a wreck. I sat bouncing my knees and clenching my sweaty hands. Suddenly I had to pee as well. An assistant pointed the way and I scampered down the hall in search of relief.

On the way back, I passed a door that was slightly ajar. True to my name I stopped and peered through the narrow opening. Inside was an opulent lounge featuring a huge buffet table covered with exotic foods. The centerpiece was an entire roasted pig with an apple in its mouth. Several of the remoras were standing around eating and drinking. They were laughing and talking about recent contestants.

"Kevin, how are things going with that girl Glimmer?" Demon Johns asked.

"We're killing it. Next month we'll be rolling out Glimmer's Greatest Honey in Jitney Jungle grocery stores nationwide," Kevin— the self-proclaimed Mr. Wonderfull—replied.

"Good for you."

"I don't know anything about bees, but the honey business is sweet!" Mr. Wonderfull said, toasting himself and then draining his glass of wine. A nearby server unscrewed the cap on a bottle and provided a refill.

"So what's up with tonight's wildcard pick?"

"Some kid who won the science fair."

"Seriously? Please tell me he's not going to pitch us the potato clock."

"You know the producers like to throw in a pity contestant," Mr. Wonderfull explained. "The kid contestants are always a joke. If it's anything good you know the parent is using the kid as a front."

"Oh well, we'll humor him for a few minutes and then send him packing."

They all gave a hearty laugh and swilled more booze.

The comments had me so mad I was seeing red—literally. I envisioned red laser dots from my riflescope on each of their heads. I wanted to kick the door open, but I couldn't afford to let Stone down now. I had to keep it together. To calm myself I moved the laser dot to the apple in the pig's mouth and imagined their surprise when the fruit exploded from my bullet.

I hustled back to the waiting area, unsure of what to do. Weighing the options, I decided to keep my mouth shut as relaying the story would only undermine Stone's confidence.

We waited in nervous silence for thirty minutes before finally getting the call.

"And next up in the tank: Stone Pinch, a young inventor who fancies himself a modern day Thomas Edison."

It was a nice intro, probably a bit of a stretch though.

Stone and I marched down the long hallway lined with tanks full of remoras. There were no sharks around so the fish latched onto the glass instead. Hundreds of sucker mouths slurped as we passed.

We entered the main room and Stone launched into his presentation. Despite his enthusiasm, the remoras weren't even paying attention. Most of them were munching on flavored popcorn from a prior contestant. Watching them whisper and giggle to each other was unnerving. I had to clench my jaw to contain my urge to yell at them.

I hoped they would pay attention when it came time for Stone to make his demonstration. I smiled wide when he rubbed his generator on my head and then began to charge a cell phone.

Stone finished with the requisite cheesy line. "So who wants to light up the profits with my static electricity generator?"

I thought I heard crickets chirping as the remoras looked at each other.

"Do you have samples? We expect to get free stuff for being part of this show," Marco Puerto Rican said.

We provided a unit to each of the remoras.

"All right, I'll get things started," Mr. Wonderfull declared. "I see a big problem here, kids. What if you're bald?"

Demon Johns laughed and leaned in so the two could rub their hairless noggins and hum like a pair of coneheads making love.

"Any hair will work—arm hair, leg hair. You can also use just about any carpet if it has some pile," Stone explained.

"What about back hair?" Marco asked.

Stone grimaced. "Sure."

"Crotch hair?" Barbie inquired.

"Ahhh…I suppose."

I watched as Demon unbuttoned his shirt and rubbed the device on his armpit. I forced myself not to look in Barbie's direction, afraid of what I might witness. As a whole, they looked like a group of primitive apes playing with small monoliths.

"I'm afraid people might get this confused with a stick of deodorant and my company, BuFu, is already in that space. I'm out," Demon stated. I rolled my eyes in frustration.

Marco Puerto Rican was next. "Look, Rock."

"My name is Stone."

"Yeah, whatever, kid. This would take a lot of effort on my part. I'll give you a hundred bucks for ninety-nine percent; we'll slap the Mav's logo on it and see what happens. I know more about the online space than anyone else on the planet. These ass-clowns might be able to get you an AOL keyword if you're lucky." He pulled a hundred-dollar bill from his pocket and waived it like he was offering a dog a treat.

Before Stone could even respond, Marco snapped, "I'm out!" He lit the bill on fire and used it to light a cigar.

Stone sensed the deteriorating mood and desperately spit out business buzzwords. "We've already achieved proof of concept. When you consider the scalability the opportunities are limitless. We have a robust online strategy."

Unfortunately, the remoras weren't sucking.

Barbie was squinting at her unit with one eye closed. "Can you use it to make cupcakes?"

"Huh?"

"I like cupcakes and companies in the cupcake industry. I just don't see how this little box could produce cupcakes. I'm sorry, I'm out."

Stone looked like a deer in the headlights.

I saw Robert putting his pen inside a tiny, leather notebook. "I love it; I'll make you an offer. I'll give you fifty million dollars in cash."

As with all contestants on the show, Stone basically ignored him. I gave Stone an elbow and like a zombie he said, "Thanks, Robert, we'd like to hear what the other remoras have to say."

"What? They said you suck. Weren't you listening, kid? For God's sake people! I'm out." Robert was not happy and stood up to leave. "I have to get to dance practice."

Lori Reindeer put her pen to the side of her face and looked down at her notebook. "I'll match Marco's offer of one hundred dollars for ninety-nine percent, subject to getting it produced in pink."

"Thank you, but I have to decline that offer," Stone replied.

There were two special guest remoras in the tank and the cameras panned to Bill Gates. "Stone, your generator is small and efficient. What if we made it bigger and less efficient?"

"Do what?"

"You know, add some bulk and bloat to it. That way it will be easier to make patches and fixes for it."

"I'm confused, sir. Why not make it right from the get-go?" Stone countered.

"Sure, what do I know? One of us is the richest man on the planet and the other is a punk middle schooler. I'll leave it at that. I'm out."

The second guest was a guy named Caesar Flickerman. I had no idea what his qualifications were. He was highly animated and couldn't sit still in his chair, constantly shifting from side to side. He looked like a coked-up, Italian gangster.

"Is it my turn?" he asked, his eyes widening like he was in the midst of a prostate exam. "Ha! Oooo! That *is* exciting. What have you got for us tonight, kid?"

"I just explained everything," an exasperated Stone replied.

"Yes, yes, indeed you did. So tell me, do you like movies about gladiators? Why don't you kids come sit on my lap?"

He eyed us like a pedophile and we took a step away.

Caesar gave us a pouty look and threw his head back. "I'm out."

Our attention shifted back to Mr. Wonderfull. He reclined and pressed his fingertips together. "Everyone else is out. That makes me your only option. I'm feeling generous so I'm going to make you an offer. I'll give you the hundred dollars that Marco and Lori offered for ninety-nine percent. In addition, you will pay me a royalty of fifty dollars per unit in perpetuity. Also, you and your sister will have to come to my house and clean up after my dogs once a week—in perpetuity. That's my offer. What are you going to do?"

Stone was quivering with anger. "I know what I'd like to do...but instead I will simply decline your unreasonable offer. Thank you for your time." Stone turned and walked out, leaving me alone with the remoras. I gave them all a good stink eye and stomped out through the wooden doors.

Departing, I heard them comment: "Sweet kids...She was such a doll...Hope that works out for them...Who's coming in next?" I hurried to catch up with my brother.

Stone fought back tears during the post-tank interview. He thanked everyone for the opportunity and said he would take the remoras' feedback into consideration as he moved forward—basically a pat answer. I assumed he would regroup, but at that moment I could tell Stone was crushed.

Corn and Flats were waiting for us in the next room where they'd watched the filming on a monitor. When they caught Stone in a big hug he broke down. Burying his head against them, he cried like a baby.

"I'm sorry, Flats. I let you down."

"No, Stone, you didn't let me down. You did a great job; they're just a bunch of idiots. I'm proud of you, son."

Flats was even a bit choked up. It was the most emotion I could remember him showing. He had always been opposed to Stone's ideas, but that night he could see how much it meant to his son.

"Don't worry about it," he said, patting Stone and rubbing his back. "Everyone has to experience some failures on the way to success. This was your first time. Next time you'll do better."

The car ride home was quiet as Stone stared out the window, the gears in his head grinding busily. He barely ate any dinner and then went down to the basement to be alone. It was one of those occasions when only time could heal the wound.

Before bed Stone stopped by my room.

"Spy?"

"Yeah."

"Thanks again for helping during the presentation."

"No problem. I'm sorry it didn't work out. Those people were flaming assholes. I know you'll show them how stupid they were for disrespecting you."

"Maybe. The spite will be a good short-term motivator. It was probably too soon to take it on the show anyway; they couldn't see the potential. What I need to start doing now is thinking big. I need to achieve a grander scale and go after a larger market. I have lots of ideas and I'll start working on them tomorrow."

I knew he was not about to let it go. Like a tenacious dog, he'd sunk in his teeth.

"Goodnight, Stone."

"Goodnight, Spy."

13.

If you fell down yesterday, stand up today.
~ H.G. Wells

Spring break was soon upon us and I was ready for a respite from Miss Fisher. I couldn't wait to get out to Pinch's Point and wrap my hands around my rifle. I had some serious pent up anger in need of release. Several times before we departed I reminded Flats to pick up extra ammunition.

The Point was never the same without Uncle Jacques, but at least Corn would be with us for the week. Having her there with Aunt Em always created an interesting dynamic. Corn was essentially our surrogate mother and Em liked to dictate to Flats how we should be raised. They both wanted what was best for us, but occasionally their ideas for accomplishing it were at odds. Stone and I tried to keep the peace by showing them both plenty of love.

My brother was still in his isolation mode and spent his time sitting on the porch working on his computer. I kept urging him to go into the woods, but he put me off.

Flats didn't like for me to go too far on my own, so for the first few days I was content with target shooting near the barn. As I lined up random objects to obliterate, a metallic glint from across the yard caught my eye. There was a new, silver lock on the angled doors leading to the tornado shelter. Juxtaposed against the old and weathered doors, the new hardware was even more noticeable.

Flats had always warned us to not play near the shelter, which of course piqued our interest in the forbidden spot. Similar to things in our neighborhood, we made up crazy stories about what was beyond those doors. I postulated that it was the entrance to a massive concrete silo where thousands of people lived underground. They'd moved their entire civilization down there and were plotting to one day rise back up and overthrow Pander. Instead of Area 51 we nicknamed it Area 13—just silly kids' stuff.

Over time our fascination had faded, but that day something rang in the back of my mind. I wondered if there was a link between the shelter and the rift between Aunt Em and her brothers. I certainly wasn't going to question Flats on the topic so I let it go and went back to shooting.

On Wednesday Stone and I finally headed back into the forest together. We had been in touch with Dale and Cattricks and were planning to meet up with them. The shooting we did on the way to the lake was half-hearted. We were both more interested in seeing our friends, particularly Dale.

We tracked them down by whistling to each other. I now recognized the four melodious bars were from the intro theme to Cattricks's online show. Once reunited, we exchanged hugs and caught up for a few minutes. I was hoping they would go shooting with us, but soon discovered everyone else had already agreed to an alternative agenda for the day. Dale and Stone would be returning to Vic's factory to work on my brother's invention. I would be spending the day with Cattricks. Somewhere along the way I had been taken out of the loop and when they brought me up to speed I slouched, crestfallen.

"Why can't we all go to Vic's," I suggested.

"We are going to be working there. It'd be boring for you to just stand around," Dale explained with a smile.

"I won't be bored. I can help."

"We're going to be doing technical stuff, kinda above your head, Spy," Stone added. It made me feel like I was two-years old.

"But..."

"Come on, Spy. You're going to hang out with me today. We're going to do all kinds of super-fun things," Cattricks assured me.

"I guess," I said, knowing my plans weren't going to change.

We headed off toward the Nub and like last time Cattricks walked in front. I was thankful to at least spend a short time with Dale.

"I'm glad to see Cattricks likes the bird and arrow pin I gave her at Christmas time," I said.

"Yeah, that was really nice of you, Spy. She's become very attached to it, almost like it's her emblem."

"Every time we watch her show she has it on."

"I think she got the idea from her sister."

"What do you mean?"

"Her sister, Prynne, always wears some kind of adornment on her shirt or jacket. Lately she's been wearing a scarlet letter A and everyone knows her by it. Cattricks liked the idea and now people are connecting her with the pin."

"Oh, I see. Maybe you should get something, Dale."

"Nah, I'm content to be in the background. Cattricks thrives on attention and I'm happy for her to get the limelight; I try to be more low key."

Once again I didn't understand what was so special about the girl up ahead. I thought Dale was far more interesting and wished I'd given *him* my bird pin.

When we made it to Vic's factory we said goodbye and I hopped in Cattricks's car. She put me in the back, while her dog Butterfinger rode shotgun. Driving away it dawned on me that I was leaving with someone I barely knew. By that point I was reasonably familiar with her Internet persona; in real life we'd only met once. I was relying on the fact that she was a certified online celebrity and knew I could always flame her if she did anything wrong.

Attached to the dashboard was a bobble head version of her dog. Although its head swayed randomly with the car's motion, I was mesmerized at how well the plastic creature seemed to keep the beat with songs on the radio. When the new Baha Men song came on I bobbed my head in sync with the doggy decoration.

Our first stop was a nearby mall where Cattricks picked up a few items at H&M and Rue21. I did my best to feign interest as she talked fashion and style. She didn't like it when I became inpatient and whistled the four notes of her theme song followed by the tune from final *Jeopardy*. It was a fun combo, kind of a whistling tongue twister. And who could blame me—Rue was totally dead.

Corn always said I was a tomboy, but would probably grow into a girly-girl at some point. Clearly I hadn't arrived there yet.

Back in the car, the swaying Chihuahua head triggered a serious taco craving. Cattricks indulged me and we stopped at Taco

Bell for some Mexican eating.

From there it was a boring ride to the fashion district. We were headed to an area called the Hem, just south of the Seam. Finally, Cattricks pulled into a plaza and announced, "This is it!"

"The Tigris Salon and Day Spa?" I asked.

"Yes! We're going to have so much fun. You can watch me get my hair done and maybe pick up a few tips. I'll do a mani-pedi and we'll have them paint your nails. My gang all work here, you're gonna love 'em. Come on, Spy." She grabbed Butterfinger and then yanked me from the back seat.

When we walked through the front door you'd have thought Cattricks was the Queen of England or maybe Norm entering the bar on *Cheers*. Everyone stopped, looked her way, and called out her name. They didn't even notice me standing there. I was just an accessory.

The salon was a narrow, deep space with rows of black chairs lining the sides. Numerous mirrors provided an illusion of added space and the smell of hairspray crawled up my nostrils.

A woman who'd been sitting in one of the swivel chairs walked over to greet Cattricks. "Look who's here! Our shining star."

"Heybitch!" Cattricks said, hugging the woman. "This is my pal, Spy. She's like my groupie for the day. Can you say hello, Spy?"

"Uhhh…nice to meet you, Miss…Bitch…" I said, nervously looking up at the lean woman towering over me. Her figure was wrapped in a shimmering, spandex unitard and stiletto heels sent her soaring even higher toward the ceiling. Her dark face was a melting pot of different ethnicities, further camouflaged by heavy makeup.

"Oh, you can just call her Heybitch," Cattricks assured me.

"Isn't that kind of rude?"

"Nahh, I came up with it myself," the woman replied. "It was a screen name I used back in the early days of the Internet. I was a star in the era of dialup service."

"What's dialup?" I asked.

"Way before your time, little girl. It was shortly after the dinosaurs departed."

"Heybitch is kind of like my mentor," Cattricks explained,

taking a seat in the stylist's chair. Heybitch started primping Cattricks's dark brown locks and they were soon lost in conversation. Every once in a while they'd lob a question my way and I would nod in agreement. I was still obsessing jealously about the fun I knew Dale and Stone were having.

Cattricks eventually moved to the foot spa area and I was next up in the chair. My nerves tightened as Heybitch combed out my hair.

"Don't worry, sweetie, I'm just going to style you. Maybe cut some of these frayed ends. You've got girl hair now, but soon you'll have woman hair and will need to take better care of it."

I nodded in consent. This was a new experience for me and I started to enjoy the attention she was giving me. Heybitch was quite knowledgeable about hair—an artist working on a blank canvas.

"So how do you know, Cattricks?" she asked.

"My brother and I were hunting down in the woods at Christmas when we ran into Cattricks and Dale."

"How about that Dale? He's a good looking young man, mmm, mmm, mmm," she said as though she was savoring an indulgent dessert.

I gave a sheepish grin and blushed a little, not knowing the appropriate response.

"I think Cattricks should make up her mind once and for all and pick Dale. He's good looking and he's got his head on straight," Heybitch opined. "That boy Chip is cute and rich, but he ain't right in the head. He keeps stringing her along and she follows like a kitten chasing a ball. Sometimes he's so in love with her and other times he wants to kill her. When they're together she's the same way. Dale keeps her on an even keel, but she seems drawn to the instability."

"I like Dale too," I whispered.

She smiled and winked at me in the mirror. "He's got a younger brother, looks just like him. Maybe when you're a little older Dale will introduce the two of you."

My cheeks flushed again and I squirmed in the chair.

"Anyway, Cattricks is like the pied piper. She has a way of gathering followers," Heybitch continued. "I keep warning her to be careful. There are so many online stalkers. Most of them are hapless nerds, but you never know when one of them might decide to get bold."

"I noticed. Still, I don't get it. What does everyone find so special about her?" I said, turning my eyes to see if Cattricks was listening. She was busy yammering away with another salon employee.

"For whatever reason she has the 'it' factor—the look, the walk, the talk. Next year maybe it will be something different. Right now it's the package people are interested in. We call her the BreakingGay."

"The what?"

"She's the BreakingGay. The one girl even gay men would consider switching teams for."

More blushing on my part.

"She needs to enjoy it while it lasts, because trust me, girl, it never lasts!" Heybitch said. She told me more stories all the while fussing over my hair. She was a real character and I quickly took a liking to her.

When Heybitch proclaimed that I was finished I moved on to the next member of the team. Cattricks introduced me to her pedicure technician.

"Spy, this is Sinna."

"Nice to meet you. Everyone here has an interesting name," I said.

"So says the little girl named *Spy*."

"I used to sneak up on people. How did you get your name?" I asked, taking a seat and kicking off my Mary Janes.

"Are you kidding me, child? Look at all this," she said, her hands presenting her body. "It's a sin to kill a mockingbird and it's definitely a sin to look this good."

I couldn't argue the point. Her taught body was on full display in a gold lamé midriff top and miniskirt. The jewel dangling from her pierced belly button winked at me in the bright salon lights. Sinna's hair fell in tight curls that reminded me of spiral pasta and she too had a heavy façade of makeup, but would have been gorgeous even without it.

"I thought it had more to do with the number of sins you've committed. Adultery, fornication, envy, drunkenness, pride. The list goes on and on..." Cattricks sniped before walking away.

"Hmmm...maybe next time I'll give her an 'accidental' slice on the cuticle and then spill a few drops of alcohol in the wound. We'll see how the peacock struts then." Sinna growled.

"That sounds like wrath," I noted.

"I'll give you wrath, little girl," she said, laughing and tickling the bottom of my feet. "You've got some dirty paws down here, Spy. Let's get these nasty things cleaned up."

She had me dip my feet in a shallow tub and turned on the jets. The water whooshed around in all directions and I felt the effervescent tingling of tiny bubbles. I spread my toes and let the streams blow out the spaces in between. I couldn't help but wonder why I hadn't done this before. If we'd had one of those things in our bathroom I would have happily cleaned my feet every single night.

Sinna made me take my feet out before they turned to prunes. Hesitantly, I removed them and she wrapped them in a soft, warm towel. The drying processed tickled and I wiggled on the seat. This of course inspired her to more tickling.

When she finished and removed the towel I looked on with amazement. "Wow, that's a vast improvement." My feet were cleaner than I'd ever seen them.

After she used odd tools to do detail work, I selected a deep purple from her rainbow palette and we moved on to the painting phase. We talked while she worked and discovered we knew some of the same people. Somewhere in the conversation I mentioned that Corn used to work for the Jeffersons.

"Really? My mom, Roxie Willis, lives in the same building as the Jeffersons," Sinna said.

"Oh, I just love George and Weezie."

"And my mom's cousin does the weather on the *Today* show."

"No way! Willard Scott is your mom's cousin?"

"Not Willard. The other guy, Al Roker."

"Sorry, I get those two mixed up. Anyway, that's so cool."

Sometimes it was such a small world after all. I was relaxing comfortably in the chair when Butterfinger drew my eye. He had escaped from Cattricks's purse and was wandering around on his own. I watched as he licked the floor and ate clumps of fallen hair.

"Excuse me, Sinna, do you think Butterfinger should be eating hair? I don't think it's healthy for dogs."

"Hmm, I've never seen him do that before. Hey, Butterfinger, stop it!"

The dog looked up at us; he appeared to be grinning. His jowls twitched, exposing a foamy crust as he hissed.

"Cattricks, I think something's wrong with your dog," Sinna hollered.

Cattricks glanced his way and shrugged. "He'll be fine."

Butterfinger was soon in the corner coughing and convulsing. He yacked up soggy globs of hair and shook his head violently. I knew cats spit up hairballs, but had never witnessed a dog do it, especially when it wasn't even his hair. I thought about Cattricks tongue-kissing her dog and it gave me the willies.

Before I knew it, two hours had passed and we needed to get back to the Nub to meet Dale and Stone. On the way out Cattricks let me share a few beams of her spotlight. I stopped in front of a full-length mirror and spun around in circles so everyone could see the final product.

"Oooo! Look at the new and improved Spy—a hot little pot of honey. That girl is on fire," Sinna said.

"You guys did a great job, but I wouldn't quite say on fire yet. Maybe smoldering. We'll get there, though," Cattricks said, wrapping her arm around my shoulder. I gave everyone a big goodbye hug before departing.

Cattricks was carrying Butterfinger on her forearm like a running back gripping a football. As we walked down the sidewalk to her car, something caught Butterfinger's attention and the dog bolted. In the air his stubby legs were already running. It reminded me of Rudolph pumping Santa's sleigh across the sky. He flew from her arm and hit the ground in a full sprint. The Chihuahua was around the corner and out of sight before Cattricks even knew what had happened.

"Butterfinger!" she cried, attempting to give chase in her heels and tight skirt.

When we made it around the side of the building we saw the dog scampering toward a fenced-in property. Near the gate was a sign that read: Gulch's Recycling and Scrap and I heard the high-pitched squeal of grinding metal. *Oh, this can't be good*, I thought.

We made it to the gate and Cattricks stopped to decide what to do. She looked down at me with puppy dog eyes. I knew I could easily outrun Cattricks, but had no desire to deal with her dog.

"You go after Butterfinger and I'll wait here and catch him if he tries to escape," I said.

"Good idea, Spy. Here, hold my purse."

Cattricks trotted into the complex with a sense of purpose. She wobbled like a staggering drunk across the dirty and rutted ground. I found it positively entertaining and thought about taking out my phone to film it. Considering the nice makeover she'd given me I decided against it.

A minute later I heard screaming and debated calling 911 or going back to Tigris for help. While I waited in indecision, Cattricks reappeared in the open yard with Butterfinger. She had him pressed tightly in her cleavage and his head bobbled with every uneven step. He looked like the toy on Cattricks's dashboard and I couldn't contain a giggle.

Right behind her was the source of the yelling. A hook-nosed, old lady was chasing Cattricks with a broom. "I keep telling you meddling kids to stay out of my yard! I'll get you, my pretty! And your little dog too!"

The lady was elderly and slow so it was like watching two sloths race to the top of a tree. Cattricks started pulling away, though I knew she would be in trouble if a heel broke.

"Henry, close the gate! Close the gate!" the lady yelled in a gravelly voice.

I heard a motor actuate and the chain link gate started to roll shut.

"Hurry, Cattricks, it's closing! You only have a few seconds or you'll be trapped." I tried to push against the sliding barrier, but it was too strong and my shoes skidded across the dirt.

The gap was narrowing and Cattricks ran through just before it clinked shut.

"Wow, that was close," I said.

Bent over and panting, Cattricks nodded. When the old lady finally reached the fence she banged it with her broom and cackled, "No! No! No!"

Cattricks turned and gave the now confined old lady the finger and a long stream of obscenities.

The lady shot back, "Exactly what I'd expect from a piece of trash. You're not even worth the effort. Time to get back to my melting."

Walking to her car, Cattricks talked to Butterfinger in a cooing voice, "What got into you, precious?"

Butterfinger's tongue flicked in and out like a lizard and the foaming was getting worse.

"Ahh, maybe you should get him checked out," I suggested. "He might be sick. If the Peacekeeper's animal unit catches him on the loose...or if mean ol' Mrs. Gulch catches him in her yard again...it might not turn out so well."

"He'll be fine. Nobody better lay a finger on my Butterfinger. He's not just my BFF, he's my BFFF—Butterfinger Furry Friend Forever."

I shuddered as she gave him another round of Eskimo kisses.

Riding back to the Nub, Cattricks filled me in on the gossip about each of the friend's we'd met. "Heybitch has a serious drinking problem."

"Really?"

"Big time. She loves the shine. Her family runs stills up in the hills so she basically grew up drinking the stuff," she said, using her hand as a bottle and emulating a gulping motion.

"I wouldn't have guessed."

"She's high functioning. Probably only buzzing a little bit today. Don't worry, Spy, I wouldn't have let her get too close to you with scissors if I thought she was wasted."

"Thanks." I liked being in on the scoop, feeling like part of the club. She was winning points with me and perhaps I was falling under her spell like everyone else.

When we arrived, Dale and Stone were talking and joking around outside. The two were gravitating toward each other with Dale assuming a big brother role. Their budding bromance added to my latent jealousy of Stone. The day had improved my relations with Cattricks; still, I was enamored with Dale when he complimented my new look.

We followed the normal route back to Pinch's Point, but

something felt different. It was as though Stone and I were following new paths. We were both in good spirits and eagerly recounted the events of our day. Stone told me he'd solved several of the problems with his invention. A new energy surrounded him and it was clear the *Remora Tank* episode was behind him.

At the house Flats didn't seem to notice Stone's improved mood or my new look. He was engrossed in his research, his glasses hanging on the end of his nose, which was buried in a thick, bound volume. I saw he was studying Blackstone's *Commentaries on the Laws of England*. The treatise was considered a rational explanation of the law—something Corn said was an oxymoron.

She gave us the "don't bother your father" look and walked us to the kitchen. There we scarfed down warm cookies Aunt Em had just pulled from the oven. Corn complimented my new hairstyle and listened patiently to our stories. Meanwhile, Aunt Em cast suspecting stares our way as she washed dishes. I don't think she approved of our new friends.

14.

It's not the size of the dog in the fight; it's the size of the fight in the dog.
~ Mark Twain

As with most historic homes, Pinch's Point was a museum of antiques. The rooms were filled with dark wood tables and ornate chairs; the walls were covered with a menagerie of adornments gathered over the decades by members of the Pinch clan. One of the more interesting items was a telephone located in the sitting room. It was so old the handset was attached to the main unit with a cord! Over the years I'd forgotten it was anything more than a prop. The household was jarred out of its mid-morning quiet when it rang the next day. Even in the adjacent room, the repetitive metallic ringing rattled my bones.

Aunt Em answered and listened to the caller before asking my father to come to the phone. "Flats, come quick. It's Mrs. Johnson from down the road and she's in a tizzy. She says there's a rabid dog out there and it's headed our way."

Flats grabbed the phone and listened as Mrs. Johnson brought him up to speed.

"Okay, calm down, Harriet. I'll take care of it. Just stay inside and keep the door closed." He hung up the phone and rubbed his chin pensively.

"What is it, Flats?" I asked.

"She said there's a mad dog on the loose. Said she saw it attack Mr. Abernathy's big tabby cat, Morris. Tore the thing to shreds."

"Oh, dear! What do we do?"

Aunt Em answered, "You'd better call the Peacekeepers, Flats. At least get them to sign a release before you go shooting anyone's dog."

"There's no time for that, Em. Who knows where it could go by then. We need to take action and shoot it now before it can infect anything else. We'll have to take the legal risk."

That wasn't something Flats would typically say so I knew the situation must be dire. I turned to Stone and he nodded. We both ran for our guns and returned in a matter of seconds.

Flats looked at us and shook his head.

"Please, Flats, can *we* shoot it?"

"No, too dangerous, kids. And you have the wrong guns for the job anyway. I prefer a shotgun for this kind of work." He walked to the gun room and returned with a weapon as long as I was tall. Flats inspected the single, massive barrel and loaded a shell into the chamber. He dropped a handful of additional cartridges into his pocket. "Okay, let's roll."

We walked out together and Flats told us to wait on the porch with Corn and Em. The air was still and an eerie quiet surrounded the house. We scanned the horizon and detected no sign of movement. Tense moments passed before we finally saw an animal headed down the driveway.

"There, Flats!" I screamed.

"Yep, I see it."

I watched in horror as the mammoth beast chugged our way. When the dog came into better view I could see it was a St. Bernard. It was easily two hundred pounds, the biggest I'd ever seen. His fur was wet and matted and his muzzle was covered with froth and dirt.

"Shoot it, Flats!" I yelled as the monster neared. When he lowered his gun I thought my dad was a coward. I also thought he was about to be eaten.

If Flats couldn't handle it then I knew it was up to me. I shouldered my rifle, but Aunt Em pushed it down before I could sight the laser.

"I have to stop it, Aunt Em."

"No, Spy, that's not the rabid dog."

"Seriously? Look at it, the thing's disgusting."

"That's Mr. Camber's dog. He always looks that way; the breed slobbers a lot."

Seconds later the dog entered the front yard and, to my

surprise, flew right past Flats. My father ignored it and maintained his focus on the road.

"What was he running from?" I asked, my innards twisting tighter.

"Look! There!" Stone shouted.

From the same direction, I could see a tiny animal weaving unevenly toward us. It was maybe the size of the St. Bernard's head at most. As it entered a sunny patch on the driveway I recognized the dog and my eyes widened. "Butterfinger," I whispered.

"That little runt?" Corn scoffed.

"Get back inside," I warned, pulling Corn and Stone and closing the screen door behind us.

"Oh please, I'll whack it with a fly swatter and we'll get on with the day," Corn said.

"You don't understand, Corn. That dog's got teeny, sharp teeth and a vicious streak a mile wide. It's the most bad-tempered Chihuahua you've ever set eyes on."

She looked down with a doubting scowl.

Movement on the driveway refocused my attention. I saw a blue uniform and realized it was the mailman. He'd been napping by one of the pecan trees and was now approaching Butterfinger.

"Nooo!" I yelled, but it was too late. The tiny dog launched from the ground and clamped onto the man's neck. He staggered and swatted at the attacker. When he finally pulled it free a geyser of blood squirted from the hole in his neck. As the mailman crumbled to the ground, the dark fluid continued to shoot out like water from a fire hydrant on a summer day.

"Oh, poor Mr. Meara," Aunt Em cried. "That's why mailmen hate dogs."

Meanwhile, Flats was holding his ground and aiming the gun. He was fiddling with his glasses and finally flung them to the ground in frustration.

"Run away, Flats! Run away!" I called.

He ignored my pleas and held steady. After taking a few more bites out of Mr. Meara's face, Butterfinger returned to his course. Beads of sweat slid down my temples as he closed the distance to Flats.

"Oh, just shoot him already," I said.

"Don't worry, honey. Flats knows what he's doing," Corn assured me. She had a strange look of excitement and was licking her lips in anticipation.

"What if he misses?" I thought about the fact that I'd never actually seen Flats shoot a gun before.

She laughed. "Flats? I don't think so, sweetie. He never misses."

My gaze swung back to Flats just in time to see him pull the trigger. The deafening blast was followed by a kick that rocked his body. A short distance in front of him a red spray appeared and then dissipated. The tiny demon had been vaporized.

Flats picked up his glasses and casually paced forward to examine his work. He gave a satisfied nod and walked back our way.

"Stay away from the red puddle. Splattered entrails can be just as dangerous as the live dog," he said as he came up the steps. He went right past us without another word. His level of calm was amazing; he wasn't even breathing heavy.

Aunt Em called the waste collection department and that afternoon T-bone the garbage man showed up in a white hazmat suit. Stone and I watched from the porch as he sprayed the dog's remains with a chemical solution and then used a wide shovel to scoop up the mess. T-bone placed the final remnants of Butterfinger in a red biohazard container and waved good-bye.

As I replayed the events of the morning over and over in my head I was having a hard time reconciling them with the prior assessment of my father. I wondered if he was changing or perhaps it was my view of him that was in flux. Maybe Corn had been right and Flats could do things besides sue people. Maybe my father wasn't a pussy after all.

Corn was rocking nearby on the glider.

"Can I ask you a question?" I said.

"Sure, baby, shoot...I mean...go ahead."

"How did you know Flats wouldn't miss?"

She grinned and then looked around to make sure he was out of earshot. "There are lots of things you don't know about your father. Someday when you're older he'll be the one to tell you. As for the shooting, he was a highly skilled marksman when he was younger. 'One shot, one kill, Pinch' they called him."

"Really?" Stone said, surprised as I was.

"Yes, indeed. But don't let him know I told you," she warned.

"Okay, it's our secret." It was like she had given us a single piece to an incomplete puzzle and now we wanted more. "What else can he do?" I prodded.

"Oh, your daddy can do all kinds of things." She had the wry smile on her face that I saw many times growing up. Only later when I became a woman did I understand its real meaning.

15.

Too many good docs are gettin' out of business. Too many OBGYNs aren't able to practice their…their love with women all across this country.
~ George W. Bush
(I swear I didn't make this one up. Scout's honor.)

Over the next few weeks, the level of angst in our house rose like steady floodwaters. Flats was evaluating a high-profile case and was dropping hints of turbulence ahead, especially if it went to trial. As always, Flats kept a lid on his emotions, but we could sense his tension—underneath the pot was boiling.

Through all of his past cases, I'd never seen him so conflicted. There seemed to be an added weight of importance to the decision he had to make. Corn cooked a steady stream of Flats's favorite meals, while Stone and I did our best not to bother him. Meanwhile, the situation at my school was deteriorating and I felt like I was alone on a sinking island.

One night I was walking past the study where Flats was reading and in my peripheral vision I could see him leaning in close to the materials he was studying. It was as if he was trying desperately to find an answer hidden among the words on the page.

I hurried past, not knowing if he'd seen me or not. Then something made me stop. He didn't say a word, but somehow it felt like he was calling for me. After a few steps in reverse I peered through the doorway.

"Hey, Flats."

"Oh hey, Spy," he said without looking up.

"Is everything okay?" I asked.

"Sure, sure, fine."

"Okay, I was just checking."

I shrugged and walked away again.

"Spy, come on in here."

This time I stopped because he *had* called me. I turned around and entered the study. He motioned to the chair next to him and I hopped on up.

"Am I interrupting, Flats?"

"No, I need a break, Spy. Tell me about your day."

Given the circumstances I didn't intend to burden him further. My days were still owned by Miss Fisher and she'd become a shell of a human. "The usual. Working diligently toward the big year-end test."

He didn't buy my blasé attitude. "Is your teacher getting you to the level necessary to be prepared for the examination?"

"Well..."

"Please tell me the truth, Spy."

The look in his eyes when he said the words was like a parental trigger that set off reactions deep inside my brain. I tried to stop the waterworks, but he'd tapped an emotion center tied to a pre-programmed response.

"Miss Fisher is a mess and I'm so afraid I'm going to get stuck in fourth grade, Flats." I could already taste the salty tears tickling the corners of my mouth.

He knelt down in front of me so our faces were at the same level and put his hands on my upper arms. "Oh, Spy, why would you say such a silly thing? You're an intelligent young lady, I'm sure you'll ace the test. However, if Miss Fisher isn't doing her job we can get you help. We'll get a tutor and the rest of the family will pitch in—all of us."

"Seriously?"

"Of course."

"We did learn a lot during the first part of the year so maybe it'll be enough."

"Do I need to go down there and talk to her?" he asked, handing me a handkerchief.

"No, you better not. I don't want to make her mad. Hopefully she'll get it together now that we're in the final stretch."

"Okay, I'll do whatever you need, Spy. You need to let me know, though. I'm sorry I've been so busy, I don't want you to feel like you can't come to me if you have a problem."

"Thanks, Dad, I feel better already." A puffy grin broke through the subsiding rain showers and I leaned forward to give him a hug. Surprisingly he didn't seem to care that I called him dad. It sounded foreign coming off my tongue. "What's troubling you, Dad?"

"Oh, this? It's a big case I'm trying to get my arms around."

"What happened?" I asked.

Normally he wouldn't have told me, but he probably knew it would distract me from my troubles.

"Unfortunately a baby died, Spy."

"That's terrible. I hope you get whoever did it."

"Yes, but that's the tricky part. No one killed it. It's not like a child was stabbed, or bludgeoned, or blown up. No hand-to-hand combat—that would be horrible. No one wants to read stories or see movies about things like that. Anyway...the baby died during childbirth."

"Was it sick?"

"There were a number of complications."

"*Complications?*"

"Yes, things that weren't the way they should have been. Even healthy newborns are fragile. It's worse when they have health issues."

"Who's fault was it?"

Flats pondered the question. I could tell this was the crux of his conundrum. "Often times when there are complications the doctors can do things to help the baby. As best I can tell, the doctor did everything within his power. Unfortunately, it still wasn't enough."

"Then who caused the complications? Somebody has to be at fault."

"I'm not sure anyone was, however, the parents made a number of poor choices. Still, it's hard to accuse parents who lost a child of being at fault. Without getting into too much detail, Spy, having babies is tricky business. There are no guarantees, but you can do things to make sure the odds be ever in your favor. One of the biggest factors is the age of the parents."

"You were pretty old when Stone and I were born," I pointed

out. "Did we have complications?"

Flats's mouth creased upward. "I wasn't *that* old! And your mother was a fair amount younger than me. There were a couple hiccups, but things were reasonably smooth for both of you. The individuals that had this baby are powerful people and are used to getting their way. Do you know who Alma Mater is?"

"Yes, I've seen her on TV."

"She spent most of her life building her political career. Years ago she led a competitive party and attempted a political coup."

"What's that?"

"Like a rebellion."

"Oh, I get it."

"Back then her name was Alma Dime. Her attempt failed and she was going to be tried for treason until, Darth Mater, the brother of the president at that time, stepped in and begged for mercy on her behalf. He convinced his brother to spare a Dime. It turned out that Alma and Darth were secretly in love. In the aftermath she threw in the towel and went over to their side. They were married and she became Alma Mater.

"Several years after abandoning her political aspirations she decided to have a baby. They attempted to conceive, but were unable. She was already in her fifties and he was in his sixties—they should have been preparing to wear diapers, not change them. Instead of considering other alternatives, they wanted the baby to be theirs. They worked with fertility specialists and were finally able to get pregnant."

At the time I didn't understand everything he was saying. However, his internal struggle—the fight between what he wanted to believe as a trial lawyer and what he truly believed as a person—was easy to comprehend. I was enthralled and remained completely attentive.

"During the pregnancy there were a number of those *complications* with both the mother and baby. Childbirth is much safer than it used to be, but sometimes you simply can't cheat nature. The doctor did everything he could to keep them both healthy and reach full term. Still, the baby didn't survive. The Maters were crushed and when their sorrow eventually turned to anger they didn't want to accept what had happened.

"Whenever someone experiences a loss—especially involving someone young—they want answers and they want to assign blame. It's human nature and when it comes to life and death the drive is the strongest."

"Then who can you blame, Flats?"

"You're asking the same question I been asking myself, over and over."

"This sounds like a tough one."

"Yes, it is. Neither side is interested in compromising so there is going to be a lawsuit. Right now I'm caught in the middle. The doctor wants me to defend him. He's a friend and great doctor and he happens to be the man who brought you into this world. A man so skilled he was able to reach inside the devil herself and safely retrieve a perfect angel," Flats said, stroking my hair.

I smiled at the sweet compliment toward me and then frowned at his disrespect toward my mother as I processed his joke.

"Sorry, Spy, anyhow, he needs someone who knows the system to fight the other firms lining up against him. His practice delivers most of the babies in Maybach now. The others have left due to lawsuits.

"Given the Maters' high profile, the legal team going after the doctor will be swinging for the fences. Those attorneys don't want me to defend the doctor and have even offered me a cut of the settlement if I *don't* take him as my client."

"Isn't that a bribe?"

"Pretty much, yeah. And if I *do* represent the doctor they've said they'll cut me out of future deals and soil my reputation."

"Isn't that blackmail?"

"Yep, pretty much."

"What if you do nothing?"

"Then I have to live with myself, Spy. This is my job and I've never run away from tough cases in the past. I don't plan to start now. I don't think the doctor did anything wrong. It was not his fault."

"It sounds like you just made your decision, Flats."

"Yes, Spy. I think I did."

16.

In matters of style, swim with the current; in matters of principle, stand like a rock.
~ Thomas Jefferson

An early skirmish of the battle took place a week later and I was there to witness it. After school I'd walked downtown to meet Flats for an ice cream. On the way back to his office I was desperately trying to keep melted black cherry from trickling down onto my hand. Flats was tongue dueling with drips of chocolate pecan. Turning the corner onto his block we were both giggling when he stopped dead in his tracks. The sidewalk ahead was strewn with flowers.

"Oh no," Flats said, bending to pick one up.

Missing his look of dread, I exclaimed, "How pretty! Someone sent you flowers, Flats. It would've been nicer if they came in a vase, though. Look how many there are."

"They're white roses, Spy. It's a calling card and a warning. This means the Clintons are involved."

"Haven't you worked with them before?"

"Yes, but this means they've aligned with the Maters' team and they want me to do the same."

We shuffled our feet through the mat of thorny stems. Approaching the door, I heard the unmistakable growl of Maybach engines on the street behind me. I glanced over my shoulder and saw the oncoming procession: a long line of sleek, black sedans. They stopped in front of Flats's office and the rear doors opened in unison. Out stepped an angry mob made up of Maybach's legal elite. Several were carrying umbrellas with metal spiked tips and thumping them on their palms—likely because rain was in the forecast. Others were carrying oversized, legal briefcases filled with God knows what.

It didn't look good. I'd never seen such an imposing group of juris doctorates. Flats pulled me close as they formed a semicircle around us.

One of the men stepped forward to speak for the group. I recognized him as Jon Fairchild from his countless billboards around town.

"We know what you're up to, Flats. Is he up there? Your baby killer."

His comment drew my attention to the windows above. The afternoon glare obscured my view, but I thought I saw someone waving to us.

"Have you all lost your minds?" Flats asked, his eyes scanning the crowd. "Do you realize what you're doing? Do you understand what the fallout is going to be?"

"Don't try to make us into the bad guys. We didn't let that innocent life slip away. We're on the right side of this fight and this is your last chance to join us, Pinch. If not, you can see what you're going to be up against."

"Indeed, I can see exactly what I'm dealing with."

The stares hardened in response to Flats's barb.

"Flats, we're trying to be reasonable."

"The doctor is entitled to representation."

"Sure he his. Let him get some out-of-district free agent. You're one of us, Flats. You should be working with us, not against us. What do you say?" he said, extending his hand to secure my father's agreement.

Flats stared at the man, pondered the offer for a moment, and defiantly kept his hands where they were. I thought about how sticky his fingers would be from the melted ice cream. Had Flats shaken, Mr. Fairchild would have been in for a surprise.

The man lowered his arm. "So that's the way it's going to be, Flats. All right. Don't say you weren't warned. This trial is going to be very costly."

"I'm sure it will be," Flats said without blinking.

Mr. Fairchild had taken note of the worn volume tucked under Flats's arm. "I see you're reading Blackstone's *Commentaries*. How fitting for a traitor like you."

At some point Flats had told me about Benedict Arnold using the book as his key when spying against the former United States. I felt so smart understanding the reference.

"I intend to fight your hyperbole and emotional arguments with reason and a rational interpretation of the law," Flats replied. In the face of the seething mob he remained calm and collected. He was outnumbered and knew this was not the place for a fight.

"Good luck with that." Everyone chuckled.

The disrespect crawled under my skin. Anger had been building inside my body and my mouth was the easiest exit available. "Flats is going to crush you."

Even louder snickers rose from the crowd. The ones in back were surprised, not having realized I was standing there.

Mr. Fairchild glared down at me. "Go home, little girl, this is *man* talk." Several of the female attorneys in the mob cleared their throats. "Oh, sorry, you know what I meant—grownup talk."

My rage generated a focused, red laser dot on his forehead. Unconsciously, my finger pulled a trigger that wasn't there and punctured the soggy waffle cone in my hand.

Fairchild looked to Flats and then back to me as if to tell my father to hush his rambunctious child. Flats simply raised an eyebrow and shrugged like a judge granting latitude.

I was off to the races. "Sometimes people just die, Mr. Fairchild. I'm sorry for Mrs. Mater, but money won't bring her baby back. She needs to move on and not punish Dr. Jellyfinger. It was not his fault."

His expression changed to that of a boxer who hadn't seen a punch coming.

To weaken his support, I executed a flanking maneuver. Behind Fairchild was a familiar face. "I know you, Mr. Rutter. Your son Brad is in my class. He's the smartest boy there—a perfect child. Tell me. Who delivered him?"

Silence.

"Who?" I demanded.

"Dr. Jelly…"

"Excuse me, I'm way down here. I couldn't quite hear that."

"Dr. Jellyfinger."

"And what if he hadn't been there. Think about what might have happened." I tried to meet his eyes, but they were cast downward. "And you Ms. Parton. Not too long ago I saw you in the Starbucks breast-feeding a baby. Who delivered that eager little leche lover?"

"Dr. Sprettum."

"Ah! One of Dr. J's partners. No surprise."

"And you, Mr. President. When you had relations with that college cheerleader. Who delivered the baby?" I'd heard numerous Clinton stories while listening to Corn gossip in the kitchen with her friends.

This salvo elicited *ooos* from the crowd.

Someone whispered, "Damn, the girl's swinging low."

Another, "Oh hell, Slick Willy, that little lady cooked you."

The former leader of Pander straightened his neck and held his fist vertical with the thumb capped on top. "Now let's be clear. There has never been a definitive paternity test conducted."

"Sir, who delivered your lovechild?"

"Could you please clarify your definition of *delivered*?"

"Don't be evasive."

"I'm still a little foggy on what you're asking."

"For God's sake, answer the question!"

He caved. "Okay, okay, it was Dr. Jellyfinger. I flew him to Mexico on Al Gore's jet to handle the procedure."

"And yet here you are seeking blood. Pathetic."

The crowd started to disperse. With their assault in tatters there had been an unspoken call to retreat.

"That's right, get out of here," I taunted.

"Don't think this is over, Flats." a belligerent lawyer shouted before climbing back into his car.

"Hey, Clinton. Before you go clean up your mess," I said, pointing to the flowers. What can I say; I was on a roll. He hung his head and sent his Secret Service detail over to pick up the roses. I grabbed a half-dozen of the nicer ones to give to Corn.

Another attorney walked up to Flats and spoke in a quiet, reconciliatory tone. "You know this isn't going to stop them."

"Yes, I know."

"Well, no matter what happens you still have my respect," he said, offering his hand.

"Thank you," Flats replied, shaking after wiping his hand on his pant leg.

"May the juries be ever in your favor," the man said.

"And yours as well."

Flats watched in awe as the last car drove off. He seemed to be in a trance, like he was enjoying the scene so completely that he didn't want to miss a second of it. Later in life he would remind me of that moment many times. He would tell me how impressed he was with the little girl who slayed an army of well-equipped orators with only her words.

There was a pinging noise and Flats pulled his phone from his pocket. Dr. J was calling from the office up above where he'd watched the entire episode.

"Hello?"

"Are they gone?" Dr. J asked.

"Yes, but this is only a reprieve. They'll regroup and be ready to attack again."

"Have you made a decision yet, Flats?"

Flats looked down and flashed me his best proud-of-my-daughter smile. "I have. I'm going to take your case, Dr. J."

"Thank you, Flats," a relieved Dr. J replied. "Should we start preparing now?"

"No, why don't you head home. I'll get rolling first thing in the morning. Right now I need to do something else."

"Okay, thanks again, Flats, I knew I could count on you."

My father hung up, turned to me, and examined the gooey mess in my hand. "It looks like your ice cream melted."

"Yeah, sorry about that." There were reddish-white drops dappled across the middle of the sidewalk.

"Don't be sorry, Spy. It's no surprise given the fiery speech you just made. Mine didn't do much better. Let's go back and get replacements."

"You're sure?"

"Definitely. You've earned it."

We tossed the remains of our first cones in a trashcan and retraced our path back to the ice cream parlor. I switched sides and took his hand with my non-sticky one. Looking up I saw he was still beaming.

"You did a great job today, Spy. Now I need to figure out how to defend Dr. J."

17.

Wisdom is not a product of schooling but of the lifelong attempt to acquire it.
~ Albert Einstein

The episode at Flats's office was the highlight of an otherwise dismal period of my childhood. School life was degenerating by the day. Rather than tend to us, Miss Fisher preferred to let nature take over and allowed the class to govern itself. It had become survival of the fittest and a number of kids had not survived. Despite my daily fear, I refused to quit.

Each day when the starting bell rang a paranoid energy descended over the classroom—the signal that the death race had begun. Like any good prisoner, I had built up a persona of toughness to dissuade other students from messing with me. I also had a big brother watching over me. Still, you had to be careful in the "fight" spots: the locker-room, the bathroom, and behind the laundry equipment in the school basement.

Occasionally, there were altercations in broad daylight when one bully wanted to challenge another for turf rights. They intentionally did it in the open so everyone else could see. If successful they would move up in the pecking order. A failed attempt usually meant a trip to the hospital.

It was an otherwise unremarkable Tuesday on the playground when I sensed trouble brewing. Several boys were whispering to each other and each time they did they looked in my direction. At first I thought it was just something childish, like an unobstructed view up my skirt, but I had overalls on that day. I looked myself over to make sure nothing else was amiss.

Then they began to move. They gathered in one spot for a while and then shifted to another area, each time picking up another kid or two. I rallied my girlfriends and we prepared our defenses.

Eventually the pack of boys headed out to the middle of the kickball diamond. That was where they were going to make the play. A boy named Bobby Charles, stood at the front of the group and called out, "Spy Pinch! I hear your daddy loves baby killers!"

He stood proudly with his arms folded as the boys behind him shared a malice-filled laugh. I knew his mother was a lawyer and it was likely she'd been with the group at Flats's office.

Despite the show, his first hope was that I wouldn't accept the challenge. His buddies would pat him on the back and he'd score an easy win with no actual fight. I wasn't the sort of girl to buy into that plan.

Miss Fisher was of course nowhere to be seen. Tristan Yule was also missing, which seemed to happen a lot at recess. Sometimes bigger kids would intervene, but they appeared disinterested. They went on with playing cards and drinking beer, as many of them had reached the legal drinking age.

Bobby bit his lip nervously when I hopped off the tree stump and waved for my girl posse to provide an escort. I was angry, but told myself to handle it like I had the group of lawyers. *Use my smart words...*

I stopped and we sized each other up from about ten feet away, it felt like a natural distance programmed into our DNA. Near enough to read body language, but not smell each other's breath. Close enough to attack and also react. I stared at his face, which reminded me of a lumpy, uneven potato.

"What did you say about my daddy?" I demanded.

He peered around to make sure ranks were closed behind him. "You heard me. What are you going to do about it?"

Good question. He had thrown down the challenge and I had to respond. I was desperately thinking of how I could do it without a fight. I went on the offensive hoping he would blink and back down like the lawyers had. "My daddy is the best attorney in this district. The lawyers going after Dr. J know it and that's why they're so afraid. It kind of reminds me of you, Bobby." I turned and got high-fives from the girls.

"I'm not afraid," he said. The quiver in his voice indicated otherwise. He was starting to feel trapped in his own snare and was getting desperate. Backing down wasn't an option so he upped the ante, our escalations all but assuring a fight.

"Where's your daddy, Spy? At home playing a little *corn* hole?"

No response could escape my clenched teeth. Bobby was a typical dim-witted elementary schoolboy and we'd had few disagreements in the past, so I assumed he was taking cues from his parents. I considered that and tried to wear his skin as Flats had suggested. Instead, all I could think about was giving him a good skinning.

"Flats Pinch is something all right," he continued. "My momma says he's a modern-day Thomas Jefferson." I only understood the comment later. Still, from the reaction I knew he was disrespecting my surrogate mother in addition to Flats.

"You take that back, Bobby Charles!" I had to fight hard not to burst into tears as emotion exploded inside of me. I knew it would be over if I did.

Bobby went for the kill. "Is the baby gonna cry?"

"I said take it back."

"I'm not taking nothin' back, because it's all true." He punctuated the statement by spitting toward me. Most of it missed, but a few drops caught my shoes. When I looked back up the red laser dot had appeared right between his dark, weaselly eyes. *Oh snap! It's go time.*

I lunged forward, violating the neutral zone. A roar went up and he braced for impact. After locking horns, we rolled around, limbs flying, mainly slapping and pulling clothes. He was stronger, but I was quicker. Being similar in size, it was an even match.

The boisterous onlookers energized our brawl and the noise alerted the closest staff. We were still entangled and flailing in the dirt when Coach Smitty arrived. He blew his whistle and pulled us apart. We caught our breath as he stood between us wearing the requisite PE teacher uniform: tight, polyester Bike shorts and a white T-shirt with Maybach Phys Ed. stenciled on the front.

We both assumed he was going to stop us and the fight would end in a draw. Instead he was only calling a timeout and then told us to get back to it. "All right, next round. Try to keep it clean."

I looked at Bobby and he was equally confused. We thought it was a trick and stayed put.

"Come on, what are you waiting for?" Coach Smitty goaded.

Bobby and I shrugged and then charged each other. It remained sloppy, in close we could only land short punches with little impact. He took hold of the suspenders on my overalls and pinned me with an arm behind my back. Being on top emboldened him and he started taunting me again. *He's monologuing! Big mistake*, I thought. The anger erased my pain. I threw my legs to one side and spun over, pulling in my knees. After planting my feet on Bobby's chest a quick extension sent him flying backward. I was up in a flash and pounced.

He was swinging wildly so I grabbed an arm and rolled him. I was getting tired and knew I had to go for a knockout. Instead of taunting him I simply rubbed his face in the dirt—like I was trying to rebury a potato. I spun a one-eighty on his back and reached my hand down the back of his pants. My angry fist latched onto the waistband of his underwear and I pulled sadistically. Groans of anticipation rose from the crowd as the tighty-whities came into full view.

Somewhere in the background noise I heard Bobby pleading for mercy, "Please, Spy. Don't do it. I'm sorry. I take it back! I take it back!"

The audience's frenzy had seized control of my mind. *Too late…*

I grabbed the band of elastic with both hands and used my body weight to yank. The grisly sound of ripping cotton mixed with Bobby's screams of agony. Someone was pulling me off, but I wouldn't let go. It made Bobby scream even louder. Finally, enough force was applied that the fibers gave way and I fell back with a handful of severed fabric. I threw it on the ground in disgust.

I turned to see the Home Economics teacher, Mrs. Butterworth, behind me. She lifted me by my armpits and looked to Coach Smitty. "Were you letting them fight?" she asked, the syrupy timbre of the islands dripping through her words.

"Yeah, it was kind of fun to watch. Sorry. Please don't tell Principal Wilson."

"What's wrong with you?"

"Oh come on, Helen. It's not like I was wagering on it."

She gave him a parting look of contempt before dragging us off to the office.

On the walk, a parade of thoughts crossed my mind. First was the fight. I had won hands down. Or more literally—hands down his pants. Next was the fallout. My victorious exclamation point would stand out in my peers' memories for some time to come and would serve as a persuasive deterrent for anyone giving consideration to stepping to me. Given the coming trial that was a definite benefit.

My final progression was to Flats. The high racing through my body from the fight drained rapidly and I had a sudden urge to cry again when I realized they were going to call my father. Despite my reason for fighting, he wasn't going to be happy.

***

I sat in a worn chair in the main office picking at the splintered armrest. It was a fitting throne for a girl with a dirt-streaked face and scruffy hair. I felt like pure white trash as staff passed by giving sideways looks of judgment.

After only minutes the translucent door flew open and Flats strode in. He'd walked from his office and there was a light sheen of perspiration on his forehead. It was crazy how fast that man could zip around town.

He gave me a disappointed look, placed his fedora on the hat rack, and checked in with the secretary. Our principal, Mr. Wilson, appeared and recounted the details of my altercation. As he listened, Flats responded with humming sounds of disbelief.

Flats knelt in front of me. "Are you okay, Spy?"

"Yes, Flats. I got the best of him. He's in the clinic with ice on his privates." I made the mistake of letting a proud smile crease my lips.

"Spy, I'm glad you're not injured, but I'm very upset about this."

"I know, Flats. I'm sorry." I should have left it at that, but felt like I still had to make my case. "He was saying mean things. I couldn't let him get away with that in front of the other kids. It wasn't my fault."

"You said you weren't injured, Spy."

"Huh? That's right."

"Well, the last time I checked words can't physically hurt you."

I paused, realizing he'd caught me in one of his word traps. "I know, Flats, but it still hurt inside. He said things about you and Corn."

When I mentioned Corn his eyebrow twitched upward. It was a flash of anger, which quickly passed.

"I know it's tough, Spy. Still, if you let them get to you then they've already won the fight."

"I tried words again, Flats. Honest. It just wasn't enough so I had to call in backup," I said, putting up my dukes. "Plus, the stress is really building up in here, Flats. It's like a rubber band stretched to its limit."

He kissed my fists and gently pushed my hands down.

"I know."

"I'm trying, but it's tough to deal with these ignorant kids."

"Spy, that's not just a school lesson to learn, it's a life lesson. You're a bright girl and you'll have to deal with many dimmer lights along your journey."

"But shouldn't the cream rise to the top?"

"It does, but it takes time and there are lots of caveats. It's not like you can move off to a secret compound hidden in the mountains and live only with likeminded people."

"What are caveats?"

"Times when the rules are imperfect—school for instance. You can get perfect grades, while a lesser student squeaks by with the bare minimum. Even though you put in significantly more effort, you both move to the fifth grade. Life is often like that, but you can't let it stop you from trying to stay on top. Don't let a bar set too low bring you down to mediocrity.

Mr. Wilson seemed troubled by what Flats was saying, but wasn't inclined to give a rebuttal. He made me promise not to fight again and sent me home with my father. Flats went easy on me, given the cause of the confrontation. I only hoped that my decisive schoolyard victory would allow for smoother sailing ahead.

***

My fourth grade avalanche continued to rumble downhill the following week. Mild spring breezes were blowing as Stone and I rode our bikes around the neighborhood after school. Passing a row of cars parked along the side of the street, we heard the suspension on one of them making squeaking sounds. Curiosity caused us to turn around and I realized the wobbling vehicle was Miss Fisher's.

Through the dirty window I saw her distinct profile. There was someone else inside, but I couldn't see his face. Miss Fisher was sitting on his lap running her fingers through his hair. Then I recognized the hair—it belonged to Tristan Yule.

Given how close they were, I assumed they were studying intensely for the upcoming test. I was glad they were both committed to his success. Perhaps he would finally move on to fifth grade.

Tristan was whispering something into her ear and he must have been getting all the answers right because she kept yelling, "Yes! Yes! Yes!" while the squeaking noise increased in pace and volume.

Stone had pulled alongside me and was watching with wide eyes.

Miss Fisher slammed her hand against the window and I shrieked in surprise. She saw me and yelled, "Jean Luc Pinch, get out of here! Now I see why they call you Spy."

"I wasn't intentionally spying. I swear."

There was a flurry of movement inside and when Tristan saw me he started laughing.

Stone was also laughing. He and Tristan must have been in on a joke that only boys understood. My brother grabbed me by the arm and dragged me away.

As we pedaled off I remained confused. "I don't know why she was so upset. I think it's nice that she's spending extra time studying with the Yule boy. She's working hard to fill him with knowledge."

"You've got it backward, Spy. *He* was the one doing the filling and I don't think it was knowledge."

"I wish I got that kind of attention," I lamented.

"Trust me, Spy, if a teacher at school gave you that kind of attention they'd be arrested. You've got a lot to learn, little sister. And it's not the kind of stuff you learn in school...except maybe in Miss Fisher's class..."

***

Later that week we had another unexpected encounter with Miss Fisher. It would prove to be the last time I ever saw her.

Stone and I were watching TV when we heard Corn call out, "Flats, get on out here. There's something going down at Mrs. DuPont's house."

Flats jumped up from his desk and hurried to the front porch, Stone and I close at his heels.

"Look down yonder," Corn said, pointing toward the developing scene.

"What do you suppose is going on over there?" Flats asked the evening air.

Swirling red and blue lights painted the large trees lining our street and the facades of nearby houses. The source was a jagged row of Peacekeeper cruisers parked in front of the DuPont home. Interspersed were black, unmarked SUVs. There was a buzz of activity as Peacekeepers and agents from the DEA-keepers—wearing their omnipresent, navy blue windbreakers—scurried about.

Flats was instinctively drawn to the unfolding drama. He floated down the steps and told us to stay put. We promptly ignored his instructions and followed him down the sidewalk.

142

He stopped across from the DuPont house and I almost bumped into him as my attention was drawn to the spectacle of law enforcement. Realizing we had disobeyed him, Flats glared at us, but didn't say anything. He knew we weren't about to stand alone by the Baddley property again like on Halloween.

As other neighbors gathered, Stone and I couldn't help but steal glances at the Baddley place, hoping the commotion would draw out the occupant. We were rewarded with not so much as an illuminated porch light or drawn curtain—nothing.

"What do you s'pose is going on?" Corn asked, refocusing our attention.

"I'm not sure. Apparently Mrs. DuPont has run afoul of the law," Flats said.

His assumption was confirmed when the door burst open and Mrs. DuPont appeared dressed in a dingy, white tank top and baggy pajama bottoms. The gaunt woman writhed like an angry animal as an escort of several officers struggled to drag her by the tattoo-covered arms cuffed behind her back.

A cameraman was documenting the arrest, shining a bright light on Mrs. DuPont's face. Her legs and lips were in constant motion, making feeble attempts to kick him and lashing out with a rant of profanity.

When the rabid creature made it to the lawn she noticed the neighbors watching. "What are you losers looking at? Piss off and mind your own business." Then her eyes connected with my father. "Hey, there's my lawyer: Flats Pinch. Flats, make them stop. They're using excessive force. This is cruel and unusual punishment. They didn't read me my rights."

The officers paused for a moment wondering if Flats was going to step in.

"Flats, do something!" she demanded.

"Sorry, Mrs. DuPont, you'll be assigned a capable public defender," Flats said with a dismissive goodbye wave.

"You lazy, worthless bastard!" Mrs. DuPont continued her bitter tirade as they stuffed her in the back of one of the waiting vehicles and slammed the door. The well-insulated car provided a sudden silence.

"My-oh-my, she was certainly fired up," Corn said, enjoying the show.

"Yeah, whoever gets stuck with her in their cell will be the one suffering cruel and unusual punishment," Stone said.

Mrs. DuPont was the leader of a sad parade. The front door opened repeatedly and the authorities brought out an odd array of people in various states of dress and mental awareness.

"How many people are in there?" I asked.

"I'm as surprised as you are, Spy." Flats answered.

"Who's he? He looks familiar," I said, scrutinizing the next arrival.

"That's Mr. White, the chemistry teacher at Maybach High School."

"Hmm, I wonder what he was doing there."

There was, however, no question about the identity of the final person to emerge from the home.

"Oh no," I cried. "It's Miss Fisher."

"Your teacher?" Corn said.

"Yes. She reads stories to Mrs. DuPont. Why are they arresting her?"

"Spy, I don't think she was reading in there. I also doubt you'll be seeing her again this year," Flats said.

"I'll never pass our test now." My tears blurred the scene as Miss Fisher, still wearing her sunglasses, walked with a bowed head to a waiting car.

"Don't worry you'll be fine," Flats assured me, placing a hand on my shoulder.

Hell Tate appeared on the front porch and, after giving orders to his subordinates, made his way in our direction.

"Evening, Flats."

"Evening, Hell. What was old Mrs. DuPont up to?"

"Running a little business in there."

"Let me guess: chemicals."

"Meth."

Flats shook his head.

I couldn't help myself and blurted, "What's Meth?"

Stone punched me the way he did when he thought I was being a stupid little sister. Flats looked down and gave me his "the grownups are talking" face before continuing his conversation.

"I knew she had problems, but figured she was just a user. I didn't realize she was dealing. She always had boarders taking rooms so I didn't pay much attention to the people coming and going."

"You never know. Are you doing okay, Flats?"

"So far. I've got a big one coming up."

"That's what I've heard. Let me know if things get sideways for you."

"Will do, Hell."

"Well, I better get back to cleaning up this mess."

"Take care."

The officers continued to come and go, removing boxes of evidence from the house. When the cruisers began to drive off with Mrs. DuPont's crew and my teacher we traipsed home.

The rest of the night I had trouble relaxing, I fidgeted on the couch while watching TV in hopes of taking my thoughts off school. The tension built up and when I did land between the sheets my mind was racing at full speed. It was one of those nights when I probably fell asleep in ten minutes, but it felt like I tossed and turned for hours.

I woke up in a fog and struggled to get my bearings. Focusing on the black hands of the clock next to my bed I saw it was already late morning. Another reminder rang in the back of my brain: *It's test day!*

After pulling regular clothes on over my pajamas, I raced downstairs and sprinted out the door. Peacekeeper cars still lined the street in front of Mrs. DuPont's house and the spinning lights made me dizzy. Hell Tate stood statue-like and our eyes met as he glared down over the rims of his gold, aviator sunglasses. He didn't say anything, but I could read his mind: *You're late, Spy Pinch.*

The school's main entrance was eerily quiet when I bounded up the front steps. The "No Running In The Hallways" sign was a blur in my peripheral vision as I blew past it. Given the circumstances I couldn't afford to be concerned with hall monitors.

Panting and dripping with sweat, I was seriously regretting the decision not to ditch my PJs. I yanked open the door to my classroom and found Miss Fisher reclined in the chair at her desk with a cigarette dangling from the corner of her mouth. She didn't even react to my appearance.

Examining the room I saw nothing but rows of empty desks—another cardiac hiccup. "Where is everyone?"

"Oh, they're all gone, Jean Luc."

"Gone?"

"They've all finished and moved on to the fifth grade."

"What? All of them?"

"Yep. I've got a sweet bonus coming my way and big plans for spending it this summer."

Miss Fisher stood up and adjusted her skirt. There was an unsettling noise and Tristan Yule crawled out from under her desk. "How's it going, Spy?" he said.

"What about him?" I yelled, further incensed by the fact that Tristan always seemed to have a smile on his face.

"Oh, he passed the test!" Miss Fisher said, taking a deep drag on the cigarette before shoving it in Tristan's mouth. "He turned out to be my star pupil."

"Can I still take the test?"

"Sorry, Jean Luc, too late."

"So I have to stay back?" I stammered.

"Stay back? No, no, sweetie. You're going to jail."

"Are you kidding? You're just messing with me again, right?"

"This is no joking matter, young lady. We should probably give that hair a trim before they take you away," she said, snapping her scissors and advancing toward me.

Feeling for the doorway, I backed into the hall. After turning to run, I stopped in my tracks. In one direction Hell Tate waited with his arms crossed, behind him a wall of DEA-keepers in windbreakers and shades. A gang of hall monitors wearing neon yellow sashes blocked the opposite end. They were holding pink referral pads and ballpoint pens, which they clicked open and closed. The chorus of pens sounded like an angry rattlesnake.

Both factions descended upon me. I was swallowed by groping arms and hauled off to prison. There, I was led down a long, stone hallway with cells on both sides. It looked like a dungeon.

I passed a cell where a middle-aged man with thinning hair stood with his arms behind his back. He was wearing a plain, khaki jumpsuit and his mouth was covered with what looked like the lower half of a hockey mask. I assumed he had an eating disorder. Although most of his face was obscured, his eyes were frighteningly expressive. "Hello, Spy. Have you silenced the Chihuahuas?" he asked.

"Huh? I didn't kill Butterfinger."

"Are you sure?"

I was certain I hadn't been the one who shot the dog, but the way he said it made me question my memory. I walked on with a furrowed brow.

"Sorry, didn't mean to upset you, Spy," he called, his voice now far less sinister. "I'll save you a seat in the cafeteria at lunch time."

I pleaded with the guard over my shoulder, "Why am I here? I need to speak to my father, Flats Pinch—the lawyer."

He chuckled and pushed me forward. When we finally arrived at my cell he took out a ring of thick, iron keys and tried several before finding the correct one. The space was dark and appeared empty. It smelled like the corners of our basement. I shuffled in and watched the guard slam the door shut. The sound of his boots echoed down the corridor as he strode away.

I was still gazing through the bars when a voice from behind startled me.

"Well, well. Look who's here."

It was familiar in a bad way.

From the shadows, Mrs. DuPont appeared like a scary, white trash apparition. She was flexing the lean muscles on her tattooed man-arms.

"Are you going to beat me up?"

"Nah, not yet at least. I need you."

"You do?" My mood brightened knowing I wasn't going to get rolled.

"Yeah, since I'm stuck in here I'm going to need some mules." She pulled a wad of plastic baggies from her pocket. "Snatched these from the mess hall. Miss Fisher is my conduit. She's a volunteer teacher in the prison library and smuggles my product hidden inside hollowed-out books."

"That's terrible—from both a literary and legal standpoint."

147

"Oh please, little girl. Nobody reads books anymore. Now I'm going to need you to drop your drawers and bend over, see what kind of capacity we're working with."

I turned, grabbed the bars, and screamed, "Flats! Corn! Get me outta here!" I blinked and realized I was staring at my bedroom wall. A cold sweat wrapped my body and my hands were clamped onto the bars of my wrought iron headboard.

The door flew open and Corn raced into my room. "What is it, sweetie?"

"Oh, Corn, I was having the worst dream. Mrs. DuPont was there, and Miss Fisher, and Mr. Tate. And Hunk, and Zeke, and Hickory, too!"

"Who the hell are Hunk, Zeke, and Hickory?"

"I have no idea..."

"It's okay, Spy, it was just a dream. You're safe." She stroked my hair and pushed back my bangs.

"They were going to put me in jail for failing my test. What day is it?"

"Don't worry about that silly ol' test. You've still got a few weeks to go and I know you're gonna do just fine."

"I hope so."

"Why don't you get changed and I'll make you breakfast. It was a little crazy last night. That's why you had a bad dream."

I took some deep breaths and my heart rate gradually returned to normal. Growing up I didn't have many nightmares; however, bad things in my neighborhood had a way of invading my nocturnal psyche.

As expected, Miss Fisher was nowhere to be seen when we returned to school the following Monday. Principal Wilson arrived and told us not to worry; we would be getting a competent replacement soon. In the meantime, the only sub they could get on short notice was, Mr. Willey, our school's groundskeeper. The next week we were introduced to Mrs. Crabapple, a former kindergarten teacher they brought out of retirement to babysit us. She was older than dirt and had problems controlling her bladder.

It didn't matter to me as my family pulled together to help me prepare. Corn worked with me in the morning, Stone helped out after school, and Flats carved out some time for me each night.

Many of my fellow students weren't as lucky and simply resigned themselves to the fate of another year in the fourth grade.

On test day I was beyond nervous and worried about controlling *my* bladder. When the exam was over I ran from the building to breathe fresh air; it felt like I had been suffocating inside. I was confident in my performance, but would have to wait several weeks for the results to learn my fate.

Sitting at the dinner table that night, Flats casually mentioned that he'd seen Miss Fisher's name appear on the courthouse docket. He was confident her teaching certificate would be revoked and young minds would never be left in her incompetent hands again. I was glad the ordeal was over. It was a traumatic time in my life, but one that I learned from—wasn't that the point? Most of all I was ready for summer vacation.

18.

Then followed that beautiful season...Summer...Filled was the air with a dreamy and magical light; and the landscape lay as if new created in all the freshness of childhood.
~ Henry Wadsworth Longfellow

Freedom arrived sooner than I'd expected. I dropped the metal door on our mailbox one afternoon and tucked between the attorney solicitations was correspondence from the Maybach County School Board. Even though it was addressed to Flats, I tore open the official-looking envelope and scanned the text. Grades: fine. Cumulative test: passed. Result: promoted to grade five. My eyes looked to the sky and I spun an exultant pirouette. Unlike the poor Simpson boy, I would be graduating from the fourth grade after only one attempt.

I wallowed in glory for a day or so before reality hit me: I had nothing to do for the summer. Stone had thrown himself back into his project and made it clear he didn't want to be disturbed.

The result was endless hours lounging on the couch watching game shows, my mind softening faster than a banana in a bag. After what I'd been through it was a pleasant state of comfortable numbness. Still, I knew it couldn't last. One morning while speculating as to what was behind door number two, I heard a knock on the door. The sound shook me from my stupor. Corn had gone grocery shopping so I knew the responsibility for answering it was squarely upon my shoulders. I wiped the little drool-icicle dangling from the edge of my mouth—a known side effect of watching too much television—and shifted my atrophying legs to the floor.

When I got to the door there was no one there. I wondered if I'd imagined it or perhaps had confused a noise from the TV. I walked back to the living room and settled my posterior back into its couch groove. A moment passed before there was another, more urgent knock.

"Oh, all right," I groaned.

Once again, there was no one waiting for me so I kicked the door open, stepped onto the porch, and scanned the yard. I immediately suspected a neighbor boy known for his childish pranks. "If that's you Johnny Appleweed, you're going to get a good whoopin' when I catch you!"

Anger overwhelmed my apathy, forcing me to take action. After walking back inside, I raced through the house and slid out the back door. Picking my way along the hedge bordering our property, I moved to where I could see the front yard. Our steps were bordered by bushy, mint-tone evergreens and there was a lattice-enclosed crawlspace under the porch. I detected motion and gradually a figure emerged.

I bum rushed the perpetrator at full speed and sent him sailing into the prickly bushes.

"Damnit, Spy!" he yelled.

With my adrenaline rushing it took me a second to recognize who it was.

"Pyckle!"

"Yeah, thanks for the friendly welcome," he said. I reached into the shrubbery to help free him. "Was that necessary?" he asked, picking thorny barbs from his hands. "I guess the hoodie should've been a clue. You need to stop wearing that thing during the summer; it makes people suspicious. This could have been avoided—you were the one playing childish games. Obviously you still haven't grown up."

"Sorry, honey, I tried. This is all I could achieve," he said, gesturing to his body.

"That's not what I meant." I punched him on the arm and all was forgiven.

After picking the dried needles out of his cherub-like face and brushing off his clothes we went inside together.

Pyckle flopped down like he owned the place. "I got stuck with my aunt again."

"Oh, it's not so bad. She's a sweetheart. Just think if Mrs. DuPont had been your aunt."

"I heard they busted her."

"It was quite the scene."

"I figured she was dishin' ice down there. Too many zombies coming and going."

"Why didn't you alert the Peacekeepers?" I asked.

"Not my job and I'm not going to mess with someone's livelihood unless they're messing with mine. Advice you should heed, Spy. It'll keep you out of trouble. Speaking of livelihoods, what are we going to do this summer? My aunt sleeps all day so I'll have lots of free time and I need to scrape together a little green."

"I've been thinking about that. Now that you're here we can brainstorm new ideas."

"I was thinking it would be easier just to steal someone else's good idea."

"That's an option, too."

"We'll come up with something. Where's that no good brother of yours?"

"He's down in the basement in full invention mode. He says he's working non-stop, but I think he's doing other things too."

"Hmm—teenaged boy—I can think of a few things he's probably doing down there. I'll interrupt him later."

"With school being out he's hoping to have his current prototype operational by the end of the summer."

"Good for him. I hope he makes something to shove down the remoras' throats."

We were watching TV when Corn arrived home at lunchtime. She was carrying a bag of groceries and stopped to check on me.

Pyckle sat up and pumped out his chest. "Hello there, sweetest peach on the tree."

"Oh, hey there, Trouble." Corn replied as though she'd only seen him yesterday.

"How was shopping?" I asked. "Any good gossip from down at the Jungle?"

"Nothing much. People were mostly asking me about your father's case. This one has become very polarizing. People are either for or against Dr. J with no middle ground."

Her comment triggered a sinking feeling in my stomach.

"Hey, Trouble, why don't you make yourself useful and grab some groceries," Corn said.

Pyckle was more than willing to oblige and sprung up like a scared rabbit. I grudgingly assisted as well. When we got to her car Pyckle hoisted a giant bag of potatoes from the trunk. The contents shifted and he almost fell over.

"Do you need a hand?" I asked.

"Don't be silly. I got this, Spy." He wobbled a bit more and then steadied himself. "Damn it, this is a lot of potatoes," he muttered.

"I only needed a couple, but they didn't have any loose so I had to buy a whole bag," Corn said. "I guess I'm going to have to find some recipes to use all the extra, or else ya'll are going to be eating a lot of potato salad this week."

In the kitchen Pyckle dropped the sack of potatoes like a bag of dirt, put his hands on his hips, and arched his back. He looked down at the spuds and rubbed his chin. "You know, Spy, that gives me an idea. We could do something like last summer."

"Potato juice? Yeah, that should be a winner. At least we can be sure no one will be mad about us stepping on their turf."

"No, not juice. We'll share our potatoes with others. If we found someone who needed potatoes, but had extra apples we could arrange the transfer. We charge a small transaction fee for the trade."

"*Our* potatoes?" Corn questioned.

"Come on, sister. You said there will be plenty of extra, no reason to let them go to waste."

"I'll put them down in the cellar and they'll be fine until I need them," Corn said.

"But Stone's working down there. No need to interrupt him."

She gave him a doubting look so I stepped in. "You know, Corn, he may have a good idea. It wouldn't hurt to try. Is there anything else you need?"

"I could use some...Brussels sprouts."

My eyes grew wide. "Brussels sprouts? Maybe this isn't such a good idea."

It was too late. Pyckle had already ripped open the bag and was off-sorting the spuds. Unfortunately, Corn wanted me to stop being a couch potato so she bought into the concept. For our first transaction Corn paid us with lunch. Pyckle called it proof of concept and that day our newest enterprise was born: a food sharing business. We called it Tuber.

I honestly never anticipated the demand, but it turned out to be a brilliant idea and took off right away.

Early on I was able to work the cute, industrious kid angle and score lots of freebies. Some people were glad to have us take extra produce off their hands or if we picked up fallen fruit from their trees we could also take some of the good stuff. We soon had scuppernongs coming out the wahzoo. However, when word of our profits spread we had to primarily trade for inventory.

Our client list grew and we met new people while expanding our territory. Most folks were welcoming, with a few exceptions. All new businesses have stumbles along the way.

One morning we were working a new street when a little old lady answered the door. She appeared harmless and sweet, swaddled in a lavender sweater that looked like she'd knitted herself.

The woman mentioned having extra eggs and seemed open to our sales pitch until she pulled on the glasses dangling on a chain around her neck. The thick lenses said it all. She reexamined us—seeing us now for the first time—and then gave me a queer smile. Her expression turned to a scowl as she considered Pyckle.

My ever-thin-skinned friend responded characteristically. "What? You got a problem lady?"

I elbowed him and took my smile from beaming to radiant, hoping she hadn't heard him clearly. "What he meant to say was: maybe you have a problem with surplus produce that we can help with."

"I'm sorry dear, but to answer *his* question, yes, I do have a problem."

Always one to jump to conclusions, Pyckle said, "Oh, so you don't want to deal with us because I'm black. Is that it?"

She scooted her glasses further up the bridge of her nose. "Black? No, I don't have a problem with that."

"Seriously?"

"No, I'm open to interracial relationships. We've made great progress here in the STD. I was even an Obama-mama back in the day," she said with a strange sense of pride.

154

"Then what's the issue?" I asked.

"I don't like midgets marrying underage girls to make themselves look taller. That's simply reprehensible."

"What!?"

I thought Pyckle was going to lunge at her. After choking down a giggle I slid between them. "I'm sorry you feel that way, ma'am, but my fiancé and I are very happy together and that's all that's important. Sorry to have bothered you."

I took Pyckle by the hand and started down the stairs, knowing we would not be doing any business with the woman.

Pyckle shook me off and glared over his shoulder. "Stop it, girl. You're going to get me in trouble."

"You're overreacting."

"Easy for you to say. You won't be arrested or dragged behind a pickup or strung up from a tree."

"The Peacekeepers don't do that any more. Only the occasional public beating."

"Okay, a beating then."

"Let it go, Pyckle. Don't let her ruin our day. Some people aren't meant to be customers."

"Yeah, you're right. Besides, she wanted to trade eggs—too dangerous. We need to stay away from eggs. They're fragile and I once saw a guy get whipped for poaching eggs."

"You're lying. Who whipped him? Foghorn Leghorn?"

"Hmm, come to think of it, it wasn't eggs. It was a turkey."

I was still incredulous. "A turkey? Who poaches turkeys? Come on, let's go."

19.

In the depth of winter I finally learned that there was in me an invincible summer.
~ Albert Camus

Our ship once again hit turbulent waters a few weeks later. On a balmy afternoon we crossed over 9 Mile Road and were trolling unfamiliar streets in the neighborhood known as Little Mexico. It was a charming area with taquerias, piñata stores, and an Estrellabucks on every corner.

We were rolling along with our wagon full of produce, whistling tunes to the birds perched in the trees, when a voice called out from a recessed doorway. "Hey, little girl. And you, little man. Where are you going?"

A dark-skinned woman wearing an ornate, red silk dress emerged from the shadows and blocked our path. "Hey, I'm talking to you." Her finger was so close to my nose I went cross-eyed.

"Let me handle this," Pyckle said, nudging me to the side and facing down her quivering digit. "We're here doing business. And that's none of your business."

"I already know what you're doing," she said, looking past Pyckle. Our bright, red wagon overflowing with crates of fruits and vegetables was rather conspicuous. "I just wanted give you a friendly warning."

"We don't have to listen to you. My father is Flats Pinch and he'll have you in court faster than Speedy Gonzalez if you try to interfere with our commerce," I piped in. I knew Flats was far too preoccupied to worry about Tuber trade disputes, but thought it was still a solid bluff.

"Maybe you'll listen to him then," she said, pointing over my shoulder and making an insane laugh. "Say hello to my *leeetle* friend!"

We cowered as a behemoth of a man waddled toward us. He was slapping an ax handle against his palm and there were rusty nails protruding from the business end. I noticed Pyckle was now hiding behind me, his chivalry having disappeared like cervezas on a hot day.

"Hey, let's not get all crazy up in here," he said from behind his human shield. "We don't want no trouble so why don't you put the lumber down."

"What? This? I found it on the street," the man said. "I'm going to take it home and pull out the nails so nobody gets hurt. This has tetanus shot written all over it."

I was shocked by his falsetto voice; it was higher than mine.

"So you're not going to rough us up?"

"No, we were just going to tell you to be careful down the street in Little French Canada—a nasty bunch down there. They're serious vegetable pullers and they don't like outsiders. Plus, the bastards refuse to speak English!"

"Ahh, okay," I said, the tension easing.

"You didn't have to get up in our grills," Pyckle complained.

"Sorry, it's a cultural thing. We're close talkers," the woman said.

"I guess we had some mixed signals. We thought you were going to harass us. We figured you saw us as a threat to your business," I explained.

"What do you mean?" she asked.

"Well we assumed you were probably tomato pickers or something."

"Just because we're Mexican you assumed we were migrant workers?"

"Well..."

"Good thing for you we're not all criminals and rapists. We're in the garment business. Feel this," she said, grabbing my hand and rubbing it on her thigh. "Real silk, nice, eh?"

"Yeah, like I said, just a little mix up on our part."

"Indeed. It's best that you take your racial biases and move along, little girl, but beware!"

Pyckle and I hurried away from the awkward situation. We

still had product to move and didn't think Little French Canada could be all that bad. After a few blocks the peppy salsa beats wafting through the streets faded away and were replaced by the somber drone of French café music being played on accordions. A damp fog started to envelop the streets and obscure the sun.

I sensed we were being followed and turned to see a beret-wearing, mustachioed man shadowing us at a fixed distance. Another man soon joined him, and then another. They were slapping loaves of hardened French bread on their palms in a menacing way. At least there weren't any rusty nails protruding from the baguettes.

"I don't like this, Pyckle."

"Yeah, me either. We should've listened to Esmeralda and Quasimodo. Let's get out of here."

We quickened our pace.

Suddenly a white-faced mime appeared in front of us.

"Jeez! What is with these people?" I blurted.

The mime smiled and bounced side to side while sliding his thumbs up and down his black suspenders. "We love surprises."

"I knew I shouldn't have sampled those mushrooms, Spy. I think I'm hallucinating."

"Wait a second, mimes aren't supposed to talk," I said.

"Damn. Talking mimes? No more 'shrooms for me."

"You don't make the rules around here, mademoiselle," the man said, giving me his angry mime face.

"Huh?" I was getting dizzy from watching the frenetic movement of the man's black and white striped shirt.

"You're a stranger. What brings you to Little French Canada?"

"Can you please sit still?" I pleaded.

"NO!" My request only increased his jittering. "I see you have a cart full of produce. Did you steal it?"

"No."

"Then let me see your receipt."

"We trade it and take a transaction fee; it's all app-based. We were hoping to do some business here."

"If you want to trade here you must be a union member. Please show me your union cards. Both of you."

"Come on, we're just a couple of kids trying to make a few

bucks. Give us a break."

"Boo-hoo, poor babies " he taunted, while rubbing his fists in front of his eyes. "I just came from my mother's funeral."

"Oh...I'm so sorry," I replied.

"Eh, no big deal really. I didn't shed any tears. I didn't want to mess up my makeup. Anyway, where are your cards?"

"We don't have any, but my name is Jean Luc Pinchot," I said, ethnically enhancing in the style of my Uncle Jack. "Does that count?"

"No. That's a ridiculous name and means nothing. I must take your wagon and escort you to jail."

"Hey, Marcel Marceau, who put you in charge? Let's see *your* identification," Pyckle said.

"Certainly. How's this?" he replied, pulling a revolver from behind his back.

"Oh, hell. I didn't see that coming," Pyckle groaned.

Things were escalating and we had to flee. I looked back over my shoulder and realized the group of men had stopped and were arguing amongst themselves. My opportunity arose when the sun emerged from behind the fog. I used the screen of my phone to reflect the light into the mime's eyes, temporarily blinding him.

"Aarrggg!" he yelled.

Pyckle sucker punched him in the crotch.

"Ouch. I didn't think guys were allowed to do that," I said.

"Hey, I couldn't reach his face. Run!"

We flew past the mime who was bent over on the ground. Through his pain he yelled to the men, "Get them!"

I heard them holler in response, "Nous sommes en grève." I Google translated it later and realized they'd gone on strike. Lucky for us it was the one thing you could count on the French to do.

Sprinting down the sidewalk I tried in vain to look at the map on my phone. I was pulling the wagon and our merchandise was spilling everywhere. Pyckle's little legs were pumping as hard as they could.

I looked back and saw the mime had made it to his feet and was giving chase. He tried to point the gun, but hit a patch of our bananas and slid like he was on ice. Bullets rang out, but sailed off in random directions.

People above saw the scuffle and began to pelt us with random items. We bobbed and weaved between the rain of potted plants, dishes, and moldy fruit. Someone even heaved a cat. Seriously, who throws a cat? At least it landed on its feet.

We made it to a major cross street and looked for a sign, hoping to find a route back to 9 Mile. I saw one with an arrow that said: 14.5 Kilomètre.

"What do you think, Pyckle?"

"I don't know…wait, that's fourteen and a half kilometers—about nine miles. Go! Go! Damn the metric system! This is Pander for God's sake!"

We ran until we were safely on the other side of the highway and collapsed in a shady patch of grass. We munched on two of the remaining apples in our nearly empty wagon.

"We lost almost everything. That's going to cut into our profits," I said.

"Spy, we could have lost a lot more. That dude was crazy."

We sat quietly for a moment reflecting on the afternoon's events and then Pyckle started laughing. His chuckle grew and eventually became uncontrolled.

"What's so funny?" I asked.

"Did you see that bitch slip on the bananas and go down? Besides the fact he was trying to kill us, that was one of the funniest things I've ever seen."

I giggled as the memory replayed and the laughing became contagious. "Yeah, that was hilarious." We rolled until our sides hurt.

Eventually we gathered ourselves and trudged home to clean up. Combined with the memories of our lemonade stand, I contemplated the extensive hazards of entrepreneurship and began to appreciate why Flats had so many concerns. From that day on we committed to staying on our side of the tracks.

20.

We must be free not because we claim freedom, but because we practice it.
~ William Faulkner

Between the long hours spent on Tuber we did find some time for fun that summer. One highlight was the Fifth of July celebration. It was a national holiday when Pander celebrated the end of The War of Secession. The districts had risen up against the central government, but then ran out of money and had to sign truces on the fifth of July. As a reminder of their fiscal imprudence each district had to submit an annual tribute to Capitropolis. It was made in the form of a large parade float constructed of chicken wire and cash. The floats were used in local festivities before being driven to the capital where the money was harvested and used to fund secret prisons in the Caribbean.

The people of Maybach celebrated at picnics and ballgames. It was an idyllic day all wrapped up in nostalgia. After lunch we went downtown to watch the parade. Leading the way was the STD's tribute—a giant dragon. Instead of fire, however, it breathed candy. Kids in the crowd along the route ran out in the street to gather the sweets randomly vomited from the great creature's mouth.

Next, we walked to Lee Park where there were rides, games, and activities. Many people wore costumes and I saw skipping kids dressed as princesses, baseball players, and newspaper boys. We spent most of our time on the midway lined with groaning machines staffed by carnies. Pyckle was just tall enough to go on the Zipper and we rode the rusting death wheel over and over again until *we* were ready to puke up candy.

As the sun's rays crept lower through the branches of the magnolia trees, we met up with Flats and Corn for dinner. Corn had packed a basket full of Southern favorites—fried chicken, mashed potatoes, cornbread, biscuits and more. Unfortunately, I was so jacked full of junk food I could barely stuff another morsel in my distended belly.

I'd tried to make it past the corndog stand, but was rendered helpless when the enticing aroma infiltrated my nostrils. The sound of gurgling oil was like beautiful music. Inside the rickety shanty I saw the metal vats with corndogs dancing on the surface. Stone warned me not to ruin my dinner, but I had passed the point of no return—I had to consume a golden log of cholesterol.

I shook him off and slammed a wad of crumpled bills on the counter. The clerk gave me a wide smile of "summer" teeth—some're there and some ain't—before handing me the impaled meat amalgam. I pinched the thin stick tightly between my thumb and fingers. Two years earlier I had dropped my dog and cried hysterically until a Good Samaritan bought me another one. Now I was skilled in hefting the weight of the magnificent culinary creation. My eyes closed involuntarily as my teeth breeched the buttery crust. "Oh, that's heaven."

Flats and Corn were content to sit in their lawn chairs and stake out our prime spot for fireworks viewing while Pyckle, Stone, and I walked off into the crowd. It was good to spend time with my brother, but I was a little jealous, as he and Pyckle gravitated toward each other making me the third wheel.

The dynamic changed again when we arrived at the reflecting pool and met up with Cattricks and Dale. We hadn't seen them in a while and Pyckle had never met them, although he'd seen Cattricks on the Internet. He'd been eagerly awaiting the introduction all day—just another worshipper.

Dale was dressed as Uncle Tom. The character was an iconic symbol of one of the crushed districts, which was now subservient to the leaders in Capitropolis. He had a flowing white goatee glued to his chin and wore a suit and top hat of red, white, and blue—the colors of the deposed district.

Cattricks, meanwhile, was dressed as Lady Oppression, a national symbol of Pander. Lady Oppression was a massive, rust-red statue of a robed woman with a hammer in one hand and a copy of Mein Kampf in the other. It had been a gift from the North Koreans.

When it first arrived, the towering creation was clad in shiny, silver steel, but the skin quickly rusted when leaders placed it on an island in a damp harbor.

"Hey, guys, how are you doing?" Dale asked.

"Wow, I barely recognized you," I said, as we exchanged hugs.

"I'm dying in this outfit," Cattricks said, fanning her face with the fake book she was carrying. "The way I've been sweating I can't believe my makeup is still on."

"Those are great costumes."

"Thanks."

Pyckle cleared his throat.

"Oh, sorry, this is our friend Pyckle."

He shook hands cursorily with Dale and then turned his attention to Cattricks. "Hello, beautiful, patriotic lady." His eyebrows bounced as he ogled her.

"Nice to meet you, Pyckle."

"I've seen your show on the Internet and I'm a big fan."

"Thanks."

"Yeah, you and a hundred million other followers," I scoffed.

"The one good thing about this costume is that it serves as a good disguise. No one has recognized me here tonight."

Pyckle, however, was still staring. Even covered in rust-face, he was digging her. He was standing so close I thought he might leap forward and latch onto her leg.

"Take it easy, big fella'," I said, tugging him back by his shirt. "Don't make me put you back on your leash." He yanked away from me.

"That reminds me. Did you ever find your dog? I remember those missing dog banner ads on your website," Pyckle said.

I looked sideways at Stone and his eyes widened. It was a topic we'd intentionally avoided whenever we saw Cattricks. Stone and I had pinky promised that we would never say anything about what had happened at Pinch's Point.

"No," she said, choking up a bit. "My sweet Butterfinger never came home."

I kicked Pyckle in the ankle and scowled when he looked back at me.

"I'm sorry to hear that. When I was a kid I had a pet frog that ran away and I cried for days."

"Can a frog *run* away, Pyckle?" I asked. "Wouldn't he have to jump away?"

Pyckle ignored me and took the opportunity to move closer to Cattricks.

"It's been tough, but I'm coping."

"She got a new dog," Dale said. It seemed even he was tired of hearing about Butterfinger.

"You did? Oh, that's great!" I said.

"Yes, I've been keeping him out of sight for now. I'm worried someone dog-napped Butterfinger and I don't want anyone stealing my darling Snickers. Tonight I left him at home because I didn't want the fireworks to frighten him."

"It should be a great show," Stone said, steering the conversation away from dogs. "They're celebrating the anniversary of the *Wizard of Oz* and using it as the theme."

"I hope it's better than last year," Cattricks said. "I was disappointed with their salute to Harry Potter. But let's be honest, he isn't in the same wizard league as the great and powerful Oz. Right, Spy?"

"Actually, Oz was a complete fraud..."

"Yeah, I guess you're right. Still, I'm sure it'll be better. Afterwards we're going to a big party. That's why we're dressed up."

"A party? Sounds like fun. Can we go?"

"Sorry, it's only for grown ups, kiddo." She patted the top of my head and I felt like a kindergartener.

"In that case, count me in," Pickle announced.

"Don't you need to check with your aunt? She'll be expecting you to come back with us," I reminded.

"My aunt will be fine."

"We'd love for you to join us, but I don't think they'll let you in, Pyckle," Dale said.

"Oh, I see. So one of those kinds of parties. No blacks allowed."

"No, that's not it."

"No little people then? Real nice!"

"Relax, dude. You don't have an invitation. It was invite-only so we can't bring anyone else. No plus-ones."

"Oh…"

"Is he always this tense?" Cattricks asked.

"He likes to project his perceived shortcomings into the minds of others. I think he'd be about six foot two if he didn't have such a big chip on his shoulder weighing him down."

"You don't know my struggles, Spy."

"On the contrary, you point them out to me every day. Why don't you let them go so we can enjoy the rest of the evening." Pyckle gave me his pouty Gary Coleman look, but at least he shut his mouth.

"So, Stone, how's your project coming?" Dale asked.

"It's getting there. My prototype is performing even better than I expected. One of Flats's associates is working on a conditional patent and once it's in place I want to have a big reveal, something to really get people's attention."

"And stick it to the remoras for disrespecting you?"

"You bet."

"I can't wait. Let us know and we'll be there. Cattricks can promote it and we'll bring a crowd."

"That would be awesome."

The lights around the park dimmed indicating the fireworks would be starting soon.

"It's time!" I declared. "We've got a great spot saved down by the water where there's a nice breeze."

"A breeze?" Cattricks said, venting her sweaty robe. "I'm so there."

We rejoined Flats and Corn and settled in for the show. The fireworks were still a traditional display, but technology was added to augment the production. The fiery opening salvo created a huge screen of smoke in front of us. Then the face of an evil, bulbous-headed, bald man appeared in the cloud. The image towered above and glared down at the audience.

"Why have you come?" the man in the smoke demanded.

"For the fireworks!" the crowd yelled in unison.

"Well in that case. On with the show."

The flotilla of barges in the river unleashed a wave of missiles. The echoing explosions and splintering bursts of light reflecting off the water created a unique kind of magic. The show was like a song with ups and downs and a constant background beat.

Excitement built as the tempo increased leading up to the finale. The sky turned bright white before a flaming hot air balloon rose and then faded into the distance. There was a chorus of *oohs* and *ahhs* as the remainder of blue smoke drifted across the contented viewers.

The beeping of text notifications on Cattricks's phone interrupted my dreamlike state.

"Oh no," she said, staring at the screen.

"What's wrong?" I asked.

"It's Snickers. Something happened. The neighbors were lighting off fireworks and Snickers got so scared he jumped out a second story window."

"That's terrible."

"It was good to see you guys, but I need to get to my baby. We need to go now, Dale."

"And miss the party?"

She didn't even answer him. She grabbed her props and started to march away. Dale didn't look concerned, but followed her obediently. "Bye guys," he murmured.

"She's not having good luck with dogs," I noted.

"I think she should get a pet rock," Stone said.

It was a peaceful night in Maybach, but dark clouds were looming on the horizon. Not to be outdone, Mother Nature kicked off her own show in the distance. As the fireworks ended, lightning began to flash. Most of the audience was content to stay put for an encore performance. It was the dramatic kind of display you get in the summer when the absorbed heat of the day battles with the cool night air. The airborne flashes crawled across the sky like cracking glass. The downward bolts were spindly fingers probing the ground—the gods fondling the earth.

Stone was particularly captivated and had a eureka moment. "That's it!" he blurted. "Now I know how to reveal my invention."

21.

The oldest and strongest emotion of mankind is fear, and the oldest and strongest kind of fear is fear of the unknown.
~ H.P. Lovecraft

A month later we were back in Lee Park for the unveiling of Stone's latest creation. His machine was now bigger, but also vastly more powerful. The rectangular unit was about the size of a coffin and painted metallic black. It had a control panel on top and a variety of connectors located on the ends. Instead of just charging consumer electronics, it had the capacity to run an entire city block. With scalability, a network of the machines could completely remake Pander's power grid.

Stone's excitement had been growing and he claimed he was going to change the world. I knew his invention was cool, but had chalked up his claims as hyperbole. Harvesting static electricity was not a new concept, yet no one had been able to do it effectively. Somehow my teenaged brother had put together the pieces of the puzzle and now he was ready to show everyone his solution.

A diverse crowd had assembled and the different factions were roaming around in cliques. Cattricks and Dale were there and they had convinced hundreds of her local followers to attend. I was surprised to see Snickers with her. The poor little dog had casts on his front legs and a little wheelchair-like device strapped to his hindquarters. He could sort of drag himself along the ground by wiggling back and forth. It was tragically sad and hilarious at the same time.

A podium area had been set up and there were several rows of seats for VIP guests. As family members we were front and center. Also included were venture capitalists from the technology district and a cadre of local politicians. I saw Pyckle talking to one of the tech guys and noticed they were both wearing the same hoodie.

Just outside our inner circle of seats I saw a group of ratty-looking men with unkempt beards and grubby little hands. Surprisingly, they were wearing neatly pressed and tailored suits. "Who are they?" I asked Flats.

"Patent trolls. Litigators looking for inventors to sue for coming up with something too close to an existing patent."

"So they are looking out for other inventors."

"Ahh, no. They only do it for the money."

"What about those guys in the red and green striped shirts behind them?" The men were pale-skinned and had gray, crooked teeth. As we watched, they put their arms around each other and cupped one another's butt cheeks. Periodically, they would burst into well-rehearsed chants.

"Soccer hooligans."

"What are they doing here?"

"I'm not sure, but I'm guessing they thought it would be a good place to find a fight. It's offseason for soccer."

On the periphery were random loners and dregs of society. They seemed more curious than dangerous.

The faction that concerned me the most was a group of latecomers: the religious freaks. Their clothes were varied and eclectic; however, they were all wearing identical Guy Fawkes masks. The visage had always creeped me out. They were carrying protest signs with a mix of slogans: The End is Near, Don't Play with God's Fire, Repent Now!

They weren't getting the attention they wanted so the leader raised a bullhorn and began preaching. His first few sentences were garbled by feedback. In frustration he shoved the equipment toward a follower who fiddled with a knob and gave it back.

"Listen to me. This is madness and must be stopped. Let us refer to the Bible for guidance."

He ran a finger across the screen of his Kindle, scanning for a bookmarked section. He read random verses about the apocalypse from Revelations before turning his wrath toward my brother.

"This supposed child before you today is no child at all. Heed Matthew 7:15. He is the wolf in sheep's clothing! This wolf intends to steal power from the sky, from the kingdom of God. He is a lightning thief! Theft from fellow man is both a crime and a sin. That's Commandments 101. What about theft from God? It is a sin above all others. If you follow him you too will be guilty of his sins. And God shall have his vengeance."

Although the mechanics were still a secret, word had spread about what Stone intended to do with his invention. We tried to ignore the preacher, but he soon became the center of attention. His boisterous followers provided him with "Praise Jesus" and "Hallelujah" as punctuation to his statements.

Corn was a religious person, but by that point she wasn't feeling the love for her fellow man. "Is that fool talking about Stone? I'm about to go back there and smack that plastic mask off his face. And then I'm gonna shove it up his..." She stopped short when she saw my eyes growing wide.

"I'm not sure that qualifies as free speech. Hopefully he'll settle down," Flats said.

Unfortunately, the sermon had just begun.

"John 10:10 warns that the thief comes only to steal and kill and destroy. If you follow this thief you shall bear the consequences."

The preacher had worked himself into a lather and I found myself clinging to Flats's arm.

"And then what? Second Peter 3:10 tells us the answer. But the day of the Lord will come like a thief, in which the heavens will pass away with a roar and the elements will be destroyed with intense heat, and the earth and its works will be burned up. And when Stone Pinch burns, you'll burn with him!"

That pushed Flats over the edge. Not only was it referring to the killing of his son, but the death penalty was to be decided in a court of law, not handed out like a flyer in the park by a dime store prophet.

Flats told a nearby Peacekeeper that the preacher was violating the terms of our permit to use the park. The officer agreed and confronted the man, asking him to stop.

In defiance, the preacher put the bullhorn in the Peacekeeper's face and continued. "See how they try to silence the truth! This is..."

169

His words were cut short when a baton cracked against the side of his skull. The Peacekeeper clubbed him into unconsciousness before returning to his post like nothing had happened. He gave Flats a nod indicating it was okay for Stone to proceed.

Shaken, but not deterred, Stone took the podium and began his presentation. "Ladies and gentleman, boys and girls, children of all ages, thank you for coming today. On the stage next to me is the latest version of my static electricity generator. I call it: The Gamechanger. Power is key to everything we do and its availability and reliability are crucial to economic growth. Currently, the STD has a single source of power and many residents have inconsistent, limited supplies. Prepare for all that to change.

"Many of you may recall my appearance on *Remora Tank* several months ago where I demonstrated a small, portable electric generator. While functional, it was basic and limited. I went back to the drawing board and developed this new prototype. It takes the idea to a whole new level. This version won't simply provide convenience; it will change lives for the better. It'll bring power to those in the dark.

"I could stand up here and talk all day about my machine's potential. However, I believe actions speak louder than words. Please give me a moment to prepare my demonstration."

Pride and confidence infused my brother's voice; he'd grabbed the attention of every person in attendance. Even high school kids were staring at Stone instead of their phone screens.

Stone pulled a cord and released a large balloon tethered behind the stage. It rose slowly and stopped about fifty feet in the air, secured by a glistening metallic wire.

"Now let's gather some electrons," he declared. He flipped a switch and an external meter on The Gamechanger showed the electricity starting to flow. The crowd was completely silent as the numbers counted higher. "See! The electricity is sitting up there waiting to be harnessed. And the process is safe and environmentally friendly."

People gasped when he grabbed the wire and gave it a modest tug, causing the balloon to sway. "No worries. The only shock will be to the establishment. It's highly scalable and can be networked to share power across large areas.

"Inside are high-efficiency batteries capable of holding power to be used day or night, rain or shine. It can gather thousands of kilowatts in a matter of minutes. Enough to run dozens of homes for days."

The readout showed the charge continuing to build. Stone plugged a small table lamp with no shade into an outlet on his invention. He twisted the switch and the bulb lit brightly.

"Soon I'll be raising capital and I hope you can see the potential and decide to help me change the world. At this point I'm going to defer any specific technical questions, but will be happy to address any general inquiries."

A number of hands shot up in the crowd.

"Yes, you in the front, ma'am."

"I'm Glinda from the South Power Company. As you probably know we oversee the One Dam Authority and, therefore, run the primary source of power for the entire district. It appears this could impact our monopoly and I think your idea sucks."

"Is that a question?"

Her fists were clenched and her cheeks burned tomato red. "No, I just don't like it. Based on what you've done here today, it looks like we're going to have to spend a lot of time and money interfering with your plans and destroying your business. And that means more work for me."

Stone looked justifiably confused by the crazy lady. "Wouldn't it be better for everyone involved if we worked together? We both profit while helping your customers and humanity in general."

The woman snickered. "Oh, you have all the answers, don't you, young man. Why do you hate me?" She burst into tears and sat back down.

"Ahh, next. You, sir," Stone said.

"I'm Ned Ludd from the League of Concerned Scientists With No Real Job."

"The what?..."

"It's a rather long name, I'd rather not repeat it. My question is: are you able to quantify what impact your fancy gizmo will have on the atmosphere? We are already facing an existential crisis of

171

global de-electrification. Your machine appears to be the final nail in our coffin."

"Global de-electrification? I've never heard of such a thing."

"What? You think you can just take electricity from the air without ramifications? It's all outlined in the book: *7-11, A Convenient Store*, the bestseller by our Chief of Rhetoric, Al Gore. For every action there is a reaction, young man. If you take power from the air we will be vulnerable to all kinds of threats."

"Such as?"

"Solar radiation, ozone depletion, polar reversal, meteorites, and alien attack. Basically the sky will be falling."

"Well, thank you for your concern, Henny Penny. We'll look into that stuff."

"Aliens are real!" the man shouted before sitting down.

"Let's move on. You sir, toward the back."

I turned to see one of the patent trolls standing on his chair. "Mr. Pinch, can you tell us how this doesn't infringe on patent #86-75309?"

"Our legal team has done extensive research and we are quite confident there are no infringement issues."

"Ha! You seem awfully confident."

"Yeah, I just said that, dude."

"Better be careful what you say. Don't perjure yourself."

"I'm not under oath! I can say whatever I want. It's not perjury. You're a hack, how many box tops did you have to send in to get your law degree? Next question."

"Back here. I'm twelve-term District Senator, Storm Thermal. If I heard you correctly, you are seeking to enfranchise the disenfranchised."

"Sure, with electricity will come opportunity for many people who don't currently have it."

"Whoa, whoa, hold it right there. Who gave you permission to do that?"

"I didn't know I needed permission to help people."

"It kinda sounds like you're angling to do our job."

"Maybe because you're not doing it."

"Listen, son. All this gamechangin' flimflam sounds dangerous. There's safety in the status quo, I can tell you from experience."

Stone threw up his hands and shook his head. "And here I thought *Remora Tank* was just a bad night. Is the world really this full of frightened idiots? How do you avoid running from your own shadows on sunny days? What are you afraid of?"

After several more minutes of inane questioning, the crowd grew restless. The soccer hooligans were stirring the pot, moshing around with wicked, in-need-of-whitening grins on their faces.

Stone was wringing his hands. "Maybe you people don't deserve this. Maybe I shouldn't help you."

"Now, you're making some sense, boy," Senator Thermal yelled.

Another voice rang out from behind. "Hear how the thief taunts you!" The preacher was awake and back on his bullhorn.

"Oh, seriously?" Stone groaned.

The crowd was swirling with waves of movement. Flats could sense the deteriorating situation and pulled me to the side while waving for Stone to join us. Corn had disappeared and I wondered if she'd gone to sodomize the preacher with his own mask, or potentially the bullhorn.

Another group wearing the melty-white, *Scream* masks had infiltrated the park and were joining ranks with the Guy Fawkes zealots. The Peacekeepers were outnumbered and beat a hasty retreat. The park was in chaos.

"Free electricity? A modern day perpetual motion machine? It sounds too good to be true to me. There has to be a cost. Or else it's a fake.

"What do we have to fear? The unknown! There are too many unknowns. Are we to believe this child is some kind of prodigy alchemist bringing us gold from the heavens? I say he's a witch and we should burn the witch!"

The sermon had gathered steam and the mob approached the stage. The frenzied followers began chanting, "Burn the witch."

Running down the back steps, I heard someone with a tiny bit of sanity left say, "Wait, we probably shouldn't kill the kid. And his dad is Flats Pinch so you know we'll get sued."

"Okay, let the witch live. Destroy the machine!"

The group of rabid disciples swarmed across the stage like angry insects, assaulting Stone's invention with sticks, baseball bats, and golf clubs. One man began prying at the generator's control panel with a crowbar.

"No! Don't open that while it's charging!" Stone yelled, trying to protect them, despite what they were doing to his work.

The man didn't listen and there was a sudden *pop!* The shock sent his body flying backwards through the air. When he landed his hair was sticking up and smoking.

"See, it *is* dangerous. Bring it down," the preacher said, pointing to the sky. A gang of people seized the connection wire and used their weight to lower the balloon like a doomed zeppelin.

We crossed a grassy area and headed for the closest street. Stone and I were running. Flats was only walking, but damn that man could walk fast when he was in a hurry. Out of nowhere a black flash appeared before us. It was one of our Maybachs and Corn was at the wheel.

She jumped out and snatched me, her grip like a metal claw. With a quick toss she flung me into the back seat. Flats and Stone hopped in and slammed the doors.

Corn shoved the transmission into drive, but couldn't move. Another mob—dressed in suits—had surrounded the car and was banging on the windows.

"We're going to stop you, Stone Pinch."

"Your death machine will never see the light of day again."

"Jeez, they're like zombies!" I cried, as a woman put her teeth against my window.

"Damn lawyers," Flats hissed. "I have an idea." He opened the moon roof and stood up. Between the savage cries outside I heard the sound of approaching sirens.

Flats pointed. "Look! Ambulances! Go chase them. Hurry!" The lawyers looked at each other before peeling off the car and sprinting down the road. Several were trampled in the quest for potential clients.

Corn gunned the engine and we finally made our escape. Through the rear window I witnessed the blanket of anarchy covering the park. Stone's machine was a pile of scrap, the stage was on fire, and the soccer hooligans were chasing half-naked women.

A procession of additional Peacekeeper vehicles had arrived and I saw Hell Tate coordinating the men dressed in full riot gear. The arching smoke trails of tear gas canisters filled the skies and the Peacekeepers began marching toward the pandemonium. I hoped our friends had made it out safely, but was comforted to know the preacher was about to get clubbed again.

"Boy, that escalated quickly," Flats observed.

"There's an understatement," Corn replied. "You scared those people good, Stone."

My surprisingly stoic brother looked out the window. We drove in silence for a long time before he finally said something. "They can't stop me, can they?"

Flats sighed. "Well, that depends. Next time we'll fight them someplace more civilized—in court."

I feared my brother's dreams had been crushed along with his machine and waited for him to go completely berserk. When we returned home, he revealed the reason for his unexpected calm: reinforcements. Stone hadn't been building a single prototype that summer; he had completed multiple units. Vic saw the device's potential and had secretly been providing my brother with equipment and working capital. The backups were secure in the basement, kind of like in *Ironman 3*…or was it four?

22.

A jury consists of twelve persons chosen to decide who has the better lawyer.
~ Robert Frost

The backlash continued as lawyers representing an assortment of special interests joined together and filed suit to block approval of Stone's patent. Without the patent protection, Stone would not be able to shield his brilliant idea from wanton theft. Additionally, it would scare off investors and potential partners. Flats wanted to help Stone, however, Dr. J's case was rapidly approaching on the docket and would require all of our father's energies in the near term. He also thought it best to keep Stone under the radar for the time being, allowing the fury to settle down.

With the end of summer came the end of our time with Pyckle. We said our goodbyes and shut down Tuber. Once again it had been an educational experience for me, while Pyckle was content to achieve his personal profit goals. When school started I was relieved to discover my fifth grade teacher, Mr. Smith, was boringly sane. For the survivors of the Miss Fisher debacle it was a welcomed change. He assured us he was not on drugs or sleeping with students, at least not yet.

The lawsuit involving Dr. Jellyfinger seemed to move in waves. Following our downtown showdown, the parties pulled back to work on their cases. Then it reared its head again during the summer when the trial date was announced. Both sides held press conferences in an attempt to sway the court of public opinion.

The media was initially behind the Maters and their dream team of attorneys. However, when Flats and Dr. J started to look like underdogs, support swung back in their direction. Flats had enlisted the help of his longtime friend, Mr. Overwood, the editor of the

Maybach Times. At the time it was still a viable newspaper, although it eventually became a flyer for peddling coupons.

After reviewing the evidence, Flats was surprised the opposing lawyers had taken the case. However, the Maters had called in favors in order to secure their representation and were paying upfront fees in addition to any contingency. Flats's greatest concern was the possibility that the Maters would be able to buy off the judge and jury.

When the trial began I ditched school and watched the events from the public balcony above. All the seats were taken so I squatted on the floor next to Corn, looking down through the wooden balusters in the rail. I split my time between listening to the statements below and eavesdropping on the color commentary provided by Corn and her friends.

The case had been assigned to Judge Lance Zigler, a sedate looking Asian man with shrewlike features. His round, black glasses, dark mustache, and triangular goatee combined to make it look like he was wearing a dime store disguise kit. Flats was pleased with the choice, calling Zigler a legal pragmatist.

My attention turned to the Maters' vast legal team and a younger member of the group caught my eye.

"Who's that?" I whispered to Corn.

"Which one?"

"The young man on the end of the table."

"Oh, that's Henry Blythe, a junior attorney with the rose firm. I can't believe he became a lawyer. He's had a rough go of it."

"How so?"

"Well, everyone knows he's another one of Clinton's love-children. Look at him with those Bassett Hound eyes and pink cauliflower nose; looks just like Bill did at that age. His momma ran a 7-11 store in Little Rock. Died of suspicious circumstances—said she was drunk and dancing with a train—right about the time Bill's political career was taking off. Just a coincidence?...uh-huh...So he was raised a bastard by his grandma."

"That's sad."

"Yeah, word has it Bill had a PAC funnel money to put Henry through law school."

"What's a PAC?"

"A political action committee, a slush fund. A place where wealthy people route their money for nefarious purposes."

"What's nefarious?"

"Not legit. Under the table."

"At least he made good for himself."

"On top of all that, he's mixed race."

"Huh? He looks pale as a ghost."

"He doesn't have much, but it only takes one drop of black blood. You can always tell by the hair, though."

"Really? You need to be at least one sixty-fourth to get Indian casino money. One drop seems rather extreme."

"That's just how it is, Spy. Unfortunately, they've always had trouble fitting in on either side. For a period in the early twenty-first century they put 'em in a place called the White House. Ironic, huh? It made people feel better about themselves. Maybe someday skin colors will finally blur and meet somewhere in the middle."

"You mean the tanning of Pander? I thought that was due to global warming."

"No, that's just a myth."

"Which? The tanning or the warming?"

She was distracted and didn't answer the question. "Shush, girl. I want to hear this."

The trial began with opening statements and the Mater's lead was a partner named Mr. Bogle. He was a pudgy, bald man who had a problem with foamy spittle collecting at the corners of his mouth. Occasionally, during particularly strenuous oration, chunks would shoot off like small moons breaking free of their home planet's gravity. His suits appeared expensive, but they fell short on tailoring as he was constantly pulling up his pants. He reminded me of a prisoner who wasn't allowed to wear a belt.

Flats had anticipated a vigorous attack, however, Bogle and the rest of the Mater team made it personal—literally. In fact, their arguments had nothing to do with the law. The comments were laced with Biblical references and old school Southern bromides intended to resonate with the jury. It was even beyond the excessive level of hyperbole commonly heard in civil trials.

After wandering around on a variety of tangents, Bogle began a character assault on Dr. J. As the diatribe progressed, the doctor grew fidgety. Flats tried to calm him, not wanting the judge or jury seeing any behavior that might imply guilt.

Then, amazingly, Bogle decided to direct his vitriol at my father. Mr. Bogle, who sounded like he was delivering a sermon, pounded the table and pointed at Flats. "And look who Dr. Jellyfinger has chosen for counsel. Another sinner! A man who lives in sin with his dark-skinned servant."

Flats scratched at his ear, questioning if earwax had distorted what he'd just heard. Now it was Dr. J who was attempting to calm Flats.

Friends also had to restrain Corn. She shot up and I was afraid she was going to pounce like a professional wrestler coming off the top ring rope.

"Oh, hell no! Tell me he didn't go there!" she howled.

The statement threw the entire gallery into disgruntled murmurs and the judge pounded his gavel for quiet. I wondered why people were always picking on my sweet Corn.

"Your Honor!" Flats interjected, glaring at the plaintiffs. Bogle just shrugged as though he hadn't said anything in the least bit inflammatory.

"It's opening statements, Mr. Pinch. Please don't interrupt. You'll get your chance to lie, smear, and slander shortly. As for the rest of you, you'd better pipe down or else I'll clear this courtroom," Judge Zigler said.

When the plaintiffs concluded, the tension was palpable and the judge called for a short recess. The window allowed Flats to cool off and refocus.

Outside, I wanted to give my father a hug, but he was preoccupied, typing furiously on his phone. He was making adjustments to his opening and clearly needed to gather information during the break.

Judge Zigler brought the court back into session and Flats waited for total silence before standing and taking a dramatic, audible breath. He gradually moved to the opposite side of the defense table, his dance perfectly choreographed. After looking flustered earlier, he was back in the zone.

I'd seen Flats in court many times before, but that day he had an aura around him. He appeared to be in motion while the rest of the courtroom was a still photo. After parting neatly on one side, the wave of dark hair crested his forehead, while the horn-rimmed glasses framed his inquisitive eyes. Flats was dressed in a monochromatic three-piece suit and tie, which made him look like an actor in an old black and white film—maybe Marlon Brando or Gregory Peck.

At just the right moment he began. "Ladies and gentleman, as you have already been told, this is a civil trial. In a civil proceeding the burden of proof is on the plaintiff. The key word being: *proof.* Listening to the plaintiff's opening statements I didn't hear even a hint of proof. With none to provide, they have instead decided to create fabrications.

"Dr. J did nothing criminal, no charges were ever filed. He also did nothing negligent. Their entire case is about spite and avoiding responsibility. Their strategy is to distract you and draw your attention from the truth. I intend to *focus* your attention on the truth.

"There have unfortunately been numerous frivolous cases brought against Dr. J and his colleagues. Many doctors in his field have left the district. This suit, however, has to be the most egregious. Dr. J did everything in his power and did everything right.

"Alma Mater did everything wrong. She's not a doting prospective mother; she's a manipulating traitor. Given her behavior, she clearly had no understanding of the responsibility pregnancy entails. So why have a baby? The advice of her attorneys. They crafted the strategy and forced the birth of this child. The real reason was to produce an heir and attach to the Mater family fortune. This pregnancy wasn't driven by maternal urges, it was greed!"

There was a collective gasp from the gallery.

"But, she couldn't even do that. Alma Mater failed at her insurrection against the government and failed in her attempt at motherhood. And ladies and gentleman, this case against Dr. J will soon be added to her list of failures."

Flats was standing tall, pleased with the vibe he was receiving from everywhere in the courtroom, except the plaintiff's table.

It was a strong start and then Flats decided to stir the pot a little more. "And since we are setting the tone by discussing legal representation, let's see who they've brought to the table. Their team first tried to strong-arm me, hoping weaker representation for Dr. J might lead to a quick settlement. That tactic didn't work. Now they've attempted to undermine my position with personal attacks. I can take the insults, but prejudicing the jury is not fair to my client. So, who have the Maters selected to help sell their lies? A liar of course."

Behind me I heard Corn make a noise like she was getting ready to enjoy a tasty slice of pecan pie with ice cream on top. "Ummmm, hmmmm."

Flats turned and pointed to the opposing counsel. "Mr. Bogle has cultivated a respectable image during his successful legal career. The profile on his firm's website says he's a church-going man whose interests include masculine activities such as bow hunting and skeet shooting. His favorite pursuit, however, seems to have been omitted."

Another dramatic pause.

"Mr. Bogle is a cross-dresser!"

"That's ridiculous. How can you make such an outrageous allegation?" Bogle protested. The top of his bald head was now bright red and there was sweat in the tufts of hair at his temples.

"Unlike you, sir, I wouldn't do it without evidence. Ladies and gentleman, please direct your attention to the monitor. I must forewarn you, what you are about to witness is quite disturbing." Flats clicked a remote control and the image of an overweight man in women's underwear appeared on the screen. It looked like an albino walrus caught in red netting.

Cries of shock and disgust filled the courtroom. "Turn it off! It burns my eyes!"

Bogle stared in stunned silence. One of his co-counsels' finally spoke. "Your Honor, I think you've let this go on long enough."

Judge Zigler gave her the hand. "Ya'll had your turn..."

Flats stood stoically, letting the picture say a thousand words, while every eyeball in the courtroom turned and focused on Mr. Bogle.

"Mr. Bogle, would you like to show everyone what you have on under your suit today?" Flats asked.

Bogle snapped and ran out like a cat on fire.

Flats let a slight grin slip out before continuing as if nothing had happened. He switched off the monitor and the courtroom breathed a collective sigh of relief. "A good lesson for everyone: be careful what kind of photos you take on your phones. Anyway...I'll conclude now ladies and gentleman. I believe in the courts. Everyone is due his or her day, but in this case we are discussing pure fiction. I hate to waste my time and yours so I will destroy their deceitful charges and do it quickly."

"Whoo-hooo!" Corn hollered.

Zigler's gavel pounded.

The takedown of Mr. Bogle was a nice early volley for Flats, but the rest of the Mater team was still dug in for the fight. They kicked off the next phase by calling their witnesses, which Flats called a parade of pigeons. Several of them were people who had an ax to grind with Dr. J, such as disgruntled hospital workers. The remainder were "character references" including members of the Mater's paid housekeeping staff. One was a mute Avox who wrote his answers on a large dry erase board. They had nothing to say regarding the case against Dr. J and Flats didn't even bother with cross-examination.

Finally, Mrs. Mater was called to the stand. Attorney Dewey Cheatum was conducting the questioning and fed Mrs. Mater a slew of leading questions, painting her as the grieving mother. They were hoping emotions would swing jury votes and he closed with what they saw as their key statement.

"Mrs. Mater, you had a number of discussions with Dr. Jellyfinger over a span of months. At any time during the pregnancy did he provide you with some type of guarantee regarding the birth of your child?"

"Yes."

"What did Dr. Jellyfinger tell you?"

"Dr. J assured me that quote: 'Every little thing was gonna be all right.'"

"He said those exact words to you?"

"Yes, he did." She sat up straight, giving the impression of confidence in her statement.

Flats looked to Dr. J in surprise. The doctor was shaking his head and shrugging.

Mr. Cheatum continued. "*Every little thing?* Wow, that sure sounds like a guarantee on his part. But every little thing wasn't all right, was it?"

The tears began flowing. "No."

"It's okay, Mrs. Mater, take a moment."

Mrs. Mater was sobbing and Mr. Cheatum consoled her, looking over his shoulder to be sure they were getting the full amount of attention they were seeking. The judge granted a recess before Flats would be allowed to cross-examine.

When court returned to session Flats was ready to pounce and came out swinging. After the emotional display, Flats wanted to repaint Mrs. Mater. He approached the witness box and scrutinized Mrs. Mater like a bird hunting an insect. He then looked to Mr. Mater, who was seated at the plaintiff's table.

"Ladies and gentlemen, these two individuals are no longer *yutes.*"

Judge Zigler leaned forward, "They're no longer what?"

"Oh sorry, my mouth's a little dry. These two aren't *youths.* Look at 'em! Beneath all that plastic surgery is an old woman and God only knows what he looks like under that shiny, black helmet, probably shriveled like a prune. Their prime reproductive years are well past. It shouldn't take a doctor to know that every little thing *wasn't* going to be all right.

"During the break, I discussed Mrs. Mater's statement—made under oath—with my client, Dr. Jellyfinger. Initially, he claimed to have never said those words to her. Then it dawned on him. He had indeed said them."

There were whispers in the courtroom and the plaintiffs looked excited by the admission. It didn't last.

"Mrs. Mater, you said Dr. Jellyfinger told you that, 'Every little thing was gonna be all right.' Correct?"

"Yes."

"Where were you when he said that?"

"Well…let me think…I don't recall…"

"You don't recall? You can remember the exact words, but don't know *where* he said them? Seriously?"

She turned to her attorney with a frightened look. "Mr. Pinch, stop pressuring me."

"Oh, sorry. Please take your time, and then tell us where. Was it in his office?"

"Well...no."

"Hmm, was it perhaps at the gym downtown? A facility where you were both members."

"Umm..."

"Yes or no? Was it at the gym?"

"Yes."

The gallery groaned.

"And where was he when he said it?"

"Umm..."

"Where was he?"

"On a treadmill."

"Really? How interesting. Was there anything in his ears at the time?"

"Yes..."

"What?"

Her eyes were on the floor. "Earbuds."

"So he was running on a treadmill with earbuds in when he made this statement to you. Had you even asked him about your child?"

"Not exactly, but he said that to me. I swear."

"Well, that I can't argue against. He did say those words to you."

"See, I told you."

"For God's sake he was singing! It had nothing to do with your child or your prognosis. It's a lyric to *Three Little Birds* by one of his favorite artists, Bob Marley."

"How should I have known?" Mrs. Mater mumbled.

"Okay, now that we've cleared up that silliness, let's move on with how you handled your pregnancy. Having a child is a great responsibility and it starts with proper prenatal care. For someone as old as you the required standards are even greater. Did you ever drink alcoholic beverages during your pregnancy?"

"No, I did not."

"You're sure? You are under oath."

"I do not recall consuming any alcoholic beverages."

"Oh, you do not recall. I see. What about illicit and off-label prescription drugs? Did you take anything that might fall into those categories?"

"No. I don't recall doing anything of the kind."

"What about bungee jumping?"

"Nope."

"Any heli-skiing trips?"

"Ahh, not that I recall."

"Your name is Alma Mater, right?"

"Of course."

"Just checking...No further questions for Mrs. Mater at this time."

"You may step down," the judge instructed.

"Your Honor, my first witness is Ms. Janie Fox."

A waifish girl in her twenties with jet-black hair and tattooed arms walked up from the gallery. She sat down and accepted the oath with an annoyed look on her face, rolling her eyes and chewing gum.

"Thank you for coming today, Ms. Fox. Could you please tell us where you are employed?"

"I tend bar at the Wild Groosling Saloon."

"And during your shifts at the establishment do you ever remember seeing Ms. Mater at the bar?"

"Yeah, she was in there all the time."

"Did you serve her alcoholic beverages during that time?"

"No."

"So she never drank any booze at the Saloon?"

"I didn't say that. I just didn't serve it."

"Please elaborate, Ms. Fox."

"She would order her drinks 'virgin' and then when we were tending to another customer she would reach over the bar and add her own alcohol."

"You can't be serious."

"Sad but true."

"Shameful behavior. Did you do anything about it?"

"I told my boss. He was hacked, but said to let it go given who she was. He didn't want any trouble—no sudden surprise inspections by the Healthkeepers."

"I see. And did you ever discuss it with her?"

"At first I called her on it. I said: 'Aren't you pregnant?' She said: 'No, just putting on a few pounds over the holidays.' I knew it was total BS."

"Hmm...so Mrs. Mater claims to have not consumed alcohol during her pregnancy, while you've told us you saw her engage in exactly that activity. It kinda seems it's your word against hers. It would help if there was some way to prove it."

"There is, Mr. Pinch. The surveillance video my boss provided to you."

"Oh, that's right. Let's take a look at that."

Flats picked up a remote and started the video. The footage from a security cam showed Mrs. Mater looking around nervously until Ms. Fox was distracted. Mater then reached over the bar and grabbed a bottle. She dumped a long pour into her previously virgin drink and then took a slug directly from the bottle before replacing it.

"Oh dear, what kind of manners are those? And what was in that bottle, Ms. Fox?"

"Vodka. You can tell by the shape of the bottle it's Heavenstea."

"One more question. What about her tipping?"

"Cheap, cheap, cheap, especially since she wasn't counting the booze she'd pilfered."

"How disappointing."

"Tell me about it."

"You've done an excellent job today, Ms. Fox. I appreciate your time and would give you a large tip if it were permissible."

Mater's team had no questions and wanted Ms. Fox off the stand as soon as possible.

"Next, I call Dr. Alejandro Luna."

A stocky, Latino man in green surgical scrubs wove his way to the stand and was sworn in.

"Thank you for coming today, sir. Dr. Luna, is Mrs. Alma Mater—seated over there—a patient of yours?"

"Ahh, no. She is not a *patient*."

"No? Well, has she visited your office on multiple occasions over the past several years?"

"Yes." Dr. Luna focused on my father, avoiding eye contact with anyone else in the room.

"That's odd. Please tell the court what type of doctor you are, sir."

"I'm a veterinarian."

"A vet, eh? So your *patients* are animals?"

"Yes."

"What was the purpose of Mrs. Mater's visits to your office?"

"She was requesting certain prescription drugs."

"Such as this one?" Flats said, pulling up an enlargement on the screen.

"Yes."

"This is for a drug called, Equizax."

"Yes."

"And what exactly is that drug, Dr. Luna?"

"It's a horse steroid used to reduce inflammation in the hind quarters."

"Does Mrs. Mater have a horse?"

"I don't know."

"So is there another reason she may have been seeking this drug?"

"Well...our office saw a rise in demand after a story in the *Pander Enquirer* said models were taking it to reduce muffin tops."

"Muffin tops?"

"Yeah, the fleshy batter that spills out over the top of tight jeans."

"Ahh, definitely something you have to worry about when pregnant. Let's look at another one. In November of last year you provided her with a prescription for Gerbatol. What's that approved for?"

"It's used to treat anxiety in hamsters and gerbils."

"Is that a real problem?"

"You know, sometimes they start running in their little metal wheels and just won't stop. It can be very hard on them."

"Again, did you ever see Mrs. Mater's hamster or gerbil?"

"No."

"Then why would anyone possibly want such a drug?"

"People started clamoring for it when a blog post in Japan said it supposedly helped to reduce wrinkles."

"Magical anti-aging properties? Any studies to back that up?

"Not that I'm aware of."

Flats ran through the drill for several others including bird laxatives, turtle amphetamines, and snake oil. "So you provided an array of animal pharmaceuticals to Mrs. Mater during the time she was pregnant?"

Pause.

"Dr. Luna?"

"Yes."

"Why would you do that?"

"She's an influential person and put a lot of pressure on me. Also, she paid full street rate for the meds. I was just trying to make a living."

"She pressured you?"

"Yeah! And her husband, Darth, was breathing down my neck too. Literally. Listen to him, he makes that scary, deep breathing sound. It can be very intimidating."

"Thank you for your testimony, Dr. Luna. It has been quite enlightening."

Dr. Luna stepped down and walked straight for the exit with his head down.

Over the following days the defensive deluge continued. Flats brought a procession of witnesses and provided documentation to contradict Mrs. Mater's testimony, including the bungee jumping and heli-skiing. The evidence of her misbehavior and irresponsibility was overwhelming—she was clearly a woman who'd spun out of control and her baby became collateral damage.

After finishing with his final witness, Flats stood and addressed the court. "Judge Zigler, given the facts we've presented, my client, Dr. Jellyfinger, would like to declare that Mr. and Mrs. Mater have *not* proven their case. We are making a motion for directed verdict."

The move triggered a flurry of huddling and whispering at the Mater's table. At the time, I did not understand the legal maneuver and asked Corn, "What's Flats doing?"

"He's forcing the judge into making a decision now in order to keep it from going to the jury. He's going for the kill shot."

"Do you think we'll win?

"Oh, we'll win. He shredded that worthless bitch."

I looked at her with wide eyes.

"Sorry, sweetie." She rubbed my ears gently as though she was attempting to wipe off some dirt.

Flats had put the judge in a corner. Zigler leaned back for a moment and pondered his decision.

"In all my years on the bench I have seen a wide variety of cases, plaintiffs and defendants of all stripes. Never, however, have I seen someone as narcissistic and self-involved as Mrs. Alma Mater. You only cared about one thing during your pregnancy: yourself. And now you're unwilling to take responsibility for your actions. Instead, you bring this 'case,' hoping the defendant will settle or you'll get a sympathy vote from the jury. I will allow no such thing to happen."

Judge Zigler hammered his gavel. "Motion granted! Case dismissed!"

The courtroom erupted and I saw Flats shaking hands with Dr. J. My father had a broad smile until Mr. Cheatum walked past. He leaned in and whispered something, causing Flats to scowl.

We made our way out the side exit and met Flats on the courthouse steps where a media circus was waiting. In addition to the press, there was a crowd of protestors. My father told me they were paid to be there by the Maters.

Flats emerged with Dr. J and stopped front and center to make a statement to the waiting throng of microphones. He spoke in a loud, clear voice to be heard over the boisterous protestors.

"We're obviously pleased with the outcome and I would like to thank Judge Zigler for making the appropriate decision. Dr. J would like to make a brief statement."

The doctor moved forward to a chorus of boos and hisses. The demonstrators were being held at bay by a small group of Peacekeepers, but I was nervous they might become violent.

"I would first like to thank Flats Pinch for providing such a capable and competent defense against a powerful and unscrupulous adversary. We are pleased with today's victory, unfortunately, this was the last straw. There are too many lawsuits and I feel like I now spend more time in the courtroom than the delivery room. The next time I might not be so lucky. Therefore, we will be closing our practice and leaving the Southern Trial District."

"Where will you go?" a reporter asked.

"Not sure. I'm considering establishing a practice in Mexico."

There was more yelling as the Mater team came through the doors and hurried past to a line of waiting Maybachs.

Dr. J's statement began to sink in and the protestors stirred in confusion. One of the women—wearing a signboard that said: Baby Killer—grabbed a bullhorn. "Dr. J, if you leave who will deliver our babies?"

"I guess they will," he replied, pointing to the team of departing attorneys. "No more questions," Dr. J said and walked confidently down the stairs. His statement doused the flames and the crowd dispersed.

Afterward, Corn had to run an errand so I walked home with Flats.

"Are you excited about winning?" I asked.

"Yes and no."

"What do you mean?"

"Anyone could have won that case—even a Tennessee monkey. It shouldn't have even been in court and showed what a joke the system has become."

"It's a shame it killed Dr. J's practice."

"So it goes."

"If that was the bad part, what was the good part, Flats?"

"Defending Dr. J gave me a feeling I hadn't had in a long time practicing the law. Like I was doing the right thing without question."

"Maybe you're growing up."

"I grew up a long time ago, Spy," he said, giving me a patronizing pat on the head.

"Maybe you're just a late bloomer."

Flats smiled.

"What did Mr. Cheatum say to you in the courtroom?"

"Oh, nothing."

"It seemed to upset you."

"He was being a sore loser. You know what they say: sour scuppernongs. Anyway, I'm glad it's over. Now I can work on Stone's case."

"I know you'll win that one as well. You're the best lawyer in the district, Flats."

He squeezed my hand and smiled again.

Over the years memories twist and fade, but my recollections of that period remain tangible and concise. Looking back, that year was a turning point. As we were growing up so was our father. He was no longer content to be a cog in the machine and knew the system, which had provided him with a successful career, had to change. There had to be a return to responsibility.

23.

Don't handicap your children by making their lives easy.
~ Robert A. Heinlein

The Dr. J case ended up being something more than just frivolous litigation against a physician. It was the first spark in a much larger fire.

The immediate backlash came as the reality of losing the district's key obstetrics practice began to set in with the populace. Expectant mothers became desperate and the market responded. New, unlicensed clinics popped up in strip malls and dark alleys. They offered delivery services along with Canadian drugs, medicinal marijuana, and fantasy football wagering. The results were disastrous and the black market for babies exploded. In a number of cases the personnel claimed the babies didn't survive. In reality, the newborns were stolen and sold to wealthy couples in Capitropolis.

The Internet was awash in terrifying stories about the kidnapping of pregnant women. The victims were invariably found in a bathtub full of ice in Las Vegas with a long abdominal scar and no baby.

Many women turned to do-it-yourself kits, which could be purchased at Jitney Jungle and The Fetus Depot. The package included towels, forceps, a bullet to bite, and a CD of music by Yanni. Apparently, it was necessary to bite on the bullet to offset the pain of listening to Yanni during delivery.

Not surprisingly the district's infant mortality rate skyrocketed. When people realized how cruel nature was, they began to protest and call for legislation to protect Ob/Gyns from wanton legal action. It was a mess. The law of unintended consequences can be so ugly.

On the legal front, Flats was being glorified, while the Mater team was being vilified. Unfortunately, many of the opposing lawyers in Stone's patent case had ties to the Mater attorneys. It made them even more determined to destroy my brother and his invention, regardless of the benefit it would have for all of humanity.

On the way to the courthouse for his hearing, Stone stared silently out the car window. I'd avoided him the best I could, knowing this dispute was weighing heavy. Instead, I turned to my father to drum up enthusiasm. "Do you have some tricks up your sleeve for today, Flats? Something to knock their legs out from under them?"

"If the facts are on your side you don't need smoke and mirrors, Spy."

"But they're still angry about Dr. J's case. Won't they be fighting dirty?"

"Yes, likely so. I saw Mr. Fairchild a few weeks ago and he was still hot as a district summer. So many special interests are involved that we have to be prepared for attacks from every conceivable direction. It'll be an uphill battle, but one we can win."

"I know you'll do it, Flats. Stone is going to change the world."

Stone grunted in acknowledgement.

Flats continued without looking up from the document he was reading. "I feel like the tide is turning. Colleagues have been quietly giving me hints that people are ready for a change. Still, this is a patent case so it will be argued before a judge. He's an appointed official and it means only one person has to be *influenced* to affect the outcome."

The proceeding was held in a small courtroom and the atmosphere felt completely different. Clad in dark, ornate paneling, it was claustrophobic and solemn. Stone and Flats huddled at a table well below the judge's bench. The Honorable John Holmes sat above looking more like a king than a judge. Behind him was a massive painting with a gold, baroque frame. I Googled the picture and discovered it was *The Light of the World* by William Holman Hunt. The door Jesus was knocking on in the painting symbolized a closed mind, probably not a good omen.

Unlike Dr. J's trial, Stone's was completely devoid of emotion. The team challenging his patent made their arguments with monotone voices, never so much as looking in our direction. It was unsettling and unexpected. They were simply going through the motions; they didn't need theatrics this time. Over the course of the next several hours the reason for their approach became clear: the judge's decision had already been made. Flats was fighting for a cause that had already been lost.

Judge Holmes rendered a swift and brutal verdict. "Stone Pinch, you're a young man with no track record and therefore no business creating a machine such as this. The opposing counsel has shown that any benefits of your device are more than offset by its dangers. Your publicity stunt caused a riot resulting in numerous injuries. You should be ashamed of yourself. In the future I hope you consider focusing your energies on a more reputable career, such as law. Your patent application is hereby denied."

He pounded his gavel and departed.

I was surprised he hadn't taken the added step of declaring my brother a witch and ordering him to be burned at the stake.

We sat in stunned silence while the opposing team filed out. There was no gloating. They'd gotten their revenge and were content with their ill-gotten victory.

On the way home, Flats offered to take everyone for ice cream, but there was no interest. Stone was crushed and went straight to his room. Flats gave him time to cool off before knocking on my brother's door. I had to lean close to the wall to listen in on their conversation.

"I know what you're going to say, Flats, but don't bother. We tried. Maybe the judge was right. I should follow in your footsteps and focus on being a lawyer."

"I think that's a terrible idea, Stone."

"Really?"

"Yes. Your talents would be wasted in a courtroom. You were meant to create things in a garage...or basement. Real things. Things you can see and feel and touch. Things that do something."

"Yeah, but maybe I need to let it go or at least scale back my ambitions. Maybe I should just give the technology away."

"Nonsense. You should be rewarded for your hard work and ingenuity."

"It was too much for people to handle and upset the status quo. Change is good, but excessive change is sometimes bad."

"Then the world needs to adapt to you. Pulling back in reaction to what Judge Holmes said would be the easy route, but I'm not going to let you take that path, Stone. This is not over."

***

Flats made an immediate appeal and was granted a hearing before appellate Judge Grisham who reportedly had an eye for courtroom intrigue. It would be heard in the federal court up in Big Rock. The court was housed there as a concession to the Clintons when they brought Arkansas into the district. The city was formally known as Little Rock, but that was eventually found to be too diminutive for such an important locale.

Our family rode the PanTrak train, which had a direct route from Maybach Junction to Big Rock. It was shockingly slow and our trip was interrupted when another train derailed over a river in our path. It was a tragic accident and all three passengers were killed. We were transferred to a bus, which got us to the courthouse just in time. It would've made a lot more sense to simply drive.

The stately courthouse rose from a base of broad marble steps. Passing through the façade's numerous fluted pillars Flats explained that only half of them actually held up the roof, the rest were slightly short, leaving a small gap at the top where they should connect. The architect and builder initially planned fewer pillars knowing it would provide adequate structural support. The building review committee, however, disagreed. When it became clear that legal action was the only way to challenge the committee, the architect revised his plans. They built all of the columns as instructed, but only engaged the necessary ones. The others were there just for show and literally carried none of the weight. Only after the building was completed did the modification become known.

Inside, the courthouse was alive; the circus-like feel had returned. In addition to scads of lawyers, there were a disturbing number of politicians. Flats assumed they were there seeking free media time, but it soon became clear a bigger game was being played.

The courtroom was buzzing with white noise. We found our seats in the gallery and Corn pointed out various politicos in attendance. When Judge Grisham finally entered and saw the crowd he laid down the rules. "Let me be clear. This is a courtroom not a taping of the Wendy Williams show. There will be no outbursts, no cheering, no booing. If anyone's phone rings I'll hold them in contempt."

Everyone sat up straight and phones were switched to vibrate.

Once underway, things proceeded smoothly. To our surprise, Flats's arguments met almost no resistance. He regularly looked to the opposition table with a confused stare when he expected a challenge and got none. They almost seemed to be helping Stone win.

The appeal was over in a few hours and Judge Grisham pronounced Stone the victor. His patent had been granted.

Flats was pleased, but reserved. The fight had been too easy. I, however, was brimming with enthusiasm as we walked back outside. A large crowd of reporters had gathered on the steps and standing at a podium at the top was Senator Wind preparing to give a speech.

Standing between the faux pillars, Flats said, "Ahh, here's where the real decision is being issued."

"What do you mean, Flats?" I asked. "Judge Grisham said we won."

"It's a chess game, Spy. We take a piece only to find our opponent sacrificed it in pursuit of his gambit. The initial trial in Maybach City was a stall tactic; they were buying time to fire up the political machine. Listen to what Senator Wind has to say. I doubt we're going to like it."

He was right.

"Ladies and gentleman of Big Rock, I'd like to thank all of you for coming out today. I also want to thank my colleagues in the Senate for working together on the groundbreaking legislation I am here to announce. It took a lot of determination and fortitude, but we were able to get it passed in a late night session. We took it directly to President Rain, who signed it into law.

"Today's announcement is timely as we have a case being decided here at the federal courthouse that falls under the scope of the new legislation. Directive WD-40, subsection 10-289 requires that all patents deemed to be of *public interest* be signed over to the government. It would be hard to find anything more in the public's interest than a new alternative source of energy."

"What does that mean, Flats?" I asked.

"It means they allowed the patent to be granted so they could steal your brother's invention."

"I just got hosed, Spy," Stone added.

"Sir, what are the benefits of this new arrangement?" a reporter near the front asked the senator.

"Too many to even list in the time we have today. As an example, the patent for Stone Pinch under the old rules would make only one person massively rich—an unscrupulous concentration of wealth. Others would have to wait for their slice of the pie until they came up with something of value. Now they won't have to wait. All we are asking is for people like Mr. Pinch to share some of their pie."

The comment triggered thoughts of Corn's scrumptious pecan pie. I certainly didn't like sharing *my* slice with anyone else.

Wind continued, "It's only rational to spread the real value to everyone in Pander. Stone Pinch's attempt to control our right to electric power was selfish. On the other hand, I'm looking out for the greater good, the general population, the *voting* population." His sleazy grin grew broader as he spoke.

"Given that the technology originated here in the STD, it makes sense for us to implement it first. We can finally free ourselves from relying on a single source of power."

"So you're not proposing a Pander-wide rollout?"

"We don't want to rush things. Let us work out the kinks first. The other districts should be thankful we're agreeing to be guinea pigs. Let me be clear: all districts are equal, but some are more equal than others."

"Will public or private companies be handling the development?"

"I'm sure there will be some subcontracting. However, our power company has the expertise to handle this. We can't put private businesses in charge; they can't be trusted. We must maintain control."

"So it will still be a monopoly?" asked a reporter.

"A fun, family board game from Parker Brothers? No. Next question."

"Can you give us some other benefits?" asked another.

"We plan to give the power away for free."

"Really?"

"Yes. Isn't that wonderful? Now, there will of course be government taxes, surcharges, and fees. But the power will be free."

The reporter looked unconvinced.

"Even better, this law applies retroactively. The Department of Homeland Repression will be examining the current portfolio for other patents to be re-appropriated."

"Re-appropriated?" I asked.

"Another fancy word for stealing," Corn replied.

"There are countless things that will be far better under our control. I mean, come on, just look at the Pander Postal Service and PanTrack rail service—stunning marvels of efficiency."

The audience collectively rolled their eyes. The winds were indeed shifting and they were sweeping us up.

A congressional aide intercepted us and began whispering to Flats. I tried to hear what was being said, but could only grab bits and pieces. He took Flats by the arm and led him toward the podium where Senator Wind was still pontificating on the glories of the government.

"And here comes the Pinch family now…" the Senator said, spreading his arms toward us. "Mr. Pinch is a talented attorney and we know they are fine, law-abiding citizens." He tried to reach down and shake Stone's hand, but Flats stepped forward and blocked the attempt.

Wind looked nervously toward the aide who nodded as if to confirm everything was going according to plan.

Returning to the microphone, Wind let everyone in on the real plan. "To demonstrate the beauty of this program, we prepared the necessary paperwork required by Directive WD-40 and today we will have our first transfer. Stone Pinch was just granted a patent for his static electricity generator. Being a minor, his father, Flaticus Pinch, will sign on his behalf." Wind handed the papers to my father and ushered him to the podium.

Flats leaned into the mic. "I'm glad we have such a large crowd here today. I do have something to say." He paused briefly, looking down at Stone. "Unfortunately, my eyes have been closed for too long. Today they've been pulled wide open and I can see the endgame of the government's machinations," he said, holding the papers above his head.

"This provides no benefit for us and, despite the rhetoric, it will not benefit you either. The only people it will reward are Senator Wind and his cronies. They blindsided us with this press conference and are attempting to blackmail me into signing this document. The directive violates my son's rights and I will not sign this authorization of theft. Tomorrow I will file suit with the Supreme Court of Pander contesting this act of seizure."

"But you must sign, Pinch. It's the law," Wind pleaded.

Flats threw the papers in his face, took our hands, and started down the steps.

Wind gathered the papers and chased after us as the cameras flashed. He tried to block our path, but Corn reared back preparing to bitch slap him. He took the hint, held up his hands, and stepped away. As our surrogate mom, Corn was always the perfect blend of June Cleaver and Mr. T.

24.

Our enemies are innovative and resourceful, and so are we. They never stop thinking about new ways to harm our country and our people, and neither do we.
~ George W. Bush

The incident in Big Rock unleashed a maelstrom and Flats was the man who'd kicked the hornet's nest. Flats kept a close watch over us and spent every evening in his oak rocking chair on the porch with his rifle resting across his lap.

A few days later, Hell Tate stopped by to make sure everything was okay. I was in the front parlor and listened in on the conversation. Once a spy, always a spy.

"Evening, Hell."

"Evening, Flats."

"Looks like you're out in a new cruiser. All black, very intimidating."

"Yeah, it's a nice machine."

"Is it stick?"

"No, automatic."

"Nice."

Corn heard the voices and walked out to the porch to see who it was. "Well, Mr. Tate. How are you doing this fine evening?"

"Just fine, Corn. Thanks."

"You look hungry. Is that wife of yours feeding you enough?"

"I'm eating plenty, probably just stress taking its toll."

"How about I grab you a thick slice of pie?"

"That would be wonderful, Corn."

After retrieving a plateful of Southern goodness, she handed it to Mr. Tate and left the two men alone.

"How are things going, Flats? Any trouble?"

"So far they're only fighting a war of image. I don't think they're violent, but I'm not taking any chances."

"You've really started something, Flats. Politicians are scared, there's hope on the streets."

"Things have been headed in the wrong direction, but I believe we can bring Pander back."

"I don't know, Flats. That guy Wind is a moron, and President Rain, he's a joker with an eye for the theatrical. You should try to find some dirt on him. There must be a couple skeletons in his closet. There will be escalation and you'll need weapons against the politicians."

"Yeah, I'll look into it. I know someone who can help."

"Are you sure you're doing the right thing, Flats?"

"If I don't take this responsibility who will? The system is broken and needs to be fixed; the balance is out of whack. The Supreme Court has agreed to hear the case and they're looking to reestablish power. With life terms they don't have to fear for their jobs."

They sat in silence for a few minutes contemplating the evening air.

"I need to get going. Let me know if I can do anything, Flats."

"I will."

Mr. Tate started down the sidewalk, before turning. "Oh, I never thanked you for the pie."

"And you'll never have to..."

***

Escalation arrived via the television airwaves the following week. Our normally scheduled programming was interrupted by a special presentation from P-PAN—the Pander Propaganda and Advertising Network. It was a channel dedicated to politicians indulging their egos and spreading their tripe for free. Typically it was just a boring feed from congressional conference meetings, a total snooze fest. Now and then things would get heated and a real fight would break out. Occasionally there was a punch or slap, but usually it involved a sad shoving match or shoe throwing. The politicians were out of shape and could only keep it up for about twenty seconds before giving up exhausted. The scuffle clips would end up on ESPN's nightly top ten.

The television beeped and the presidential crest appeared. We sat up and prepared for an important message, but had no idea what was coming.

President Rain was the most recent in a long string of lawyers serving as president. After building a fortune in the courtroom they wandered into politics, usually under the guise of: "It's my duty to give back to society." Society would have been better off if they'd just kept whatever it was they were giving back. These lawyer-politicians were called: *careers*. Once they obtained an office they became a permanent part of the government and no scandal or error seemed big enough to dislodge them. The careers came from established pedigree in the wealthier districts and their path to the presidential mansion was a well-worn one.

Every few election cycles the electorate would wander. One time they elected a businessman. He tried to make the government efficient and profitable. It seemed like a grand idea, but gridlock in Capitropolis proved to be the immovable object. The bureaucratic machine choked on the president's programs and everyone lame ducked it to the next election.

Another time they gave an actor a shot. He was so talented he fooled everyone. He used the prospect of millions of dead children to win a war that was never fought. It was a fun experiment, but the people went right back to the careers after that.

President Colonanus Rain appeared on the television screen and peered out at his subjects across the nation of Pander. His habit was to stand with his head leaned back, like he was looking down at you. He was endowed with the most penetrating blue eyes I'd ever seen. Eyes that made you feel like he was capable of looking at your internal organs.

With an etched face framed by flowing white hair and matching beard, he looked like the wise grandpa on a 70s TV series. However, when you knew who he really was the perception was quite different. It shifted even more when he opened his mouth. His voice was smooth, but unnerving. He spoke slowly, every word a single bullet from a revolver. When I heard him doing voiceovers for television commercials it sent shivers down my spine. I could never buy a Volvo or fly Delta.

In turn, I saw him more like a thin, evil Santa Claus—the last person I'd ever want to come down our chimney. Still, that night he was right in the middle of our living room. I clenched my hands on my knees as he began to speak.

"People of Pander, I come to you tonight from Capitropolis on a beautiful, cool evening." The camera panned back and you could see he was seated in his rose garden wearing a slate-gray smoking jacket and matching pants. "Unfortunately, as I examine the forecast I see dark clouds on the horizon. Word has come of an uprising in the Southern Trial District. An unnecessary challenge to the power of your wise and benevolent government. This is dangerous, very dangerous indeed. These provocateurs are portraying us as greedy, when in reality it is *they* who are greedy. We are simply trying to do what is best for the population of our great country.

"The agitators want to upset the peace we imposed upon Pander. A peace hard fought for; a peace so many died for. In our history as a nation we've had too many civil wars. The War of Secession, UFC #1,701, and WrestleMania to name just a few. All bloody, painful conflicts we'd do well not to repeat.

"Most of these raging conflicts started with a smaller spark. Some event that seemed inconsequential at first blush, but harbored a far more sinister core. We can't let this happen again. It must be stopped before it grows into something larger that engulfs all of Pander.

"The senile members of our Supreme Court have made the regretful decision to indulge these malcontents and hear their case challenging Directive WD-40. To defend our position, I have engaged my brother, Rectusphincter, the Attorney General of Pander."

The camera panned to the side where an equally creepy, dark-haired version of President Rain sat grinning at the camera.

"What's his name?" I asked.

"Rectusphincter," Flats replied.

"Seriously? What was their mamma thinking? Those names just invite gastrointestinal humor."

Flats raised his eyebrows and nodded.

The President continued, "We in Capitropolis are working hard to support the people of Pander and all we ask is you do the same for us. Thank you and good night."

The TV switched back to *Wheel of Fortune* already in progress. Our family sat in stunned silence as the eternal Vanna White turned letters on the board.

***

The speech rattled Flats, but he did his best not to show it in the days that followed. He redoubled his efforts to build his case, working all hours of the day preparing for our trip to Capitropolis.

One evening I walked past the study and saw him hard at work. I wanted to take some of the burden from his shoulders, but knew leaving him alone was probably the best way to help.

"Hey, Spy," he called. "You can come in."

"How's it going, Flats?"

"We're getting there. Going before the Supreme Court is a major undertaking. Legally, we have a strong case. It's the *outside* issues I'm worried about.

"I know the court is supposed to be impartial, but they still take cues from the populace. I'm afraid we might lose in the court of public opinion. Rain and his cronies are working hard to portray us as rebellious villains.

"To be honest, we could use a little help. We're getting traction on traditional media and support from businesses and the Chamber of Anti-Government, but the regime is killing us on social media. They have too much power and control.

"I'm doing everything I can on the legal side," he said, gesturing to the surrounding stack of papers and law books. "Still, this won't win over the hearts and minds of the people. I don't want to use Stone, but we need to let the younger generation know what this means for their future."

"What can I do to help, Flats?"

"I'm not sure, I wish I knew."

I pulled out my phone and started flipping through the apps. Unfortunately, I didn't have a lot of friends or followers. Most of them were kids from school. Then it hit me in the face like a Ronda Rousey roundhouse kick.

"I have an idea, Flats!"

***

Two days later we took a short drive down to the coast to meet Dale and Cattricks on a beach where they were filming. We parked and walked over the dunes to find Cattricks surrounded by a whole team of people. She gave us a quick wave before returning to her spot in front of the camera.

"Action!" yelled the director, a burly, dark-skinned man with an unkempt beard and black hair pulled back in a ponytail.

Cattricks pretended to frolic on the sand with two other girls before turning to the camera. A scared countenance shrouded her face as she looked down at her bikini bottom. I heard Stone gasp in anticipation when she tugged at the edge of the swimsuit. Exposing her pale butt cheek allowed us to see the juxtaposition of surrounding tomato-red skin. She gazed back at the camera. "Don't forget to always wear sunscreen."

The girls beside her nodded in agreement. One of them raised her sunglasses to reveal raccoon eyes, while the other one peeled back her bikini top to show her burn line. "If we burn, you burn with us!" Cattricks declared.

Stone was enthralled by the scene and was ecstatic when the director had them reshoot it several more times. The man was finally content and called it a wrap.

Dale handed Cattricks a bottle of water and they walked over to where we were standing. After exchanging hugs, I asked Cattricks, "What are you doing? A commercial for sunscreen?"

"Sort of. It's called a PSA or public service announcement. It's like a commercial, but done in order to make the public aware of a safety issue."

"Oh, that's nice of you."

"Yeah, it's a good cause. They asked me to do it because I appeal to a younger demographic."

"That makes sense. It's a shame you had to get such a nasty sunburn, though," I said looking at her inflamed skin. Stone was also scrutinizing her body closely.

"Nah, it's fake. Just makeup." She swiped her fingers along her hip and showed me the red smear.

"Oh, that's good." I noticed Dale carrying a large, feminine looking beach bag that appeared to be moving. "Is Snickers in there?"

"No," he said, offloading it to Cattricks.

She reached inside and scooped out a tawny cat. "This is my new friend: KitKat."

"He's a cutie. Is Snickers okay?"

"Snickers joined Butterfinger in the great dog kennel in the sky."

I didn't want her to get emotional so I made a mental note to ask Dale later about the circumstances of Snicker's demise.

"So what's going on with you guys? You said you had something important to discuss," Cattricks said, stroking the cat and leaving red streaks down its back.

"Yes, you know about our Supreme Court case, right?"

"Of course. I can't believe how they're trying to hose you, Stone."

He forced his eyes upward to meet hers and nodded in acknowledgement.

"Well, we were wondering if you could help us out with a social media campaign. Maybe doing something kind of like your PSA. Letting people know our side of the case and how it will impact the future of Pander."

"That sounds interesting," she said, distracted by the squirming cat.

"Would you be willing to be the face of our campaign?" I asked, hoping not to push my luck, while playing to her ego. Also, I knew how the male population responded to her. "Cattricks, you could be the symbol of our revolt."

"Hmm, sounds a little dangerous…and like a lot of work. Maybe somebody else would be better suited for the job. What about Castro?"

"Who?"

"The director," she said, pointing to the Latino-looking gentleman who was smoking a cigar and sipping a cocktail with green leaves floating in it.

I examined the surly man as he scratched wiry chest hair through his white guayabera shirt. "Where's he from?"

"Havana I think. He lives on the island over there," she said, pointing across the water.

Dale rolled his eyes at the suggestion. "Him? He can barely direct a simple commercial. We can't trust him to lead a revolution, it's sure to fail. It has to be you Cattricks. I'll handle the logistics, but you're the star." He had stroked her ego the way she was stroking that silly, red-striped cat.

"Oh, all right. Of course we'll help, Spy."

"Great," I said, hugging her. "I know you're busy, but we will be leaving for the capital in two weeks."

"I've never been to Capitropolis. Maybe we could go with you."

"Seriously?"

"It sounds exciting and would add some variety to my web show."

Dale was looking over a calendar on his tablet. "We might have to switch a couple things around, but that could work. We can do live webcasts as we go."

"Awesome!" I said. "We'll get you tickets right away."

"Well, to do this right we will need to bring the team."

Flats gave me a look indicating he wasn't excited about handling travel for an entire posse. "How big is the team?"

"Pretty much the crew here, plus a few others. And don't worry; we can get some sponsors to comp part of the costs. We just need to make sure their products appear in our clips. Right, Dale?"

"Sure, that should be no problem. I was thinking, in order to build morale we should come up with a name for our group," Dale suggested.

"How about Team Cattricks?"

"Ummm, perhaps something a little more representative of everyone."

"Okay, how about…The Patriots."

"Are you kidding? Only people from District 1 like the Patriots, everyone else hates them."

"True."

"What about the A-Team."

"Nah, people might think the A stands for ass. We don't want to be the ass team. Or be called A-holes."

Cattricks looked pouty. "Dale, you never listen to my ideas."

"No, I do *listen*, Cattricks, it's just that a lot of them really suck. That's why I'm the idea guy."

"What about using our area code—452—instead?" I said.

"I like it. Representing the 452."

"So we will be Team 452?" Cattricks asked.

"Nah, we need something jazzier than *team*."

"Jeez you're picky, Dale."

"How about Squad 452," I said.

"Snappy. I like it! Looks like we might have ourselves another idea person on Squad 452," he said, patting my head in approval. "Let's go over and we'll introduce you to everyone. We have a surprise for Cattricks, too."

"Ooo, we love surprises, don't we!" Cattricks said to KitKat as they exchanged Eskimo kisses. Lowering him, she finally noticed the streaks on the cat's back. "Oh look, he's wearing makeup now, just like his mommy. Maybe I'll rename him Red Stripe."

Our group followed Dale across the beach to a staging area with a metal frame staked into the sand. He pulled back a curtain and revealed a massive, multi-tiered cake. Written in blue frosting was: *Congratulations Cattricks! 300 Million Followers.*

"Good lord that's a big cake! Where did you get it?" Flats asked.

"Chip baked it," Dale said.

"Your show has that many viewers?"

Dale clarified the number. "Well, not exactly. She has that many 'followers'. A lot of them follow because their friends do—peer pressure. Actual viewers tend to run between one thousand and ten million."

"That's quite a wide spread."

"Our audience is ever-shifting. The young adult market is particularly fickle."

Dale gathered everyone around to make a formal announcement and we gave Cattricks a round of applause.

"Thank you all so much. I could never have hit this number without your help. This is awesome. It's hard to beat eating cake by the ocean." She grabbed a fingertip of frosting and let KitKat lick it first before she tasted it. "Umm, yummy."

When she reached for another dollop the cake exploded. I thought she'd triggered a bomb, however, when the flying frosting settled I saw a young man who'd burst through the top layers.

"Surprise!"

"Christ, you nearly gave me a heart attack, Chip," Cattricks yelled. KitKat hissed and clawed at the new arrival.

"So sorry, your highness. I damn near suffocated. Why did you leave me in there so long, Dale?"

"Not my fault. You can blame Castro for shooting so many takes."

"Is that the truth or was it a dare, Cattricks?"

"I'm sure it's the truth, Chip. Stop being paranoid." Cattricks shook her head in frustration. "Will somebody please help him out of the cake and get him his meds?"

One of the assistants helped him out and led him away.

"I still love you, baby doll," Chip called over his shoulder.

"What the Hell Tate is wrong with that boy?" Corn asked.

"This is the first time I've ever seen him," I told her. "From what I understand he was injured during a baking contest on the Food Network. There was an explosion and a flying pan hit him in the head. His mental state has been a little off ever since. He and Cattricks do the truth or dare thing as part of his rehab therapy."

"It doesn't seem to be working too well."

"No."

"She should have Flats get her a restraining order against him."

"Looks like she might need one for Stone as well."

My brother had a towel and was down on his knees wiping frosting from Cattricks's legs. His face was at the exact height of her bikini bottom.

"Oh no he doesn't," Corn said, snatching Stone by the shoulder and dragging him back. "Stay away from that girl, you hear me."

"Yes, ma'am."

"It's a good thing Pyckle isn't here. He'd be licking it right off her skin," I said.

"What's so special about that scrawny, little thing?" Corn asked.

"According to Dale, she's the 'it' girl."

"I guess. But this is starting to feel like *Something About Mary*. If Brett Favre shows up I'm going to get his autograph and then slap him straight."

We each grabbed a plate of the remaining cake and Dale introduced us to the rest of the attack squad. "This is our sound man, BeeGee. He also happens to be one of Maybach's hottest DJs, specializing in electronic music and remixes of 70s disco."

A bespectacled man turned in his chair from the control panel where he was working. His wide, brown face was centered with a jet-black goatee.

"Nice to meet you," he said shaking hands. Despite his masculine appearance, he had a silky smooth voice.

"That's a cool chair," I said, noting the large, knobby wheels.

"It's my beach wheelchair."

"Oh." I hadn't realized he was paralyzed. I felt like an idiot, but he gave me an understanding smile.

"BeeGee used to work for P-PAN and he knows how to hack it," Dale said.

"Really?"

"Yeah. He even did one of their most famous jingles."

"Which one?"

"*P-PAN. You might as well be watching us because we're watching you*," BeeGee said, the words whistling off his tongue.

"I know that one," Flats said. "Jeez, I always thought it was a woman singing."

"It's a gift."

"Over here is our ace cameraman, Polenta. He's Castro's brother. The other brother, Raúl, was sick today."

"How are you doing?" I asked.

All I received for acknowledgement was a nod and upturned lip.

"He doesn't say much, but he's great behind the lens," Dale assured us. "And over there are Croissant, our assistant director, and her assistant, Marsala."

The two pretty women in their twenties looked up from the screen they were watching and waved.

"These names are making me hungry," Corn said.

"Anyone else?" I asked.

Dale thought for a moment. "We'll need to take Sinna from the salon. Cattricks usually sees her on a weekly basis and will need plenty of styling. The last thing we'll need is some muscle. I know a few guys who can help us there. My buddy Kato is super sneaky and has wicked martial arts skills. Another acquaintance, Fresh, is a mountain of a man, he looks like a bouncer."

"Awesome. I was nervous about the trip, but now I'm excited," I announced. "This is going to be so much fun."

Flats agreed to let us hang out for a while as the afternoon sun crept toward the watery horizon. When we finally left, I had sand between my toes and a new sense of confidence about our group. We were ready to take the capital.

24 ¾.

Sometime that light at the end of the tunnel is a train.
~ Charles Barkley

Honestly, I was looking forward to our departure date more than Christmas that year. The night before we left I barely slept and was bursting at the seams in the morning. At the station I bounded up the worn, wooden ramp.

"Now, take it easy, Spy," Flats said. "We have a long trip ahead of us."

"I still can't believe we're taking a train. Why couldn't we just fly?" Stone griped.

"You know Flats doesn't like to fly," Corn answered. "And besides, this is so much easier. Look, they don't even have PSA lines to go through. You just walk right up to your train. Easy."

"Still, he could have taken the train and we could've met him there."

"Oh come on, Stone, this will be fun," I said, skipping toward the ticket office. To me it felt like we were getting tickets on the Polar Express.

Flats knocked on the glass and jarred the elderly ticket woman from a slumber.

"Huh? What? Oh, hello, what can I do for you?"

"We're here to check in for the train to Capitropolis," Flats said, handing her our confirmation papers.

"Sure, sure." She spent about two seconds looking down through the glasses at the end of her nose before pounding a massive stamp down on each ticket.

"There are ten gates and you are at the very end. Here's a little secret for you: your train will stop at about nine and three quarters. You'll see a narrow brick wall there. It'll save you a bit of walking."

"Really? Nine and three quarters? Wow, that's a great help. Thanks," Stone moaned.

"Is it on time?" Flats asked.

"Hmmm," the woman said, checking the screen. "Nope, she's already running forty-five minutes behind. Make yourselves comfortable down there."

"Thanks."

We began the long march down the desolate platform.

"There's only one train coming this morning. Why couldn't it stop here?" Stone asked, pointing to gate one directly in front of us.

"Stop trying to ruin my fun."

"I'm not trying to ruin anything, Spy. It simply makes sense."

I have to admit, by the time we got to our gate I was tired. It was a good thing the train was running late, because so was the rest of our group. Nearly an hour passed before we saw Cattricks, Dale, and their entourage schlepping toward us. Besides all of the people and the carry-on luggage they also had several carts of suitcases. They looked like a Middle Eastern caravan.

"Wow, you guys are carrying a lot of baggage," I said when they arrived at our spot on the platform.

"Literally and figuratively. Supporting Cattricks takes a lot of…stuff," Dale said. "Sorry we're running a bit behind. We had to make about ten stops."

"Did everyone make it? What about Chip?" I asked, noting his absence.

Dale nudged a particularly large trunk.

A muffled voice called out. "What? Who's there? Are we there yet?"

"Almost, Chip. Put your mouth up to the air hole. It's time for your happy pill."

"Do I have to swallow it?"

"No, you can chew these. Ooo, this one's shaped like a dinosaur!" Dale carefully dropped an oblong tablet through the opening.

"That's not a dinosaur," I said.

Dale held his index finger up to his lips, "Shhhh."

"Is he going to be okay in there? It's a long trip to Capitropolis," I whispered.

"We'll let him out to eat and use the bathroom."

"How did you get him in there in the first place?"

"He was playing truth or dare with Cattricks and took the dare."

"Ahh, well that's a plus."

In the distance a whistle sounded and everyone turned to watch the approaching train. The massive, black beast chugged into the station, belching thick smoke. When it stopped the haze consumed us and triggered a group coughing fit.

"Good lord, don't they have any trains more modern than this?" Dale asked, breathing through his sleeve.

"Yeah, it's weird. Some things are so modern while others have remained primitive. Pander seems to have so many anachronisms."

"Excellent analysis, Spy."

"Thanks, Dale." I was glad the smoke cloud concealed my blushing.

He started to load luggage and leaned Chip's trunk on edge. "Time to ride the choo-choo, Chip."

"Hoooot! Hoooot!" came the reply from within.

There was plenty of room for all our stuff onboard, as the train was relatively empty. After finding our compartment, Stone and I threw rock paper and scissors to see who got the top bunk. The beds were unlike any I'd ever seen before. They folded down from the wall like shelves. I smashed his scissors with my rock and climbed up to my victory platform.

"Oh, this is so cool! I'm glad I got the top one."

"Quit gloating, Spy."

"Just saying." I shifted to my back and stared up at the ceiling. I could feel the rocking of the now moving train and started getting sleepy. Suddenly everything went dark. I thought I'd fallen asleep, but couldn't move or breathe. Something was wrong. "Stone!"

I heard him laughing below. "A lot more room in here now. I'm glad I got the bottom bunk."

"Stone, you better let me out of here. I'm gonna scream and you'll be in trouble."

"What? Did you say something, Spy? I couldn't quite hear you."

"Now, Stone!"

I counted to three and then let loose as best as I could given my confinement. My high-pitched squeals echoed through the hollow train car.

"Okay, okay, settle down."

The latch clicked and my bed flopped back open. I was about to take a swat at him when I felt something move next to me in the bed. The sheet writhed as though a small ghost was approaching. When a rat's head appeared at the edge I let out another scream.

"What?" Stone said.

My arm instinctively swatted at the vermin and flung it off the bed. It hit Stone square in the forehead before falling to the floor. He yelled and the rodent scurried into the corner.

"Oh my God! That's so gross. Kill it, Stone."

My brother scanned the room for a weapon while making sure the rat remained trapped. He grabbed a suitcase and crept toward his prey. After slowly raising the bag he dropped it like a pile driver. Its impact was muted by a squishing sound.

I almost gagged when he lifted the bag. "Oh, that's even grosser."

He bent over to make sure it was dead and then lifted the carcass by its tail.

My sibling sense told me what was coming next. "Get rid of that thing," I told him.

His eyes lit up and he started swinging it in my direction.

"I'll scream again. I swear it, Stone."

Undeterred, he came at me. In defense I let out a blood-curdling, little girl scream. The shock wave repelled him and he eased back.

"Okay, Spy. I was just messing with you. What should I do with it?"

We looked around and saw there was no garbage can in the compartment.

"Flush it?"

"Nah, this thing's too big. It'll clog the toilet and we'll have an even bigger mess."

"The window," I said, pointing.

Stone yanked on the latch with his free hand and was able to drop the sash just enough to fit his arm through the opening. "Bombs away!" He closed the window and slathered his hands with sanitizer.

I climbed down and noticed a jagged line of blood on Stone's forehead. "Looks like he scratched you," I said, dabbing the small scrape with a Kleenex.

The sliding door whooshed open and Corn jumped inside. "What's going on in here?"

"Ahhh...nothing," I said, trading glances with my brother. "There was a bee in here, but Stone opened the window and it flew away. He bumped his head during the excitement."

She looked to Stone, who concurred with my lie.

"Okay, you two need to settle down and stay quiet. No more of that screaming."

"Yes, ma'am," we said in unison.

Corn left and we sat down together on the lower bunk. "All right, Spy. This is going to be a long trip. We need to try to get along and not drive each other nuts. And we can't add any more stress to Flats, either."

"Don't lock me in my bed again and we'll be fine."

"Spy, I'm sorry."

"Okay, it's a deal. Best behavior." We executed the contract with a pinky shake.

Seconds later the door once again was thrust open and we expected to see Corn. Instead there was a pale, red-headed boy.

"Oh, hello there," he said, with what sounded like a fake British accent.

We just stared in response.

"I was wondering if you'd seen Scabbers."

"Scabbers?" Stone asked.

"Yes, my pet rat. I'm in the cabin next door and he seems to have gotten loose. I heard screaming, which is how people often react to him."

Stone and I looked at each other sideways through guilty eyes.

216

"There's no rat in here," Stone assured him.

"Oh dear. I hope no harm has fallen upon him."

"I doubt it. I'm sure he'll turn up. What kind of name is Scabbers anyway?"

"He chews off his fur in spots and gets scabs."

"Ewww." I said, my face crinkling up in disgust.

"Yeah, that's gross, dude. Anyway, we'll let you know if we see the scabby little fella."

"Thanks. Cheers," the boy said before heading down the hall.

Stone got up to close the slightly ajar door.

"Be sure to lock it this time too," I said. "That was crazy."

"At least we didn't lie."

"Yes we did."

"Uh-uh. Scabbers is *not* in here and no *harm* fell upon him. It was a suitcase…"

***

My excitement faded along with the late afternoon sun as the train crawled down the tracks. I spent countless hours staring out the window at the sights of Pander passing me by. It was my first time going cross-country and our nation was a collage of topography and environments. There were high mountains, low deserts, icy tundra, thick timberlands, and tropical rain forests.

Pander was a strange amalgam of districts held together by history, geography, and a God-given excess of abundant natural resources. Further cementing our bond was a shared paranoid fear of people north and south of our borders. At the district level there were many differences, each was dysfunctional in its own special way.

Along the way I saw animals I'd never seen before. At one point I watched a strange turtle walk alongside the tracks. It kept pace with us and I thought it was some kind of mutant created by the scientists in Capitropolis. Then I realized it was a regular turtle; we were just going ridiculously slow.

Stone and I were glued to the window when the train passed a heard of buffalo. Random animals began tipping over and we initially thought they were falling asleep in the fields. In reality, the train was moving at such a leisurely pace that hunters onboard could take accurate shots at the furry creatures. As the bloodshed continued, I wondered when we would finally get the bullet trains that had been promised for years.

Nearing the capital, the surroundings turned urban. There was an uneven mix of gleaming new buildings and scrubby tenement projects. Endless billboards filled with government propaganda cluttered our view. However, vandals had defaced numerous posters of President Rain and red, spray-painted graffiti was rampant. There were images of hands holding up the middle three fingers and hands holding up only the middle finger. At the time I didn't understand everything, but could sense the unrest boiling around Capitropolis.

Three days after leaving Maybach we pulled into Disunion Station. Our geographically illiterate Uber drivers took us to several hotels, before finding the correct one. It was dinnertime when our motley group finally checked in so we went to our rooms only to drop off our bags. We were heading toward the elevator when, like the mom in *Home Alone*, I noticed someone was missing. "Where's Chip?"

"Oh…yeah," Cattricks said, looking to Dale.

"He should be fine, let's go."

"He's been in there a long time. We should make sure he's okay," I said.

"All right," Cattricks shrugged, handing Dale her room key. "Bring out the gimp."

We walked back to her room where Dale went in and opened the trunk slowly. When he peered inside Chip sprung out like a jack-in-the-box. "Raahhrrr!"

Dale didn't even flinch.

"Did I scare you?" Chip asked.

"Yeah, you got me good. Again."

"Awesome. Hey Cattricks, are you up for some truth or dare?"

"No, Chip. Not now. We're all hungry and we're going to dinner. Get moving."

218

He looked hurt. "Okay, honey bunch."

We hustled down the street in the chilly dusk and found a busy tapas joint. They couldn't accommodate a party our size so we went next door to a quaint bakery-bistro. The adults all sat together at one long table, while Stone and I were relegated to a short, kid's table with Chip.

The waitress brought out three sippy-cup style drinks.

"Ooo, dinosaurs!" Dale said, examining his.

"Could I get a regular-sized drink?" Stone asked.

"Sorry, sweetie, that's what comes with the kid's meal."

She also set down a loaf of bread, which Chip seized hastily. He sniffed at it and tapped it like a squirrel testing a nut. "This bread is burnt!" he yelled before throwing it like a football right at Cattricks. It bounced harmlessly off her shoulder.

"Chip, keep it up and you'll go back in the box," she said without looking our way.

"No! I won't go back in the dark." He cowered and started to shake.

Halfway through the meal Chip became agitated and his attention wandered. He opened a bottle of ketchup and started wiping it on his body like sunscreen. Then he crawled across the floor and up onto the adult's table where he spread out across the red tablecloth, shoving dishes out of his way.

"What the hell are you doing, Chip?" Cattricks screamed.

"Camouflage. This is how we'll hide from the government. You can't even see me unless I open my eyes."

"That's insane. Everyone can see you. Yep, right there in the middle of our table is an idiot slathered in a condiment."

"Hmmm...guess I need more ketchup." He reached for the bottle and Dale stabbed at his hand with a fork.

Everyone looked perturbed, but Stone and I found his gags to be hilarious. Still, we could understand why the adults didn't want him around. On the way back to the hotel, they dared Chip to jump into a public fountain to wash off. It was quite cold, but he didn't seem to mind, splashing and rolling around like a playful puppy dog.

***

The next morning we woke up early and went straight to Capitropolis Hill to begin our lobbying efforts. The members of Pander's congress were supposed to be "representatives" of the populace, but that was no longer the case. The intended role and the actual one had long since diverged.

It was a job that took money to get and keep. Once they were in, though, it took a lot to ever lose a seat. Short of murder they seemed to be forgiven for just about every other type of transgression. Lying, cheating, bribe-taking, embezzling, and philandering were regular activities. If caught, they would hold a tear-filled press conference and their sins would be absolved. Flats thought some of them even intentionally created scandals to keep their names in the press.

They were a sad sample of the population, which was no surprise as most of them had been spit out of the lawyer ranks. Although Flats now had the reputation of a renegade, he at least knew how to speak their language.

When we arrived at the capitol building it was disconcertingly quiet. I checked my phone to be sure it wasn't Sunday. "Where is everyone?"

"I don't know, maybe they're all inside. Let's go find out," Flats said.

We entered the rotunda and walked toward the main hall without encountering another soul. Finally, standing at the doors with his hands interlocked before him was an aged usher. He was so still I thought he might be a mannequin.

"Excuse me, is anyone in there?" Flats asked the gentleman.

He simply shrugged as though we'd asked a silly question.

"Can we go in?"

"Sure." He took a step to the side.

Flats opened the door and peered inside. The chamber was empty and the only sound I heard was crickets chirping.

Flats looked back to the man. "Isn't there a vote today?"

"Yeah, I s'pose there is."

"Shouldn't the lawmakers be here to cast their votes?"

"Probably."

"Well, I don't see anyone in there."

"There might be a few around. Passed out in their chambers or maybe lounging in the spa. I saw one outside filming a propaganda piece on the front steps a little while ago. He might still be out there."

"We didn't see anyone when we came in."

"Sorry," he said before shuffling away.

"Now what?" I asked.

"Let's head back outside."

We followed Flats and returned to the main entrance. The only person there seemed to be wearing a costume. He looked like a rolled up newspaper with skinny, white arms and legs sticking out. The man was humming a song and smoking a cigarette and appeared startled when our group descended upon him.

"Excuse us, sir. Are you a lawmaker?" I asked politely.

"Me? Hell no, girl. I'm just Bill. All I do is sit here on Capitropolis Hill." He looked away and returned to humming his catchy tune.

"If you're a local, perhaps you can help us. We've had a long, long journey to this city. Riding the PanTrak took forever. Our train even hit a bus."

"That's a shame, darling, there ought'a be a law to have buses stop at train crossings." More humming.

Flats was growing impatient. "Yeah, yeah, another time, Bill. We've got bigger fish to fry right now. We're looking to peddle some influence and need to find lawmakers."

"Hmmm...I hope and pray that you will, but today I am still..."

"We don't have time for this kook. Let's go." Flats broke into his power walk, flying down the remaining steps.

Despite his lack of information, I thanked the strange man and followed my father. Unfortunately, I had Bill's tune stuck in my head for the rest of the day. *Mmmm...mm-mm-mm-mm...mm-mm-mm-mm-mm-mm...*

We tried searching nearby, high-end restaurants in hopes the lawmakers would be dining with lobbyists, but came up empty. Next, we visited a number of hotels to see if they were there with high-end prostitutes. Still no luck. We did stumble upon the mayor of Capitropolis in a ghetto crack den, but he was too high to help.

After lunch we were scheduled to attend a rally and meet our supporters. Sinna and her team did our hair and make-up and we headed to the National Mall. At first it seemed like a strange place to meet as most malls had been decimated by online shopping. However, we needed a big, open space so it fit the bill perfectly.

Dale and Cattricks had been running our media campaign and were scoring great feedback. We were worried about being out of touch during the train trip as PanTrak only offered Internet service through telegraph wires along the tracks. However, at the numerous stops Dale was able to get free Wi-Fi via McDonald's and posted messages from Cattricks letting everyone know we were closing in on the capital.

Another positive was her new pet, KitKat. Now that she had a cat, there was an endless supply of super-cute pics and videos to post. One evening, she shared a picture of KitKat dangling from a bunk by his front claws. Dale Photoshoped it and added the caption: "Hang in there." Internet gold.

The huge crowd assembled at the Mall amazed me. It was a diverse mix of people with a shared interest in our fight against government repression. There were CEOs, small businessmen, inventors, doctors, and even Joe the Plumber. Voices that were still out there in Pander, but rarely heard from in the national media. I was glad to *not* see any soccer hooligans in attendance.

We were greeted with a thundering round of applause. Cattricks put on her public persona and led a pep rally from the top of the escalators, eventually introducing Flats and Stone. They both made brief speeches to additional cheers.

"This is incredible," I said to Cattricks. "Stone and Flats are receiving a stamp of approval for what they're doing. It's a mandate from the people."

"Yeah, it's almost hard to describe. Like…the…"

"Like…the tide is rising?"

"No."

"Like the wind is at our backs?"

"No, that's not what I was thinking."

"Like fire is catching?"

"Nah, never mind."

25.

One of the things I've used on the Google is to pull up maps.
~ George W. Bush

With one day until our Supreme Court hearing, tension was building across Capitropolis. Spies in Cattricks's fan base had located the absent lawmakers. They'd retreated to a secret government bunker known as The Nuts to develop a plan to stop us.

Luckily, partisan infighting foiled their efforts. Initial attempts to defund the judicial branch failed and the bickering prevented the passage of any spending bills. The entire government would soon shut down, but not until *after* our day in court.

With the lawmakers failing, President Rain shifted tactics. His press secretary informed the media of a pending stream of executive orders intended to create more legal hurdles for us. Even if we eventually won, he would keep us fighting in court until he resigned his lifetime term or died in a bloody coup.

We were so close. Failure was simply not an option. Rather than waiting for their attack, we went on the offensive. Squad 452 assembled in the hotel lobby and laid out our plan.

"What's your strategy, Flats?" Dale asked.

"We need to divide up. I'll prepare for court and the rest of 452 will go after the lawmakers."

"You're right. They feel secure in The Nuts and won't be expecting a full frontal assault."

"I'm kinda worried about doing full frontal," Cattricks said.

Chip snickered and Cattricks responded with her annoyed mother glare.

"Cattricks is our voice and vision. She needs to be seen to inspire the people. But we can't afford to lose her," Flats said.

Dale held up a roll of papers. "Don't worry. Thanks to BeeGee we have detailed plans to the entire facility. I think we can hit 'em right in The Nuts." Stone and I couldn't help but giggle. I mean, really, who came up with such a silly name.

"That's awesome. How did you manage that, BeeGee? Did you hack the government's computers? Or were they delivered to you by a small, loyal robot?" Cattricks asked.

"No, I just downloaded them from the county website. Freedom of Information Act."

Cattricks still didn't look convinced about the plan. "Yeah, but I won't really be at the front will I? It sounds dangerous, Dale."

"No, we'll have an advance team handling all the dirty work. I found some of your fans at the local Star Trek convention. They were dressed in the red shirts—you know the guys who go down to the planet with Kirk but never make it back."

"Perfect. I think I can help get us there too. I have this," she said, holding up an odd-looking item in her hand. "It's a special mapping device for Capitropolis."

"Umm…Cattricks, that's the snow globe you bought from a street vendor."

"But look at the detail." She held it close to her eyes, mesmerized by the floating, white crystals.

"Yeah thanks, we'll just use Google Maps." He tapped his phone briskly. "With traffic, we're forty-three minutes away."

"What strategies do you have to neutralize them?" Flats asked.

"We have our sabotage team led by Joe the Plumber and I have a few other ideas as well." At the side of the room, Joe nodded to confirm acceptance of his mission. Standing with him was a cadre of peculiar characters.

"All right. Corn and I will take the kids and head over to The Mock to prepare. We'll be in touch. Good luck."

The group dispersed and we headed toward the revolving door at the entrance. We stopped to wait for a man who was entering the hotel. When he emerged from the chamber, he looked at Flats and gave a smile of recognition.

And somehow I recognized the man. He was like a vision from a dream. Someone I'd never met, but knew well.

224

Flats and the man shook hands and patted each other on the shoulder.

"Do you know who this is, Spy?"

I scrutinized the tall, lean gentleman before me. I tried to put the pieces together: the short, thinning hair; the round, rimless glasses; the long-sleeve, black turtleneck; the mom jeans. "Aren't you...Steve Jobs?"

He laughed. "No, dear. He died. But he did steal a lot of my ideas and my style of dress. I was the true pioneer of this look. I was wearing this back in the 70s when I was rolling out my Orange computer line. Then he shows up with his damn *Apple*. Psshhh...coincidence my ass. There was no comparison of his Apples to my Oranges; they just had better marketing.

"Then in the 80s I was ready for my triumphant return with the Admiral 63 computer. *I* would have been the one to dominate the personal computer market if that damned Commodore 64 hadn't arrived a month later."

"Sounds like you've had some tough breaks, mister."

"Well, that's life. In the end it worked out fine. The equipment side was destined to become a commodity business. I sold out and switched to information management and applied research. My companies don't have brand name recognition, but I run most of the cloud."

"Wow. That's nice. Anyway, you look familiar, but I still can't place you. Have we ever met?"

"Yes, but under different circumstances," the man replied.

I screwed up my face and tried to picture how I might know him. Finally, Flats let me off the hook. "Spy, this is our next door neighbor: Dew Baddley."

The gasps from Stone and I were perfectly harmonized.

"The man in black..."

He smiled and patted my shoulder.

I had so many questions. "So...so...why do you only work at night?"

"Well, I don't sleep much at all. I've always been an insomniac. During the night I spend a lot of my time working with companies in Asia, it's the middle of the day over there."

"Ahh, that makes sense. What about the other people in your house? The little, dark-skinned folks?"

"Asian PhDs. They were persecuted in their homelands—places like China, North Korea, and Loompaland—so I brought them here and now they work for me. They're hard workers; they can write code for hours on end. That's the reason I'm in town: securing H1-B visas for my workers. I wish I could find more domestic talent, but that's the world we are living in."

"Well, that's nice of you. Before I forget, Mr. Baddley, I want to thank you for saving me from being eaten by the mayor and keeping me warm the night of Mrs. Simpson's fire."

"I was just being a good neighbor."

"And thanks for fixing my phone," Stone added.

"No problem."

"Oh yeah, and thanks for the iTunes gift cards in the tree."

Dew gave me an odd look. "iTunes cards? I don't know what you're talking about."

"Hmm...nevermind."

"While we're at it, Dew, thanks again for helping me gather information during the Mater trial," Flats added with a wink.

I thought back to the trial and remembered Flats on the phone before he took down Mr. Bogle. The flashback of the Bogle photos made me shiver.

"My pleasure. I know why you are here so if I can help just let me know."

"Thanks, Dew."

"And good luck to you, Stone. We're all rooting for you," he said before hustling on his way. The meeting had cleared up many mysteries of our neighborhood, but also created a few new ones.

***

Flats had arranged to use the mock courtroom at nearby Georgetown Law School. The Mock, as it was known, was a training facility for the gladiators of the bar. The room looked like an old-school courtroom, but it was equipped with high-tech training tools. Flats came off as a folksy, small-town lawyer, but he was a steely, veteran attorney and had spent many hours training in similar facilities. The session was presided over by a robo-judge and opposing counsel and witnesses were holographic images.

Corn and I took our seats while Flats and Stone walked to the plaintiff's table to begin their training. Word had spread about our arrival and soon a large crowd of law students gathered next to us in the balcony.

Flats started at the beginner level, but quickly ratcheted it up to expert. He was also able to make an in-app purchase and upgraded from standard to Supreme Court mode. The all-star panel of former judges appeared at the front of the courtroom, names like: John Jay, Oliver Wendell Holmes, Thurgood Marshall, Paula Abdul, and Piers Morgan.

My father was at his pinnacle during the trip to Capitropolis. The system threw all kinds of curves—pleadings, motions, objections—and Flats knocked them out of the park. When they produced a pair of gloves as surprise evidence he refused to let Stone try them on. It was obvious they weren't going to fit.

Stone gave an impassioned plea for justice and they didn't take it easy on him because he was a kid. Hostile witnesses threw knives, shurikens, and axes. He nimbly dodged every implement. Besides quick reflexes my brother also possessed freakish strength for a kid his age. He lifted massive Martindale Hubell law books and heaved them across the chamber to show his strength. The judges gave him high marks for the display.

Meanwhile, I worked on my shooting skills, using rubber bands to shoot paper arrows at the nerdy law students. Corn tried to reprimand me, but was too busy laughing when I stuck shots right in a student's hair. My targeting skills carried over across a variety of weapons. She also joined me for a paper airplane contest to see whose could go the furthest from the balcony.

At the end of the day we walked confidently from the building, prepared for anything the Supreme Court of Pander could throw our way.

***

Dale's team had scouted out The Nuts and the following day they prepared to launch their attack. BeeGee was streaming the action online, so we were able to watch a live feed of the assault.

The Nuts consisted of two, tunneled-out mountains. It dated back to the War of Secession and the lawmakers had it stocked with enough food and PAC contributions to last them for weeks. The facility's main entrance was located on the edge of a golf course so Squad 452 assembled on the eighteenth green. In order to blend in, the men were all wearing white pants and collared polos while the girls were sporting short skirts and sleeveless shirts. Dale had a short pencil and was making notes on a map while Cattricks practiced putting. Her stroke was very impressive.

"So what are we going to do now, Dale? Blow it up?" she asked, rolling in a breaking ten-footer.

"No, it's too strong."

"What about cutting off their air? Close off all of the vents?"

"Too slow. We need to incapacitate them now."

"Then what's your plan?"

"That!" he said, pointing to an approaching truck. Sitting on a trailer behind it was a massive green and white cake. When it got closer to the camera, I realized the cake was decorated with money. The decal on the side of the truck said: Larry the Lobbyist.

Larry parked the truck in front of a set of towering, metal doors built into the hillside. He left the vehicle running, rang the doorbell, and then ran off into the bushes. A minute later the doors opened a crack and a lawmaker's page came outside. He looked around before climbing in the truck. After tapping the horn, the doors opened wide and he drove the cake inside.

"Yes! We're in!" Dale said, pumping his fist like Tiger Woods.

"No we're not. We're still out here," Cattricks said.

"Some of us…"

"Oh, I should have known. That was one of Chip's special cakes wasn't it?"

"Yep. I told him it was a dare from you."

"Why didn't you tell me?"

"I didn't want your feelings for Chip getting in the way of the mission."

"Oh please, my *feelings* are that he's an idiot."

Dale looked doubtful.

"Anyway, do you think that was a good idea, Dale?"

"We'll find out shortly."

BeeGee changed the feed to picture-in-picture and we watched on PPAN as the cake was rolled into the main chamber. The lawmakers descended upon the offering and dug in, grabbing cake and cash by the handful. They looked like greedy ants swarming dessert on a picnic blanket.

We waited in anticipation for Chip to emerge from his Trojan horse, however, when the top flew open and he yelled, "Surprise!" it proved anticlimactic. The lawmakers barely flinched; they were in a sugar and greenback frenzy. Chip seemed upset no one was paying him any attention. After screaming in several people's faces, he went to the podium at the front of the chamber and took the microphone. He launched into a crazy, directionless rant.

Outside Cattricks shook her head in disbelief. "Great, Dale. Nice plan."

Dale watched pensively. "Wait a second..."

"Damn, he's gone cuckoo for Cocoa Puffs this time."

"No, look. He's filibustering! It's working. They're helpless." Sure enough, the lawmakers continued to gorge on the cake while Chip addressed the oblivious audience.

"I think you're right."

"Now we can turn our attention to President Rain. According to this map he operates out of the right Nut. Let's head that way. He could start issuing executive orders at any time and we need to make sure it doesn't happen."

The team jumped in golf carts and zoomed across the course to an area at the front of the second mountain. I felt a pang of terror when the PPAN feed cut to a picture of the presidential seal. The president would take to the air any second.

"Can you jam it, BeeGee?" Dale yelled.

"Not yet, I'm working on it. In the meantime, we need to cut off their power. The facility gets all of its electricity from a hydroelectric plant on the river. Is Joe in position?"

"Yes, he's there. It's hard to believe they rely solely on one source of energy rather than a diverse palette of options. What kind of energy policy is that?"

"I know, just like in Maybach City. That's why they want to steal Stone's idea."

Dale placed a video call to Joe the Plumber. In the background we saw his team crouched at the approach to the dam. I cringed at the long line of plumbers' cracks.

"What do their defenses look like?"

"Well, despite this being Capitropolis's most important strategic asset, they appear to have it guarded by about a dozen members of the Daft Punk fan club."

"Still, will you be able to get close enough?"

"Sure, Dale. They have paved walkways leading directly to its most vulnerable spot."

"Oh, come on Joe. Seriously? That's like building the galaxy's most potent weapon—say...a battle station capable of destroying entire planets—and allowing it to have an Achilles heel that one person can exploit."

"I know. Even worse would be doing the exact same thing a second time, let alone a third. A bunch of second graders couldn't write a script that bad. Anyway...where were we?"

"We need to pull the plug on President Rain. Tear down that dam."

Joe relayed the order to his lieutenants. "Mario, you take the right flank."

The mustachioed man with a red shirt and overalls whom I'd seen in the hotel lobby sprung into the air. "Okey-dokey!"

"Luigi, you take the left."

The similar-looking gentleman in a green shirt also shot up. "Mama-mia! Let's-a-win!"

The wave of surly men stormed toward their target. They went unchallenged until someone at the top of the dam began dropping wooden barrels and bananas. The plumbers easily jumped the obstacles and arrived at their objective. Mario and Luigi produced several large, black bombs from their back pockets. They wound them up, put them in position, and then called for a retreat, pumping their arms furiously as they ran.

Just as the plumbers reached higher ground a thunderous explosion shattered the dam into millions of pieces.

"Whoo-hoo!" they yelled.

"Mission accomplished," Joe said. "Environmentalists have been fighting to get rid of that dam for years. We did it in under a minute. Not only is the government's power cut off, now the Kwai River can once again flow freely."

"Nice work, Joe. Meet us back at the rendezvous point on Laurentian Street."

The attack had succeeded in cutting off The Nuts and a quiet settled over the area. "Dale, what was the point of sending Chip in if destroying the dam cut off all power? Why not just do that first?" Cattricks asked.

Dale gave her an evasive smile. "Yeah, live and learn."

Cattricks's phone rang. "Hello?"

On the other end someone was screaming. "Cattricks, get me out of here!"

She hit the mute button. "Dale, it's Chip calling. I can't believe he has a signal inside the mountain. PT&T is definitely not his provider. What do you want me to tell him?"

"Try to get him to settle down and keep the lawmakers busy. They might find a way to tap auxiliary power."

"Okay." She tapped the phone again. "Hey, Chip, truth or dare?"

Realizing the dire situation, President Rain made a short-lived escape attempt. Dale had accurately anticipated the exit route and called to let us know they'd captured him. "We've got President Rain by The Nuts." At such a tense time it provided Stone and me with a good laugh.

***

Squad 452 had proven to be invaluable. Now all we had to do was make it to the Supreme Court and argue our case.

It was a short trip so Flats insisted on walking. We trotted at a good pace in the cool air until we ran into trouble a block away from the court building. It was Bill. He appeared to be on drugs and was carrying an automatic assault rifle.

"What are you doing here?" I asked.

"Nothing…was getting done…over on Capitropolis Hill so…I decided to take the law into my own hands."

"Are you okay?"

"Just a little medicinal marijuana. Perfectly legal."

"Great, a high piece of legislation carrying a gun," Flats scoffed.

"Are you going to the Supreme Court to take away my right to bear arms?"

"No, now please move along, Bill."

"Liar! I'm not moving. I'm standing my ground." He raised the gun and we stepped back. Corn pulled us behind her.

"Easy now, Bill. Relax and we'll find you a comfy place in a nice sub-committee," Flats assured him.

"I have the right to bear arms, dammit!" he repeated, waving the gun barrel back and forth.

"Yes, but not the right to shoot innocent civilians. Why don't you drop the gun, Bill?"

"You shall not infringe. This one's for the second amendment."

I cowered, expecting bullets to fly, but the sound I heard was not gunfire. It was the squealing of tires followed by a dull thud. I looked out from behind Corn and saw Bill sprawled out on the road. A car had slammed into him and at the wheel was Dew Baddley. "Son of a bitch. Dew saved me again. He always knows how to show up at just the right moment."

"You said it, baby girl. Now don't be cussing no more," Corn said.

Flats shook hands with our rescuer. "Thanks, Dew. That was close."

"That's a nice car you've got there, Mr. Baddley. I hope he didn't cause any damage," Stone said, admiring the classic auto.

"Nah, those are real chrome bumpers. No crumple zones on this baby. This is my Ford Falcon; she's the fastest car in the galaxy."

"Well, thanks again for running down that crazy piece of legislation."

"My pleasure." Dew pulled forward and pinned Bill under his tire. "You're all clear, kid. Go win this thing and then we can all go home."

We waved goodbye and crossed the street.

Walking up the broad steps of the Supreme Court building we were supremely confident. Our path had been cleared and the goal we'd been fighting so hard for was finally in sight. We were wearing matching gold lapel pins from Dale's cousin Vic. Cattricks had ditched the silly one with a bird a long time ago. Instead, these had a lightning bolt hitting an engine. It had become the logo for Stone's business and the emblem of our fight.

Our footfalls echoed off the walls in the cavernous, marble lined halls leading to the court chamber. It was an imposing place for a little girl and made me feel so small. But I knew in my heart, like Flats had always said, this was the place where all citizens were equal.

Inside, the courtroom had an aura of authority. The wide, dark wood bench had nine seats for the justices. Behind them, towering columns climbed to the celestial ceiling. Red velvet curtains draped the back wall and each of the entrances. We found seats near the front rail and waited for the court to come to order.

As the hands on the clock reached ten o'clock, there was a flurry of activity and whispering among the staff. The justices filed out in a line from behind one of the curtains and took their respective seats. Then a bailiff walked to the front and recited a script from memory. His booming voice rolling like thunder through the room.

"Oyez, oyez, oyez! All persons having business before the honorable, the Supreme Court of Pander, are admonished to draw near and give their attention, for the court is now sitting. God save Pander and this honorable Court.

"First on today's docket: Mr. John Galt."

No one stood and the justices looked confused, shuffling through their paperwork.

"Who?" one of them asked out loud.

"John Galt. It says it right here," announced the bailiff, pointing to his listing.

233

"Who the hell is John Galt?" another justice asked.

"I don't know. It doesn't look like he's here so let's move on. Next case: Stonewall Tiberius Pinch vs. the Forcibly-United Districts of Pander."

Flats and Stone stood and passed through the low gate leading to the plaintiff's table. Pander's attorney general and his team went to the opposite side.

"Oh dear, I hate kid cases. This is a grown up court for Pete's sake," one of the justices said, tossing his pencil and rolling his eyes. The nameplate in front of him said: Simon Cowell and he had a British accent.

"Who ever nominated him?" I asked Corn.

She whispered back, "President Rain put him on the court. He's not even a citizen of Pander, but his company produces propaganda for Capitropolis and he did have a lot of judging experience."

Flats responded, "He is a minor, but I represent him, Your Honor."

"Oh, and I take it you're the dad?"

"Yes, Your Honor."

"So you're the one *really* responsible for this invention. Just using the kid as a front. I've seen it a million times. Can we go ahead and vote?" he asked, looking down the bench to the other justices.

The bald one, Justice Mandel, had other ideas. "Simon, the kid has the same rights as anyone else."

"Nonsense, Howie. You always suck up to the young ones. Giving kids everything they want. That's one of the many reasons this country of yours is falling apart. Grow a pair and learn how to say no for once."

"If it's so bad why don't you get on your hovercraft and fly back to Airstrip One?"

"Don't you dare disrespect the Mother Country, Howie."

"Pfff...those clowns don't know the first thing about running a totalitarian state."

"Take that back. We were properly repressing the populace before Pander even existed."

"Blah-blah-blah. You know, Simon, I get tired of you trying to run this show. You're not Chief Justice, Wapner is."

"Well, I get tired of your bald head and ugly face. Why don't you shut your trap before I come down there and sneeze on you."

"Listen, Limey, if you're feelin' frogish then leap."

To our amazement that's exactly what Justice Cowell did. He sprung from his chair and had his hands around Justice Mandel's neck in a matter of seconds. Mandel rebuffed the attack and they started rolling around on the bench, sending papers and water glasses flying. After a flurry of fists and head butts, Cowell grabbed a gavel and crowned Mandel, splitting his head open like a ripe melon. Mandel was stunned, but still managed to strike back with a Three Stooges-style eye poke. Cowell failed to block it and had his eyes gouged.

By the time Chief Justice Wapner got to his feet to intervene, both men were covered in blood. "This is the Supreme Court, not the Jerry Springer show."

His comment had no effect. Cowell already had his teeth latched onto his foe's ear, while Mandel had a handful of his opponent's hair. Both were letting out anguished growls.

Wapner did his best to separate the two, but he was no match for the younger men's strength. They knocked him over the front edge of the bench. As he fell, he grabbed their robes and dragged them down. All three of the men landed on the polished marble floor with a dull *thud*. They weren't moving and I was afraid they'd died.

The bailiff rushed over and confirmed they were still alive, but unconscious. He called for medical personnel and the three men were soon loaded on stretchers and wheeled out of the chambers. I couldn't believe what we were watching. When the dust finally settled the bailiff announced there would be a brief recess before the remaining justices reconvened and continued the session. We huddled with Flats to discuss what had happened.

"Oh, Flats, this is terrible. We lost three of the justices," I lamented.

"No, this works in our favor. We lost Mandel and Wapner, but it was worth it to ditch Cowell. He was obviously going to be a thorn in our side. Now we're left with a group of legal mavericks and a strong Southern bias on the bench."

"Really?"

"Absolutely. Justice Chamberlain Haller is from our district and presided over the famous cousin Vinnie murder trial."

"He sure looks a lot like our neighbor, Herman Munster."

"Yeah, you're right, Spy, I noticed that too. Justice John Taylor—the one chewing tobacco and singing—also from the STD. Judges Joe Brown and John Raulston both hail from Tennessee."

"Boy, you sure increase your odds of being on the Supreme Court if your name is Joe or John."

"Another keen observation, Spy. There have been a lot of them over the years."

"That leaves the females justices: Judge Judy and Judge Marilyn Milian. Both are pro-business and will be sympathetic to our case."

Flats's confidence buoyed my spirits and I waited nervously while the janitors finished moping up the blood. Twenty minutes later the justices returned and the court was called back into session. After everything that had happened we were finally going to have our glorious day in court. Even then I knew it was going to be a defining moment in our lives and the future of Pander.

Flats stood and began his argument.

26.

If you lose the power to laugh, you lose the power to think.
~ Clarence Darrow

The morning sun is cresting the eastern horizon, chasing me, as my bullet train races west. We are hurtling along with smooth, silent speed. The sleek machine powered by plentiful energy flowing from Pinch static generators.

My gaze is regularly drawn toward the landscape flitting past the window. The novel I'm reading has trouble holding my attention. Another legal thriller that ends in a climactic court battle—so cliché.

Seated next to me is my daughter, Nelle, her attention held tight by the game she is playing on her iPhone 84S. She always has to have the latest model. I think back to the time I was about her age riding the train to Capitropolis. It seems like a million years ago. So much has changed.

It's a short trip from the east coast back to Maybach City and I start to see recognizable landmarks. We're rapidly approaching the dump. You probably thought I meant the info dump, right? That place where authors tie up all the loose ends they forgot to include in the story and were too lazy to go back and weave in properly. Actually, I meant the trash facility down by Tristan Yule's house. The district does a great job recycling, but society still generates mountains of crap.

In the few minutes before our stop, I'll fill you in on some of the highlights since that turbulent time in my childhood. In case you hadn't figured it out, yes, we won. Flats and Stone rocked and the Supreme Court awarded us a victory.

Things got a little crazy in the aftermath of our revolt. Chip had indeed gone mondo loco. He claimed President Rain had taken him captive, injected him with bee venom, and conducted experiments on him. After they let Chip out of The Nuts, he hid in waiting on a second floor balcony of the nearby clubhouse. When Squad 452 brought President Rain back to the building, Chip dropped an enormous sack of flour, instantly killing the President. Flats was able to build an insanity defense and Chip was sent off to a nice facility in District 10 to get some rest.

In the ensuing chaos, Vice President Dick Chainy assumed power. No one had seen him in years and few people even knew he was still alive. The first thing he proposed was another fiscal reaping to be called: The Stimulus. However, before that could happen Chainy was gunned down. He was hunting on the grounds of the presidential mansion when Bill from Capitropolis Hill—recently resurrected—jumped out from behind a tree and shot him in the back. Before Bill could stand trial, he was killed in committee.

Next we elected a businessman from District 1. He campaigned on the promise to make Pander great again, but turned out to be a charlatan. He too was gunned down. Unbelievable, I know!

Finally, we elected President James Bond. People shot at him all the time, but could never seem to hit him, even expert assassins at point blank range. It was truly amazing. Over time, things in Pander began to improve. As was typically the case, the president had nothing to do with it. He just took all the credit.

It wouldn't be fair to say that we deserved all the recognition either. There were sparks across Pander, which lit the greater fire that soon raged. However, our case in particular served as inspiration on a national level. Stone fought the system and won, serving as a beacon of hope to many others.

In light of the presidential changes and the Supreme Court's willingness to reshape the landscape, the Lawmakers were the final government branch in need of an extreme makeover. Following our assault, they spewed from the Nuts and returned to the capitol, but their days were numbered. In the fall an angry mob threw the bums out. The gerrrymandered districts were restructured and new elections held, making way for a return to government of the people for the people. In this new environment, businesses returned and thrived and the economy blossomed. The animal spirits had been unleashed.

Stone commercialized his engine and became fabulously wealthy. It was the first of many fruitful inventions. Time and time again, he showed how technology and private enterprise could solve society's ills, while the government only provided lip service. As the years went on he voluntarily spread his wealth to worthy endeavors and charities of his choosing. These methods were far more efficient than those employed by the government and avoided the taxing friction of the bureaucracy.

Cattricks soon became too old for Internet stardom and moved on to other endeavors. She honed her game and became a professional golfer. A bigger blow to her flock of suitors came when Cattricks revealed she was a lesbian. During my teen years Flats taught me golf and now when I cross paths with Cattricks we try to get in a round. Our relationship is strictly platonic.

Pyckle also surprised everyone. He stopped spending summers in Maybach, but we kept in touch. He diligently worked his way through undergraduate studies and then medical school to become Dr. Clifford Pyckle Cosby, Obstetrician and Gynecologist. His new practice flourished, filling the void left by Dr. Jellyfinger. Pyckle had the added advantage of being the perfect height for catching babies.

The good doctor even delivered Nelle. Given our history, it was kinda weird in the delivery room, but by that time I was an adult and he was a professional. Although I did double-check to make sure his degree was legit.

My life has been pretty quiet. Once I finally hit puberty I caught Dale's eye in a different way and we were married on my sixteenth birthday, allowed per STD statutes. I wanted to have a career before starting a family and held a variety of jobs—army sniper, writer, and community activist—before getting pregnant. Dale is currently the producer of a TV sitcom.

I glance out the window again as the train pulls into the station. My heart rises when I see a watchman standing on the end of the platform next to a Maybach City sign.

While in town we'll be staying out at Pinch's Point. Aunt Em passed years ago. I helped Flats settled her estate and finally discovered what was in the backyard tornado shelter. Aunt Em was a "prepper," stockpiling survival items, waiting patiently for an Armageddon that never came. I sometimes think she blamed Flats for preventing the end of days in Pander—and maybe that's where we were headed.

Eventually Flats semi-retired, married Corn, and moved out to Pinch's Point. They completely renovated the place and painted it several lovely shades of grey. Our old neighborhood was rezoned and the house I grew up in was razed to make room for a frozen yogurt shop. My neighbor and hero, Mr. Baddley, also sold and moved away. Sadly, he died while testing a prototype rocket he was developing for space travel.

Nelle and I step off the train and Corn is waiting there for us with a warm embrace. She is alone. We lost our beloved Flats two years ago. In a surprising twist of fate, an ambulance ran over him. No, he wasn't chasing it. Rather, he was out for a walk when the driver swerved off the road while reading a text message.

I was glad my Nelle at least got to meet her grandfather before his death. When she was learning to speak he tried to make her call him Flats, too. We laughed so hard when it kept coming out *Fats*, instead. Corn and I worked on her in secret and the last time we left Maybach during his life Nelle gave Flats a hug and said, "Goodbye, Grandpa."

About the Author

Tate Volino lives with his wonderful family in Osprey, Florida. He has written several golf-themed novels and created works in Kindle Worlds: The World of Kurt Vonnegut. After escaping from Corporate America at a reasonably young age, he now spends his time writing, reading, and raising kids.

Made in the USA
San Bernardino, CA
14 January 2020